# Nazi POWs in the Tar Heel State

UNIVERSITY PRESS OF FLORIDA

Florida A&M University, Tallahassee
Florida Atlantic University, Boca Raton
Florida Gulf Coast University, Ft. Myers
Florida International University, Miami
Florida State University, Tallahassee
New College of Florida, Sarasota
University of Central Florida, Orlando
University of Florida, Gainesville
University of North Florida, Jacksonville
University of South Florida, Tampa
University of West Florida, Pensacola

# Nazi POWs

## IN THE

## TAR HEEL STATE

ROBERT D. BILLINGER JR.

University Press of Florida

Gainesville · Tallahassee · Tampa · Boca Raton · Pensacola

Orlando · Miami · Jacksonville · Ft. Myers · Sarasota

Copyright 2008 by Robert D. Billinger Jr.
Printed in the United States of America on acid-free paper
All rights reserved

13  12  11  10  09  08  6  5  4  3  2  1

Library of Congress Cataloging-in-Publication Data

Billinger, Robert D., 1944–
Nazi POWs in the Tar Heel State / Robert D. Billinger Jr.
p. cm.
Includes bibliographical references and index.
ISBN 978-0-8130-3224-5 (alk. paper)
1. World War, 1939–1945—Prisoners and prisons, American. 2. Prisoners
of war—North Carolina. 3. Prisoners of war—Germany. 4. Germans—
North Carolina. I. Title. II. Title: Nazi prisoners of war in the Tar Heel
State.
D805.U5B56 2008
940.54'7273097569-dc22    2007038090

The University Press of Florida is the scholarly publishing agency for the
State University System of Florida, comprising Florida A&M University,
Florida Atlantic University, Florida Gulf Coast University, Florida In-
ternational University, Florida State University, New School of Florida,
University of Central Florida, University of Florida, University of North
Florida, University of South Florida, and University of West Florida.

University Press of Florida
15 Northwest 15th Street
Gainesville, FL 32611-2079
www.upf.com

Dedicated to the North Carolina "alumni,"
especially Matthias Buschheuer, Werner Lobback,
Erich Moretti, Fritz Teichmann, and Max Reiter

# CONTENTS

# TABLES

# MAP AND ILLUSTRATIONS

# PREFACE

In the bustle of busy home-front North Carolina during World War II, they were mostly overlooked by adults. Children noticed. Margaret Sampson of Wilmington wondered about the mysterious German prisoners in the camp across from her school. She wondered who they were and how they came to be in North Carolina. As an adult she still remembered those days. And in 2002, Margaret Sampson Rogers helped see to it that the state of North Carolina placed a historical marker at that unique and memorable location. Unlike Margaret Sampson Rogers, few North Carolinians remember that there were ever German prisoners of war next door.[1] Most of those who do remember forget that their "German friends" were once all looked upon as "Nazi enemies." This book is an attempt to explain how "Nazi enemies" became "German friends."

During World War II, 378,000 German prisoners of war were held in 155 base camps and 511 branch camps in forty-six of the forty-eight states of the continental United States.[2] But their story is largely forgotten. POWs who were former U-boat mariners, "Afrika Korps" men (members of German units captured in North Africa in the spring of 1943, some of whom had been part of General Erwin Rommel's famous Afrika Korps), Luftwaffe airmen (air force), regular Wehrmacht (army) soldiers, and even Waffen-SS men (members of the Nazi Party's private army) brought an exotic element to the daily lives of American servicemen and civilians in the still very rural and provincial America of the 1940s. But their impact on the American mind has been small. The attention of Americans, then and now, has been focused on our troops overseas, not on foreign prisoners in America. That attention is not misplaced, but its exclusivity has prevented an examination of Americans as keepers of prisoners. It has also hampered the development of clearer insights into the variety, uniqueness, and humanity of the foreign prisoners Americans have detained.

There has been a trickle of academic books on the German POW experience in America over the years. Early on these included a ground-breaking dissertation; a study of the American government's attempt to reorient German POWs; and a popular, very professional general study of the POW program that appeared in 1979.[3] More recently there has been an excellent scholarly study of the "failure" of the American reorientation program, an oral history of American and German POWs, and several notable studies that have focused on the German POW program within specific states.[4]

There is a need for more state studies that recapture the imagination of contemporary Americans. The German POW experience is still "news." Few Americans were aware of their presence during the war, and since then their traces have almost completely vanished. The German POW camps nationally, including the eighteen former POW camps in the state of North Carolina, were designed as temporary enclosures and were gone within a year or two after the war. The POWs themselves, even the youngest ones, are now in their late seventies and early eighties. The generation of American soldiers, farmers, pulpwood men, and curious children who knew about the German POW presence is passing from the scene. The History Channel and popular texts focus on World War II as a European or Asian phenomenon. The home front, though not totally neglected, is not quite exotic or action-packed enough for popular audiences.

But photos of "Nazi prisoners" picking cotton on a North Carolina farm, stories of a member of the Luftwaffe who was shot while attempting to escape from a pulpwood-cutting crew in rural Carolina, or just the idea that 700 former members of Rommel's Afrika Korps were camped just four miles from a private university still can arouse public attention. The exotic touches the familiar. Overlooked history becomes vividly alive. Dead history becomes local, personal, interesting, and real.

It is time for a popular and anecdotal history of the German POW experience in North Carolina. The Tar Heel State was the first to host German POWs during World War II (survivors of the submarine, U-352, sunk off Cape Lookout on 9 May 1942). It was also the state in which the next-to-last German POW escapee surrendered in postwar America (Kurt Rossmeisl fled Camp Butner on 4 August 1945 and turned himself in to the FBI in Cincinnati on 10 May 1959).[5] North Carolina also had Camp Butner, which contained a separate compound for "Allied"

POWs, individuals who had been captured wearing German uniforms but who claimed to be nationals of states that were at war with Nazi Germany. These "Allied" POWs, whom other German POWs thought of as "deserters," were men who had been coerced into the German army though they claimed to be Alsatian Frenchmen, Austrians, Czechs, Luxembourgers, Poles, or members of various Soviet-ruled nationalities. North Carolina also had in its eighteen camps, which held about 10,000 German POWs, the pulpwood cutters and agricultural workers who were typical of the POW work program nationally and whose occasional strikes were reported in military bulletins. The Tar Heel State also had the limited numbers of escapes, suicides, and shootings that were typical nationally and that help illustrate to the contemporary reader a world now long forgotten by most Americans. The German POW experience in North Carolina is representative of the POW experience nationally. It has just enough unique differences to be worth a special retelling to North Carolinians and those interested in America's German POW experience during World War II.

When you have written a book about the German POW experience in Florida during World War II but teach history at a university in North Carolina, people seem to think that you know all there is about German POWs in the Tar Heel State. Well, I did not, and I do not. But repeated friendly queries about how many camps there were in North Carolina, where the Germans came from, what they did here, and what kind of men they were motivated me to undertake a quest for some answers. Friendly questions, personal curiosity, and an empathy, if not always sympathy, for former members of the Wehrmacht has led me to multiple trips to the National Archives branch in College Park, Maryland; the federal military archives in Freiburg, Germany; and the newspaper collections at UNC-Chapel Hill, and to conduct interviews by letter, phone, and in person with former POW residents of North Carolina still living in Germany and Austria. Everywhere I found friendly, receptive assistance in the United States and abroad. Former German prisoners of war who spent some of their captive years in North Carolina were especially friendly and forthcoming. Letters and telephone calls were enthusiastically exchanged. In several cases, I was welcomed into homes in Europe for overnight visits so that questions and conversations did not have to be limited to a brief interview period.

But there is something else that must be said in a preface to a story about German prisoners of war in America. One cannot write about German POWs in North Carolina or anywhere within the United States without confronting head-on the tendency then and now to generalize about the nature of those POWs by the use of the word *Nazi*. While good historians such as Arnold Krammer have used the word in their book titles, they have also explained that book titles and realities are not the same.[6] By way of explanation, let me present a translation of a letter from a German POW at Fort Dix, New Jersey, that appeared in a national POW newspaper, *Der Ruf*, on 15 February 1946. The headline above it read: "Are We All Nazis?" The letter brings insights that apply to German POWs in all of the camps throughout America:

In nearly all American newspapers during one recent week we could read "Captured Nazis End Lives in Automobile Accident— Nazis Buried at Fort Custer." Many of us received the report with no particular feeling; many shook their heads but said nothing. Each of us must die and in our situation not much is made of that. But is it right to designate all prisoners of German lineage simply as "Nazis"? Are we all really "Nazis"? How many of us have had our eyes opened while prisoners of war! We have shown our good will for the creation of a new humanity through the work that was demanded of us; we have put forth all of our efforts: in the cotton and sugar fields of the unfamiliar and glowing hot southern states, during the floods of the Mississippi, on the farms of all states, and in the factories. Everywhere German POWs have done their job and still work, there are contented businessmen. Many of them have even promised us that if we become free men we would be accepted and given work. Are those not good signs? How many of us have already suffered in concentration camps, had to experi-ence suffering and denial and, to their supposed rehabilitation, been sent to the Wehrmacht! How many are here who at home had to suffer chicanery! How many of us have lost their brother and father, their whole family, and all of their possessions! How many workers and simple middle class people are there among us who belonged to a left of center party and who during the Nazi dictatorship just went about their work to provide their family with bread so as not to endanger them, who simply daily just accepted this terror! Are they all Nazis?[7]

My study of the period when the Wehrmacht came to North Carolina will suggest that German prisoners of war in America were indeed not all Nazis. Its purpose is to show that amid the uniformity, regularity, and monotony of the POW experience there was a lively variety of personalities, perspectives, and experiences. The story of the German POWs in North Carolina highlights the complexity of humanity and human existence. It a study of both American and German prejudices and perspectives. Marvelously, but not surprisingly, many of these prejudices and perspectives were transformed through wartime contacts and common work experiences. Germans and Americans came to recognize and appreciate the basic humanity of former enemies. The story of when the Wehrmacht came to North Carolina, like the story of the German POW experience in America as a whole, is really the story of Germans and Americans evolving from stereotypical enemies to uncommonly fast and longtime friends. This book is dedicated to clarifying that insight and keeping its memory alive.

In the research and writing of this book, I have met many wonderfully helpful and interesting people. I cannot begin to thank them all, because they are so numerous and my memory loss is a sign of aging. Special thanks go, of course, to the "alumni," to whom this book is dedicated. Several of them have especially befriended me and have had me as a guest in their homes. I am also very grateful to the staffs of the German Federal Military Archives in Freiburg and the Modern Military Branch of the National Archives (NARA II) in College Park, especially to Ken Schlessinger who has assisted my archival research on numerous occasions. I am very appreciative of the assistance of the staff of the German Office for the Notification of the Next of Kin of the Deceased of the Former German Armed Forces [Deutsche Dienststelle für die Benachtrichtigung der nächsten Angehörigen von Gefallenen der ehemaligen deutschen Wehrmacht], who helped me find information on prisoners of war who died while in captivity in North Carolina.

I am pleased to express my debt of gratitude to my colleagues at Wingate University for their interest in and encouragement of my research over the years and for their own scholarly examples. Susan

Sganga of the Ethel K. Smith Library of Wingate University has been especially helpful in assisting me with exotic reference materials. I also thank the administration at Wingate University who through a sabbatical leave enabled my research overseas.

Special thanks goes to the University Press of Florida and to two esteemed colleagues, Matthias Reiss and Lewis Carlson, who carefully read a draft of the manuscript and whose encouragement, questions, and insightful comments have helped make this a better book. Remaining errors and oversights are mine.

Finally, special thanks go to my wife, Cheryl Beam Billinger, for all of her support. She has suffered through many drafts and my many moods. We are a more "formidable" couple because of this experience together. Bless her!

# 1

# THE GERMAN VISITORS

## An Introduction

The German POWs in the wartime camps of North Carolina were world travelers. Most had never been to America before their captivity. Some of them were not even out of their teens. But they had all seen parts of the world that most Americans had not. They had also seen and done things that most American soldiers were only beginning to imagine. They all came from a Europe that had been at war since September 1939. They had fought on the steppes of Russia, on the sands of North Africa, in the hills of Italy, and in the villages of France. When they were taken prisoner, they were transported from a world of battlegrounds to an America that experienced the war through newsreels, newspaper reports, letters, and government telegrams. They came from a shooting war to a peaceable one . . . from a world of rationing to a world of bounty. They went from train travel by cattle car to train travel by passenger car, from meatless weeks to meat three times a day. On their wartime odysseys they traveled from hell to heaven.

The men discussed in this chapter are representative of the POWs who found themselves in North Carolina during World War II. The diversity of their backgrounds, branches of service, location of capture, and ideological predispositions are key to understanding the complexity of the German POW experience in America. At first this complexity went unnoticed, but later it frustrated the Germans' American military captors.

The men to be encountered in this and later chapters include Erich Moretti from Graz, Styria. He served with an air force glider artillery regiment and was captured in North Africa in April 1943 and then spent

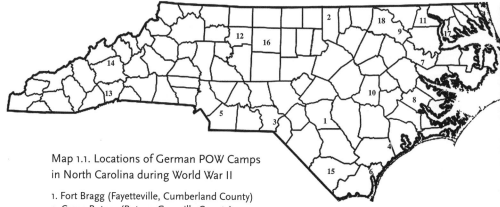

Map 1.1. Locations of German POW Camps
in North Carolina during World War II

1. Fort Bragg (Fayetteville, Cumberland County)
2. Camp Butner (Butner, Granville County)
3. Camp Mackall (Hoffman vicinity, Richmond and Scotland County)
4. Camp Davis (Holly Ridge, Pender and Onslow County)
5. Camp Sutton (Monroe, Union County)
6. Wilmington (New Hanover County)
7. Williamston (Martin County)
8. New Bern (Craven County)
9. Scotland Neck (Halifax County)
10. Seymour Johnson Field (Goldsboro, Wayne County)
11. Ahoskie (Hertford County)
12. Winston-Salem (Forsyth County)
13. Hendersonville (Henderson County)
14. Moore General Hospital (Swannanoa, Buncombe County)
15. Whiteville (Columbus County)
16. Greensboro (Guilford County)
17. Edenton (Chowan County)
18. Roanoke Rapids (Halifax County)

time in Camp Sutton and Camp Butner. Though an Austrian by citizenship before 1938, he had been raised in a pro-Nazi family and considered
himself a "German" even before Hitler's occupation of Austria. Matthias Buschheuer, from the Rhineland, was with the Afrika Korps and was
captured in Tunisia in May 1943. During his stay in North Carolina, he
got to know the only POW who was killed trying to escape from a work
party from Camp Sutton. Fritz Teichmann from Nuremberg served
with the Air Corps and was captured in Italy in July 1943. He was later
a resident of a special stockade within the POW camp at Camp Butner.
Max Reiter from near Linz, Upper Austria, fought French partisans
as a member of the Waffen-SS while still a teenager. He was captured
in Normandy in July 1944 and celebrated his eighteenth birthday as a
prisoner of war at Camp Butner. Werner Lobback was a native Saxon

and a lieutenant with an artillery unit that was captured in Cherbourg in the summer of 1944. He wound up with fellow German officer prisoners working for R. J. Reynolds in a tobacco factory in Winston-Salem. Friedrich Wilhelm Hahn and Nikolaus Ziegelbauer were former concentration camp inmates who were captured during their forced service in Wehrmacht units. They found themselves confined in North Carolina camps along with prisoners described as "Nazis."

## Erich Moretti

Erich Moretti, POW serial number 4WG-2319, was born in 1922. He was raised in Graz, Styria (until 1938 a part of Austria), and was drafted into the Wehrmacht in September 1941. He was captured in North Africa on 23 April 1943, shortly before the general collapse of the Afrika Korps, which Moretti's Luftwaffe unit had been sent to assist. Moretti, only nineteen when he was called to service, had been raised in an "Austrian" family. His father was a Greater German nationalist and illegal Nazi before Germany annexed Austria in the Anschluss of the spring of 1938. It was no surprise that young Erich thought of himself as a "German" even before his years in the Hitler Jugend and service in the Wehrmacht. Moretti, as a Styrian, thought he might have to serve in a mountain ranger unit. He wanted to be a paratrooper with the Luftwaffe, and he volunteered for that service. When he learned that there were no openings for paratroopers, he opted for membership in an airborne artillery unit of the Regiment Hermann Göring. After training in occupied Utrecht, Holland, in the late fall of 1941, he joined his regiment in Munich in January 1942. Its remnants were just returning from service in Russia. With the recuperating regiment, Moretti spent four months outside Paris, near the Longchamps racetrack. From their camp, the Styrian and his buddies could view the races through their four-meter air force sighting telescope.

From Longchamps, Moretti's unit was sent to Brittany and then to occupied southern France. It was then deployed in Tunisia in late 1943. Its job was to defend the back of the remnants of Rommel's Afrika Korps from the advancing Americans to its west. Though sent to deal with the Americans, Moretti's unit was captured in April 1943 by the famed British 8th Army. Turned over by the British to the Americans for safekeeping, Moretti and his comrades soon found themselves on trains to Oran. Then they shipped to America in a large convoy of Liberty ships. To this day, Moretti is not sure where he and his fellow prisoners disembarked, though it was probably in New York City. From there, like many of the early German POWs in America, they were sent by train to the new and recently opened German POW camp in Aliceville, Alabama. The camp was one of the largest of the new POW base camps, holding about 6,000 POWs in six separate enclosures. It was in Aliceville that Moretti got his first taste of America. He labored in wood-cutting and in peach and peanut harvests. Then, after more than a year in Alabama, he was sent to Camp Sutton, one of the new POW camps in North Carolina. His final stop in America was Camp Sutton's base camp, Camp Butner. There he did warehouse, farm, and pulp and timbering work until the spring of 1946. As an "Austrian," Moretti had the good fortune to be sent back to the recently restored Austrian state. Unlike many of his German comrades in America, who were forced into a year or more of labor in Britain or France after the war ended, he was back home in Graz by June 1946, in time to study economics at the University of Graz the following winter.[1]

## Matthias Buschheuer

Matthias Buschheuer was born in 1922 in Brühl, just south of Cologne in the Catholic Rhineland. Like Moretti, he was captured in Tunisia, in May 1943. He was already a seasoned combat veteran though he was only twenty-one years old when captured. He had served in Russia with a pioneer unit until he was wounded. After his recuperation, he was shipped to North Africa for service with the 15th Panzer Division of Rommel's Afrika Korps. Wounded by a splinter from an antitank grenade, he was captured by the British on 9 May 1943.[2] During May 1943, all of the Afrika Korps fell to the pincer movements of combined British and American forces. Within a few days, the Allies found themselves with over 150,000 prisoners. Of these, about 135,000 were sent to the United States in the summer of 1943.[3]

The "Afrikaner," as the German POWs captured in North Africa called themselves, were the first, largest, and most troublesome group of German captives on American shores throughout the war. As the first and largest group to arrive in America, they were the first to test the new American POW camp systems. They set the tone of most of the POW camps long after Germans from the Italian theater and France began to swell the numbers of POWs in America. The Afrika Korps men tended to be younger, more fit, and more self-confident than later captives, who, whether they were older or younger than the Afrika Korps veterans, had seen more German defeats than the "Afrikaners."[4] The Afrika Korps men enjoyed the reputation among their comrades and American authorities as the Germans intent on upholding pro-Nazi or at least German military loyalty and discipline within the camps. For most of the war, they sought, with some degree of success, to maintain the peer pressure within the POW camps that frustrated anti-Nazi German comrades. They constituted a major obstacle that American military authorities sought to overcome through a reorientation education program that will be the focus of a later chapter.

Buschheuer and his fellows were turned over to the Americans by the British while they were still in North Africa. They were transported to the port of Casablanca and from there were shipped to America. For Buschheuer, the trip from Casablanca to New York harbor took twenty-four days because of the convoy's slow progress through Atlantic waters infested with U-boats. Once in America, Buschheuer and his comrades were deloused and put on a train for the two-day trip to Aliceville, Alabama. During his first nine months in captivity, Buschheuer became accustomed to POW life in America. One novelty was picking cotton at a side camp in Indianola, Mississippi. From the large Aliceville camp and its side camp in Indianola, Buschheuer and 699 others were sent to Camp Sutton in Monroe, North Carolina, in March 1944. He spent about a year and a half at Camp Sutton until he was transferred to Camp Butner on 28 December 1945 and then to Camp Shanks, New York. On 6 March 1946, his convoy embarked for Europe. His long way home to the Rhineland, through four French POW camps between March 1946 and the summer of 1947, is a story for Chapter 10.[5]

## Fritz Teichmann

Fritz Teichmann, POW serial number 31G-125694, was captured near Cerbini, Sicily, on 17 July 1943 by elements of Patton's 8th Army. Born in Nuremberg on 1 January 1922, Teichmann was a music student and vocalist who found himself in the German air force by 1941. Originally assigned to an air-sea rescue unit on the East Frisian island of Norderney, he was reassigned in the spring of 1943 to a new regiment of the Hermann Göring Division in Sicily to await an Allied landing. He was assigned to serve with an officer and a driver in a radio vehicle. Their job was to listen in on and distort communications between U.S. tanks. Driving along a curvy stretch of highway in Sicily, Teichmann and his comrades suddenly found themselves approaching a group of about twenty American tanks. Though the Yanks had not yet recognized the German vehicle, which was still several hundred yards away, Teichmann's officer decided that it was time to surrender. He stepped out of the vehicle and raised his hands. Only then did the Americans notice that the occupants of the vehicle were not Americans. For Fritz Teichmann, the shooting war ended. Interestingly, as he comments, "I had the great good fortune never to have to use a weapon in this war."[6]

Teichmann's first stop in captivity after Sicily was a POW camp at Sousse in Tunisia. From there he was transferred to a camp in Algeria with former members of the Afrika Korps, who, like Buschheuer, had been captured just before the Allied invasion of Italy. Along with these "Afrikaner," Teichmann was transported by Liberty ship to Newport News, Virginia. Then it was on to Camp Gordon, Georgia, in the fall of 1943. Camp Gordon was one of the large new POW camps in the southeastern United States. Like many of his comrades in camps throughout America, Teichmann was surprised by the quality and quantity of food served. Because of the requirements of the Geneva Convention, it was equivalent to that provided to American soldiers on home bases. He, like other German POWs, was originally not required to perform work outside of the camp except on a voluntary basis. This soon changed. At Camp Butner, for instance, a group of three men with a crosscut saw and ax would eventually have to fell four cords of wood a day. "For us unpracticed wood cutters that was certainly a difficult task," Teichmann later remembered.[7]

Teichmann tells of an interesting experience he had in 1943, shortly after he arrived in the United States and was still stationed at Camp Gordon. He and a German POW labor crew were sent out to work on potato-sorting machines. As they were the first POWs in the area, a number of curious locals showed up for their own entertainment. They asked Teichmann, who spoke English, to encourage his comrades to remove their caps. When Teichmann asked them why, they said that a movie had portrayed Nazis with little horns on their heads. The Georgians just wanted to see for themselves. The film, Teichmann recalls, was an anti-German one starring Walter Slezak, an Austrian immigrant and the son of Leo Slezak, one of the Vienna opera's most famous tenors.[8]

Parenthetically, it is interesting to note that Teichmann's "Nazis have horns" story was not unique to his experience. Captain Fritz Lempp from Munich, a POW at the camp in Winston-Salem, had a similar experience. In his case, a guard asked the prisoners to remove their hats so that he could see if the Germans had horns. "He said to me seriously, 'I am really interested because I was sure that Nazis had horns and that they ate babies.'"[9] A similar incident occurred to Max Reiter, a youthful Waffen-SS man who spent most of his captivity at Camp Butner. While working on a local farm, he was introduced by the owner to a black tenant. When she asked Reiter if he was a Nazi, he smilingly responded, "Yes." She refused to believe him, saying that Nazis had horns and he did not.[10]

At Camp Gordon, Teichmann resumed his prewar musical interests. He enjoyed listening to live radio opera performances from the Metropolitan Opera in New York. But Fritz Teichmann was not content just to listen to others. He also founded a POW choir and a string trio; these were hobbies that he would later continue at Camp Butner. While at Camp Gordon, Teichmann and his musicians attracted the attention and interest of an American officer, who had them assigned to a large military hospital. In the mornings they polished windows and collected paper and cigarette butts, and in the afternoons they practiced for evening performances of chamber music for hospitalized American soldiers.

At Camp Gordon, Fritz Teichmann first ran afoul of the American authorities. One day two U.S. soldiers came into the POW camp and took him to headquarters. Several American officers questioned him about his "codes": "Schubert," "collections of songs," "musical notes," and "men's choirs." The Americans claimed that they had written evidence that he was using codes in correspondence with people outside of the POW camp. As Teichmann explains it, this was all the result of a misunderstanding. In 1938, he had had an American pen pal while he was in school. He needed musical materials for his Camp Gordon choir, so he sent a note to the former pen pal asking her for help in obtaining these materials. He offered her a small package of cigarettes by way of payment. Though he did not smoke, Teichmann, like his comrades, had received 200 cigarettes through the Red Cross. He made up a small package and asked a civilian with whom he worked at a canvas-cutting job outside the camp to take the package to the post office for him. Teichmann never learned whether it was the civilian messenger or the pen pal who went to the police. "You see that we have loyal citizens," the American military interrogating officer said.[11] This would not be the last time that Fritz Teichmann's initiative would lead to misunderstandings and have repercussions for him in American camps and in postwar England.

It got him into trouble again when he was stationed at Camp Butner in North Carolina There he gave some hard-earned PX canteen coupons to a fellow POW and found that no good deed goes unpunished. It turned out that his comrade undertook an escape from the POW camp. Among his possessions when he was recaptured were Teichmann's signed PX coupons. Teichmann was accused of helping with the flight attempt. It was an accusation that Teichmann still labels as "totally insane." "What could he [the escapee] have bought outside the camp with the coupons?"[12] Their purpose was for internal camp exchanges and they had no value beyond the German POW stockade. Teichmann believes, however, that it was because of the coupons that he found himself transferred to a segregated unit within Camp Butner, the "11th Company." An International Committee of the Red Cross visitor's report of June 1945 noted: "According to the statements of the Camp Commander, this part of the camp houses those of the prisoners considered to be National Socialists; one encounters likewise among them those undisciplined elements which the detaining power regards with suspicion from the political point of view. The [German] Spokesman denies these statements."[13] Teichmann, too, still denies any particular ideological slant among his comrades of Company 11.

While at Camp Butner, Teichmann worked in nearby tobacco warehouses with both male and female blacks. He remembers that work with white females was not allowed by American officials. He considers the German historian, Matthias Reiss, right on track with his book *The Blacks Were Our Friends*. The Germans were very much aware of the racial differences in America and felt that American blacks, a fellow repressed group, could be trusted.[14] Through dealings with blacks, Teichmann attempted to raise money for a possible escape. One way to acquire U.S. funds illegally was to use his hard-earned canteen coupons to buy soap powder to sell to blacks with whom he worked in the tobacco warehouses. They were willing to pay Teichmann hard cash for the difficult-to-acquire soap powder, which was rationed during the war. They also warned him when military intelligence people began sniffing around after whites complained that blacks had soap powder and they did not. Forewarned was forearmed; Teichmann and his buddies made sure that the army found no incriminating cash among their possessions.[15]

Teichmann discovered other means to earn illegal cash. One method was to cooperate with what he calls the "tobacco mafia." Apparently there was a rule at the tobacco warehouse that after auctions, tobacco that "accidentally" fell on the ground during transportation belonged neither to the original seller nor the buyer; it belonged to the auction house representatives. The Germans, who were in charge of transporting baskets full of tobacco to the various exits to be picked up by the buyers, were subject to bribery by both buyers and the auction house to either pick up or leave dropped tobacco.[16]

Teichmann also sold some of the paintings of a gifted POW artist to wealthy civilians who came to the tobacco market. The problem with cash, whatever its source, was that it was illegal for POWs to have it. On arriving back at Camp Butner in the evening, the POWs were searched by the camp guards. However, where there was a will there was a way. According to Teichmann, the same guard who accompanied the Germans to their day of work took care of their money while they passed through the camp gates, keeping part of the money as his handling fee. Unfortunately for Teichmann and his potential escape plans, it was his "tobacco mafia" contacts who were prepared to secure a false passport for him. When his working assignment at the tobacco warehouse ended, his contacts with the "tobacco mafia" ended too. As Teichmann noted, years later he learned that only one German POW ever succeeded in escaping from Camp Butner. Kurt Rossmeisl escaped in August 1945 and was able to successfully elude capture until he turned himself over to the authorities in 1959.[17]

Teichmann's friendship with the Butner POW physician, Dr. Gasser from Vienna, and the Nuremberger's sense of humor led to later minor repercussions in Britain during his long journey home. Because of the Viennese doctor's cultural interests and pleasure in Teichmann's musical efforts at Camp Butner, the two men often visited in the POW sick bay. There, Teichmann's fertile imagination and sense of humor led to an unusual prank. One of Dr. Gasser's assistants was a POW corpsman of Polish descent who did not speak German well. Taking advantage of that fact, Teichmann allowed the assistant to believe that he was a major and the chief German doctor in the camp. When a new arrival from one of Butner's side camps arrived at the infirmary, Teichmann would make believe that he was the examining physician and would ask the new POW patient all kinds of foolish questions. All of the other Germans were in on the joke. Only the Polish corpsman believed that Teichmann was a major and a chief doctor.

Several years later, the joke turned on Teichmann. In 1947, as a POW turned over to the English, he was working in the gasworks in Halifax, Yorkshire. Who should turn up at the same location but the Polish corpsman from Camp Butner. He recognized Teichmann at once, and he told everyone, including the guards, that Teichmann was the chief physician and a major from Camp Butner. Later during his "repatriation talk" with a British officer at one of the main camps, Teichmann was asked about the story that he was a Wehrmacht major and a medical doctor. Fortunately, he was able to convince the Briton that as a 23-year-old he could hardly have already studied medicine and risen to the rank of major in the German army.[18]

For a good bit of his time at Camp Butner, Fritz Teichmann seemed a model prisoner. As a music enthusiast, English-speaker, and organist, he worked with the U.S. chaplain. He functioned as an interpreter, the sacristan for the POW chapel, and the distributor of YMCA/Red Cross gifts at the main camp. He accompanied the chaplain on his visits to Butner's side camps at Wilmington and Winston Salem.[19] Teichmann was also a favorite of the camp commander, Col. T. L. Alexander. He had

Teichmann play the organ for American military and civilian services outside the camp on Sundays. Alexander would pick Teichmann up in his car and take him along to his church.[20] This stopped abruptly when Teichmann was transferred to Company 11 and the so-called Nazi compound. According to Teichmann, Colonel Alexander called him to his headquarters and explained that he could do nothing about the transfer because the order came from Washington. Teichmann suspects that the camp's intelligence officer, Lt. Burton Spear, was responsible for his transfer. He claims that Spear never knew of his real escapades: selling soap powder to African Americans for potential escape cash, hiding alcohol in a piano, and smuggling sweets to men in isolation. Instead, Teichmann's playing of Wagnerian music at camp concerts was misconstrued as encouraging the morale of camp Nazis.[21] And, of course, there were Teichmann's PX coupons that had been found in the possession of a POW escapee.

According to Teichmann, Company 11, the so-called Nazi camp at Camp Butner, was misnamed. The compound contained mostly Afrika Korps men, some later arrivals from France, and one "Italian."[22] In Teichmann's memory, "The whole atmosphere of the 'ill-famed Company 11' was so good that nobody ever wanted to be transferred." "The discipline at Company 11 was better than in the other compounds as we had no need for democratic and communistic ideas or struggles."[23] Parenthetically, it is important to note that sixty years later, Teichmann reflected the German soldier's desire for "non-ideological" loyalty and military discipline. For him, as for many German POWs in wartime America, loyalty to the German army and to Wehrmacht peers, not "democracy," "communism," or even "pro- or anti-Nazism" was the issue of importance. "Political issues" were important for American military reeducation specialists, "political diehards" among the Germans, and later historians, not for the average POW. Surviving in the POW camps and enjoying their experiences in America as much as possible was what was important to the German POWs. Work and its joys and frustrations remain the focus of memories long after the war.

When Teichmann was first transferred to this compound in early 1945, its inhabitants were not permitted to work outside the camp. He did not see this as the punishment that the Americans seemed to intend. In any case, the army shortly changed its mind: Teichmann and his comrades of Company 11 were sent out to work on farms and in tobacco factories.[24] For a time Teichmann worked at Willow Springs on a tobacco farm. He and the other prisoners on the detail collected the leaves and dropped them on a sledge drawn by a mule. Teichmann remembers being "driven mad" by the fact that the mule stopped when it wanted. It paid no attention to the German's cries of "whoa."[25] Such memories of Camp Butner, not the issues of "democracy" or "communism," are the ones that have lasted with Teichmann and many of his comrades in the American POW camps.

## Max Reiter

Max Reiter, POW serial number 31G-20477, was born in Naarn, Austria, about twenty-five miles east of Linz, on 30 December 1926. He was the fourth child in a working-class family, and his father died in 1937. He was schooled in Naarn and later in Perg before being selected to go to a teacher's preparatory school in Linz at government expense. In the spring of 1943, he and his classmates were told that those born in 1926 would soon be called up to military service. If one wanted a particular branch of the service he should volunteer. Reiter really wanted to join the Luftwaffe, so he hurried to volunteer. In May 1943, he reported to a basic training camp on the Attersee. There he and his fellow recruits were given the uniforms of the Hitler Youth [Hitler Jugend] and drilled by Wehrmacht soldiers whose wounds kept them from more active assignments. In July he was suddenly drafted into the Waffen-SS. His protests that he had volunteered for the Air Corps did him no good. He was told that the Führer was creating a new Hitler Jugend division and that was where he was needed. With this unit, he was sent first to Breslau and then to Apeldorn in the Netherlands. The transport was by cattle car with fifty men and a bale of straw per car. In the Netherlands, Reiter underwent very rigorous training and then took his loyalty oath to Adolf Hitler in a dramatic military ceremony.

When his training ended on 20 December 1943, Reiter was able briefly to return home over Christmas. By his seventeenth birthday, on 30 December 1943, he was on his way to the SS division Das Reich in Russia. In the middle of January 1944, Das Reich and Reiter were sent to Bordeaux, France. Then, near Toulouse, Reiter's Waffen-SS unit tangled with the French resistance. When German guards were knifed, SS retribution was swift. The Germans detonated buildings because they believed that they were the homes of members of the resistance.[26]

With the Allied landings on 6 June 1944, Reiter's unit, with its vehicles and artillery, were hurried off to Normandy. His division was soon surrounded in the area around St. Lo. It was there that Reiter was wounded by splinters from a tank shell and left for dead. His parents received official word that their son was missing and presumed dead. In fact, Reiter was alive but a prisoner of war in an English field hospital next to Germans, Americans, and Englishmen. In August, he was shipped to a hospital in England.

By the end of the month, he was sufficiently recovered to be dismissed from the hospital to a "normal" POW camp. In actuality, the "camp" was only a large area surrounded by barbed wire without any shelter. When this British temporary camp was cleared in October, Reiter and his German compatriots were shipped to New York. They arrived on 9 November 1944 and disembarked from their Liberty ship at Pier 33. Reiter recalls that when he later visited America in 1994, he realized that Pier 33 was long gone. Its location was that of the World Trade Center, as it stood before the infamous 11 September 2001 attack.[27]

After their New York arrival and immediate delousing, Reiter and a large number of his comrades were sent by train to Camp Butner. What struck him at the time was that they were transported in Pullman cars with upholstered seats. In the German military, Reiter had always been transported in cattle cars along with forty-nine others. No less surprising was their arrival at Camp Butner. After marching from the train station to the camp, each POW was assigned a white-sheeted bed upon which toiletries, underwear, and slippers were laid out.

This compensated somewhat for an unpleasant incident during the train trip. On the journey, an American officer went from car to car and assigned one German in each car to speak with their American guard on behalf of the prisoners. Because Reiter considered his school-learned English to be too modest, he did not volunteer. Later, when a question arose among the prisoners as to whether they might be allowed to smoke, Reiter asked the guard in his best English, "Please sir, can we smoke a cigarette?" The American guard exploded with anger. He called the American officer, who insisted that Reiter should have volunteered as the spokesman when originally asked. As punishment, he forfeited three meals during the train ride to North Carolina. His comrades were strictly forbidden to share their rations with him.[28]

Reiter spent the rest of the war at Camp Butner except for several work assignments of two or three weeks during harvest time: picking cotton in Alabama, fruit in Florida, and tobacco in Tennessee. After each short stay, he and his POW contingent were trucked back to Camp Butner.[29] One of Reiter's most memorable experiences at Camp Butner was his week of "vacation." Assigned to a wood-cutting unit, he and his group were picked up every morning and driven to work by an American civilian. While an American soldier sat at the back of the truck to guard the prisoners, Reiter, because of his ability in English, was designated as group leader and sat up front with the civilian driver. The driver, W. G. Hunt, lived with his wife and daughter in nearby Oxford. One day, Mr. Hunt told Reiter that he would not be driving during the next week because he was taking a vacation. Reiter responded that he would like to take a vacation, too.

It turned out that Hunt owned a small farm. He asked Reiter to see if he might be assigned to help him during his week at the farm. The American authorities at the camp approved this assignment under the condition that Reiter was back at the camp each night. Each day for a week, Mr. Hunt picked up Reiter in the morning and brought him back to camp in the evening. Each day Reiter worked hard at the farm. This work led to an additional interesting experience. One afternoon, Mr. Hunt needed to get something in town. He took Reiter along with him in his truck. After shopping, the pair stopped at a restaurant for something to drink. When several other customers complained about the presence of a German POW, the owner explained to Mr. Hunt that he could stay, but the German had to leave. Hunt argued that since he and the German were working together they ought to be allowed to have a drink together. That was not persuasive to the restaurant owner. So Hunt paid the bill, and he and Reiter drove back to the farm. Reiter still remembers with fondness his American friend, W. G. Hunt, who later sent him cigarettes when he was repatriated to Austria in 1946. Reiter still has a picture of Hunt with his wife and daughter. It is a cherished souvenir of a happy time in America.[30]

## Werner Lobback

Lieutenant Werner Lobback, POW serial number 31G-40512, was born in the state of Saxony in eastern Germany in 1920. He was a Wehrmacht coastal artillery officer who was captured in Cherbourg on 26 June 1944. Slightly older than the other POWs already mentioned, he was a career army officer. He signed on to a twelve-year contract with the Wehrmacht in 1938 in order to get schooling for a career in engineering. He became an artillery officer but received little of the schooling he had hoped for. After the war started in Poland in September 1939, he was almost continuously on the move with units in Poland, France, Russia, and then France again. After only nine months of school in Berlin, he found himself with the 645th Regiment in Caen, building battery emplacements on the Normandy coast. In light of the assumption that the equipment and organization of the German army were always excellent, it is interesting that Lobback remembers that the guns that he was forced to use were Czech and Polish artillery pieces. They had been captured during the Germans' victorious early war exploits, but it was difficult to find appropriate ammunition for them. The Germans were not as well prepared for the Allied invasion as has been believed.

When the invasion came in June 1944, Lobback and his men were surrounded in the fortress at Cherbourg. Forced to surrender, he found his American captors to be very "fair." In fact, the treatment was extraordinary. After a brief stay in several British camps in England, he and 120 fellow German officers spent thirteen days on the United States Army Transport *Brazil* on the way to New York City. The American captain told his German officer prisoners that they should not feel that they were prisoners of war but rather were "travelers with limited rights." They were free to roam around the deck and enjoy the air during the day. They were locked up below decks only at night. Lobback, visiting North Carolina as an 84-year-old tourist in 2004, shared a copy of the remarkable printed menu that was served to the *Brazil*'s German officer "guests" on Sunday, 23 July 1944: "Mixed Pickles, Soup du Jour, Fried Fresh Fish, Boston Baked Pork and Beans, Braised Short Ribs of Beef, Delmonico Potatoes, String Beans, Hearts of Lettuce, French Dressing, Ice Cream, Wafers, Cheese and Crackers, Fresh Fruit, Bread, Butter; Iced Tea and Coffee."[31]

Before being sent as a volunteer to work at the R. J. Reynolds plant in Winston-Salem in August 1945, Lobback and his fellow officers spent a short time in Camp Carlisle in Pennsylvania and about a year in the officers' section of the large POW camp in Como, Mississippi. A camp composed of four companies with a total of about 1,000 men, Como had many Germans from the Afrika Korps as well as men like Lobback who had been captured in France. He was at Como from 17 August 1944 until 4 August 1945. As an officer, he was not required to work. Instead, he and his fellow officers joined classes in English, history, and mathematics in pursuit of schooling certificates. They also enjoyed playing or watching others play soccer or tennis or they participated in theater or musical groups. The Germans received "excellent" food, Lobback recalled: fried chicken every Sunday. The prisoners joked that the American camp commander "must have had a chicken farm."

Yet life was boring. Lobback and about 200 other German officers at Como decided to voluntarily relinquish their work-free status and be transferred to the Winston-Salem branch camp of Camp Butner so they could work at the tobacco plant in that city. Lobback still possesses a certificate from the "Army Service Forces, Headquarters, Detachment #2, 1460 SCU, Prisoner of War Branch Camp, Winston-Salem, North Carolina, 1 February 1946." It states:

To Whom It May Concern:

This will certify that the following named German Officer Prisoners of War, Volunteered for manual labor in Connection with the 1945 Farm Crop, and that his work performance and Cooperation during the period of 1 August 1945 to 1 February 1946 was entirely satisfactory.

LOBBACK Werner, 2nd Lt.

31G 40512

[Signed]

A.A. Wilson

Capt. AUS

Commanding

After finishing his stay in Winston-Salem and spending the month of March 1946 at Camp Butner, Lobback was shipped back to Europe in April. He arrived in Antwerp and made two brief stops in Belgian camps. He was returned to Germany through the British camp in Munster and was released on 29 June 1946 at the American base at Bad Aibling, Bavaria. Werner Lobback, like the other four POWs already mentioned, became a friend of America and Americans through his positive experiences in American camps, especially those in North Carolina.

## Friedrich Wilhelm Hahn

Not all of the POWs who came to North Carolina were as "normal" as Moretti, Buschheuer, Teichmann, Reiter, and Lobback. There were those with more interesting life stories behind them as they traveled through the American POW system. Some were captured in German uniforms that had been given them as punishment for their opposition to the Nazis and their practices. One of these men was Friedrich Wilhelm Hahn. Captured in Europe while serving with a Wehrmacht unit, he was sent to Camp Mackall in North Carolina. As a writer for the Camp Mackall POW camp newspaper, *Die Freie Wort*, he described his sixteen months as a detainee in the Dachau concentration camp. In the 1 October 1945 issue he explained how a German POW in North Carolina had once been a concentration camp inmate.[32] While serving in the Waffen-SS, he was convicted in 1941 by a divisional court of SS Division Viking and condemned to two years of concentration camp imprisonment. His "crime" was that of "showing favoritism to Jews and political prisoners." After his sentencing, he was sent to the infamous Dachau concentration camp, whose horrors he described in his POW newspaper articles.[33] He considered himself fortunate that after only sixteen months in Dachau he was released to probationary service in the Waffen-SS Parachute Battalion 500 in Prague. He was fully "rehabilitated" on 5 May 1943 and returned to a normal military unit. After that he found himself fighting and being captured by American forces. Thus it was that a former Dachau concentration camp victim became a POW in a camp in North Carolina. This victim of Nazi "justice," through his articles in a North Carolina POW camp newspaper, became a spokesman against Nazism and a tool of an American military reorientation program that began as early as the spring of 1945.

## Nikolaus Ziegelbauer

Another unique North Carolina POW was Nikolaus Ziegelbauer of the Ahoskie camp. Like Friedrich Wilhelm Hahn, he knew something about Nazi "justice." He too had experienced concentration camp life. Living in the St. Pauli district of the north German city of Hamburg, Ziegelbauer was an open opponent of the Nazis and their SA even before 1933. When Hitler came to power, Ziegelbauer was denounced, taken into "protective custody" in September 1933, and sent to Berlin. During his interrogation in the police presidium on the Alexanderplatz, he was set upon by four whip-swinging thugs. When he lost consciousness, he was thrown into cold water and then confined for twenty-four hours in a cell in which he could neither stand nor sit. He was interrogated again and set upon with fists and feet until he was black and blue. The next day he was sent to the Brandenburg concentration camp.[34]

There, he and his comrades were welcomed with the greeting: "So you are here now, you Red pigs and Nazi-exterminators." Ziegelbauer was fortunate; because he was already bandaged, he received only a few kicks. Others, who joined him in a large hundred-man cell after a couple of hours, were covered with blood and contusions. In the camp he met the poet Erich Muehsam and the well-known lawyer Dr. Hans Luetten. The former, an older man, had his fingers broken and his facial hair ripped out. Muesham, like many others, died within the first four months in the camp.

The remaining inmates were shipped either to Oranienburg or Papenburg in Eastern Friesland. The latter location was Ziegelbauer's destination. Put to work in the moorlands, the inmates were subject to all kinds of chicanery by the SS. Individuals could be clubbed by rifle butts or even chased into the swampland to drown. The relatives of inmates who drowned in the swamps were told that their loved ones had been shot while attempting to escape. Ziegelbauer recalled that many well-known figures were confined in his camp. One was Fritz Ebert, the son of the former president of the Weimar Republic. Ebert and other notables were treated especially harshly. But the treatment of Jews was even more frightful. They were beaten with clubs. Sometimes they were forced to hit each other until one of them was either dead or lay bloody on the ground. How Ziegelbauer finally escaped the living hell of the concentration camp system and came to be a member of the Wehrmacht and a POW in America was not made clear in the article that he wrote for the Camp Butner POW newspaper, *Der Lagerfackel*. Very probably he escaped the concentration camp by joining Punishment Division 999, units of which were captured by the Allies in North Africa. In any case, the editors of the POW newspaper at Camp Butner introduced his article with a declaration of its credibility, and the man himself was vouched for by the German spokesman at Ahoskie.

Obviously not all German POWs were "Nazis." Nor did they come to America with the same experiences. Their Wehrmacht uniforms masked real differences. Those differences have become evident to historians, but they were not evident to their wartime American captors, who often did not speak German.[35] To GI captors, as to the American public and press, German POWs in America were "Nazis." The stories of Hahn and Ziegelbauer reveal, however, that some of the POWs were opponents of the Nazis both before and during their captivity in America. The stories of Austrians such as Moretti and Reiter show that neither man considered himself an "Austrian" while in America, though many POWs who were former citizens of the Austrian Republic would proclaim themselves "Austrians" during their time in American camps. Conflicts between these self-proclaimed "Austrians" and their "German" comrades will appear in a later chapter. Finally, the story of Teichmann, as of that of many of his Wehrmacht buddies, reveals that loyalty to the German army and one's peers rather than loyalty to a political ideology was the key to feelings of unity or disunity within the POW camps. Those feelings, rather than relations with Americans, most colored the experiences of the German POWs. Memories of disunity among the prisoners themselves and memories of increasingly good relations with Americans were most lasting in the minds of America's wartime guests.

# 2

# POW CAMPS IN
# THE TAR HEEL STATE

## An Introduction

There were ultimately eighteen German POW camps in North Carolina during World War II. They were located in the administrative area of the Fourth Service Command, one of the nine national service command areas. The Fourth Service Command covered the southeastern states including North Carolina, South Carolina, Georgia, Florida, Alabama, Mississippi, and Tennessee and was under a commanding general headquartered in Atlanta.[1] Because of the warm southern weather, which was ideal for American military installations and POW camps, and the agricultural demand for POW labor, the Fourth Service Command had more than its share of the national total of 155 base camps and 511 branch German POW camps. It had twenty-three POW base camps and ninety-four branch camps. In July 1945, four more branch camps were in preparation.[2] Even though the war in Europe was over and the last shipments of German POWs had been received in May 1945, there was still a need for additional POW labor in the fields and woods of the southeastern United States.

### Early Naval Camp at Fort Bragg

The first German POWs to come to North Carolina, and to the United States, for that matter, were temporary residents. They were men from the *U-352*, which was sunk off the coast about thirty miles south of

Cape Lookout on 9 May 1942, by a U.S. Coast Guard cutter, the *CGC Icarus*. The *U-352* was the first German U-boat sunk in American waters. It was on its second battle cruise and had arrived off the American coast on 2 May. The *CGC Icarus* initially became aware of the presence of the German submarine through its sound equipment rather than by sight. Shortly thereafter a torpedo from the German submarine missed the cutter by 200 yards and the *Icarus* turned to lay a depth charge pattern above its assailant. When the German commander decided to surface his vessel in order to save as many of the crew as possible, the American cutter fired upon the emerging submarine with 50-millimeter and 30-millimeter machine guns and then with a three-inch gun. Six direct hits out of fourteen shots were scored. While this was going on, thirty-three Germans tumbled from the conning tower and swam rapidly away from the submarine. The disabled sub sank within five minutes.[3]

The *U-352*'s skipper was Kapitänleutnant [Lieutenant] Helmut Rathke, a 32-year-old East Prussian native and professional sailor. His crew, whose average age was twenty-two, consisted of four officers and forty-one men. There were originally thirty-three survivors out of a crew of forty-five. Three of the survivors were wounded: one lost an arm and the other a leg during the fight. Gerd Reussel, who lost a leg, died of his wounds before the *Icarus* could land its prisoners at the navy yard in Charleston, South Carolina. He was buried with full military honors in Post Section, Grave #18, National Cemetery, Beaufort, South Carolina.[4]

The surviving U-boat personnel were landed at the navy yard in Charleston at 11:30 a.m. on 10 May 1942 and turned over to the provost marshal at Paris Island, South Carolina. He immediately took them to Fort Bragg, North Carolina, where they were placed in a "specially prepared Detention Camp by the Army." Their quarters at Fort Bragg were a section of former American barracks that had been hastily isolated from neighboring facilities by enclosure with a double barbed-wire fence.[5] An investigating unit from the Foreign Section of the Office of Naval Intelligence (ONI) that was especially trained in the interrogation of survivors of German submarines met them at Fort Bragg. The ONI group consisted of two U.S. navy officers, one of whom had done this same work in England. The third member of this group was an

English officer who had also done such interrogations in Britain.[6] The men of the U-352 were prime intelligence source possibilities in the eyes of their American captors.

The POW camp at Fort Bragg was visited on 17 September 1942 by Mr. Weingärtner of the Department of German Interests of the Swiss Legation in Washington, D.C., in the company of Bernard Gufler, assistant chief, special division, U.S. Department of State. The Swiss government functioned under the Geneva Convention as the "protecting power" for German internees during the war and the U.S. Department of State was the agency designated to maintain contact with the German government through the Swiss. At that time of this early Swiss visit to a POW camp in North Carolina only six German POWs remained at the facility.[7] Orders had come for the majority of the submariners (twenty-five out of thirty-one seamen, along with their skipper) to be sent to Fort Hunt in Virginia for further interrogation.[8] In the summer of 1942 the Americans had just entered the war and wanted to learn as much about the technology and capabilities of their enemies as possible. Submariners were the earliest German captives in America and had technical knowledge and expertise that was fresh, relevant, and accessible if a combination of cunning and good humor was exercised. American intelligence officers were particularly interested in learning what damage British commandos had caused on the German U-boat base at St. Nazaire in Brittany several weeks before. It was suspected that the men of the U-352 had been at the base at the time. In fact, they learned little, except that the crew liked to drink at La Belle in Gotenhafen (the Polish port of Gdynia near Danzig) and that the Germans were upset that a bottle of champagne now cost six marks or more at the Maritza Bar in La Baule, St. Nazaire's beachfront community.[9]

The six POWs from the U-352 who were still at Fort Bragg in early September 1942 were only the tip of the iceberg of the submariners who were passing through the North Carolina holding camp. But their situation gives hints of the larger early POW picture. Those who were visited by the Swiss delegate in mid-September 1942 had been provided with "clean and attractive uniforms for work and for dress occasions." The prisoners presented "a neat and soldierly appearance" when they lined up for inspection in their standard American uniforms, which had been dyed green to make them easy to recognize. Their leader was a noncommissioned officer, Maschinist Heinrich Bollmann.[10] The mustachioed and curly-haired Bollmann was older than his fellows, and a picture taken at the time reveals that he had lost an arm. None of the internees were ill except for their spokesman, Bollmann, "who suffers from nervousness as a result of the amputation of one of his arms."[11]

The visiting dignitaries noted that the Germans were adequately housed considering that the camp was a temporary facility. There was no need for a sports field and none existed for the internees to use. But the recommendation was made to add more space in the open air for exercise should the buildings used by the Germans ever be filled to capacity. The only complaint from the Germans was that they were bored because of the lack of recreational activities. While they had a few books and games, they asked the Swiss representative to send more books, games, and musical instruments. As there were too few prisoners to justify a special POW canteen, purchases were made for the prisoners through the post canteen. The Germans prepared their own meals at a standard soldiers' mess kitchen equipped to handle several times their number. They seemed pleased to be allowed to prepare their food according to their own tastes.

They did express to the official visitors their concern that they had not received communications from home since their capture. They worried that their relatives might not have been notified of their capture or current well-being. Both the Swiss and State Department visitors reassured them that communications had been established and that the internees would probably soon be hearing from friends and relatives.

The six POWs interviewed by the Swiss and State Department visitors in September 1942 were almost immediately transferred to Fort Devens, Massachusetts. A memo from the provost marshal, General Allen W. Gullion, ordered their transfer because of an upcoming International Committee of the Red Cross visit to Fort Devens and because of the imminent arrival of new German submariners at Fort Bragg. Later memoranda indicate that after the initial transfer of the remaining members of the U-352 to Fort Devens, Bollmann and his five comrades were sent on to Camp Forrest in Tennessee.[12]

The submariners of the U-352 were not the only early internees at

Fort Bragg during 1942. The camp was a holding facility for submariners who had been sent to the Washington area for careful intelligence screening or who, like the *U-352* crewmen, were held before their transfer to Fort Hunt or Fort Meade for such screening. In November 1942, the provost marshal general arranged for fifteen members of the crew of the *U-162*, a U-boat that had been captured in the Caribbean, to be transferred from Fort Bragg to Fort George G. Meade in Maryland. The crew had been interned originally in Trinidad before its transfer to Miami and then to Fort Hunt for interrogation in September. After Fort Hunt, they were briefly residents at Fort Bragg before their transfer back north to Fort Meade.[13] These were the men commanded by Fregattenkapitän [Commander] Jürgen Wattenberg, later made famous when he and twenty-four fellow submariners made a lengthy escape from a POW camp at Papago Park outside Phoenix, Arizona. That escape began on 23 December 1944. Wattenberg remained the most elusive of the group and was not captured in Phoenix until 27 January 1945.[14]

Fort Bragg received twenty more submariners in early December 1942. They were transferred from the port of Hampton Roads, Virginia.[15] These were the men of the *U-595*. Its officers and eighteen crewmen were sent for interrogation at Fort Hunt; the rest were sent to Fort Bragg.[16] The men of the *U-595*, some of whose officers would figure with Wattenberg in the Papago Park escape of December 1944, had been captured after being attacked in the Mediterranean by a British plane. The submarine had run aground on shoals about seventy miles northeast of Oran, Algeria. Its crew was subsequently captured by American GIs and shipped via the *Brazil* to Newport News, Virginia. From there, twenty-two of the officers and crew were sent to Fort Hunt and eighteen temporarily to Fort Bragg.[17]

It is not clear when the last U-boat prisoner left the temporary detention facilities at Fort Bragg. A June 1943 memorandum regarding POW files that remained at Fort Bragg noted that the files were "abandoned [on] June 1, 1943." The North Carolina POW experience of 1942–1943 had come to an end.[18]

## The Early "Permanent" Camps at Camp Mackall, Camp Davis, Camp Sutton, Camp Butner, and Fort Bragg

"Permanent" POW camps were not set up in North Carolina until 1944. This was a year later than the earliest major American camps, which were located "in the lesser populated sections of the country . . . encompassing 18 states from Arkansas and Alabama, across Georgia, Mississippi, Louisiana, to Wyoming, Nebraska, Oklahoma, Colorado, and Texas . . . [to minimize] the terrifying specter of escaped Nazis sabotaging and raping their way across the United States."[19] The North Carolina camps were part of the U.S. military's new policy of risking prisoner of war camps beyond the more "isolated" parts of the United States. In January 1943, the government decided to utilize POW labor on military reservations. Then in the fall of 1943 the military decided to use POW labor as contract labor in the agricultural-based areas of the civilian economy as well.[20] In the spring of 1944, POW camps were set up on U.S. military reservations in North Carolina for both purposes.

In February and March 1944 the first non-naval German POWs came to four camps in North Carolina: Wilmington, Camp Mackall (six miles north of Hoffman in Richmond and Scotland counties), Camp Davis (about thirty miles from Wilmington at Holly Ridge in Onslow County), and Camp Sutton (on the outskirts of Monroe in Union County). In May 1944, additional POW camps were set up at two of the largest military reservations in North Carolina: Camp Butner (six miles west of Creedmore and fourteen miles north of Durham in Granville County) and Fort Bragg in Fayetteville. Permanent branch camps of these original base camps at military reservations were soon established to assist in civilian agriculture at Wilmington in New Hanover County, Williamston in Martin County, and Hendersonville in Henderson County.

As part of a national program of broader POW camp distribution, German prisoners were first sent from other states to "branch camps" or "side camps" in North Carolina located on or near American military reservations. A POW camp was set up in Wilmington near Camp Davis in February 1944 with prisoners from Camp Gordon, Georgia.[21] Camp Mackall received prisoners from Fort McClellan, Alabama, on 29 February 1944 and remained a side camp of that Alabama camp until it became a base camp on 1 May.[22] Camp Davis was set up with POWs from Camp Aliceville, Alabama, on 18 March 1944.[23] Camp Sutton in Monroe opened on 26 March 1944, also with POWs from Aliceville.[24] Camp Sutton was briefly the largest German POW facility in the state with 750 men.

After a brief pause, the camp expansions in North Carolina continued. The camp at Fort Bragg was established on 10 May 1944 with 250 men from the camp at Crossville, Tennessee, and 250 from the camp at Aliceville, Alabama.[25] Camp Butner's initial prisoners arrived on 30 May 1944 from Camp Jackson (Columbia, South Carolina).[26]

The summer of 1944 saw the continuing proliferation of branch camps in North Carolina that were designed to fulfill the labor needs of American agriculture. It was a need that was certainly felt and that led to articles in newspapers such as the *Durham Morning Herald*. "State Faces Grave Shortage in Farm Labor This Season: Draft, Migration Takes Heavy Toll, Hamilton Reveals," was a headline on 10 March 1944. The article noted that Dr. Horace C. Hamilton, head of the Department of Sociology at North Carolina State, had reported that despite draft deferments, 25,000 North Carolina farm workers were taken into the armed forces, while an additional 36,000 North Carolina farm workers had migrated to other states. Hamilton estimated that in 1944, additional crop production would require 50,000 more workers than in 1943. He concluded that 806,000 farm people would be expected to do the work that required 880,000 workers.[27]

In addition to workers from the new "permanent" POW camps within North Carolina, temporary POW labor camps could be part of the solution to the agricultural labor problem. For example, from July until September 1944, a contingent of German POWs arrived for work in Hendersonville. They were sent in from the base camp at Camp Forrest, Tennessee. At the end of the agricultural season in 1944, the temporary camp was closed and the POWs were sent on to a camp in Oneonta, Alabama. A branch camp was not reactivated at Hendersonville until July 1945 and then as a branch camp of the base camp at Camp Butner. This Hendersonville branch would be in existence only through October 1945.[28] Once the local agricultural harvest needs were met, the Germans were transferred to other areas and other labor.

The two major "permanent" base camps of North Carolina were at Camp Butner and Fort Bragg. Of these two, the larger and the one with more branches was Camp Butner. Eventually it became the base camp for twelve smaller branch camps, including the original North Carolina POW base camps at Wilmington, Mackall, Davis, and Sutton. Additional working branch camps of Camp Butner were set up at Ahoskie in Hertford County in August 1944 and at Winston-Salem in Forsyth County in October. Meanwhile, the new base camp at Fort Bragg developed three of its own branch camps: at New Bern in Craven County in August 1944, in Scotland Neck in Halifax County in September through October 1944 and again in September through November 1945 (a temporary camp for the peanut harvest), and at Seymour Johnson Field at Goldsboro in Wayne County in October 1944. These branch camps were later transferred to Camp Butner's jurisdiction in November 1944.[29]

The final round of branch camp expansions in North Carolina came with five new branch camps of Camp Butner in 1945. In May, a POW camp was set up to service Moore General Hospital in Swannonoa in Buncombe County and another was created at Whiteville in Columbus County. Then in August 1945, new camps were set up in Greensboro in Guilford County, Roanoke Rapids in Halifax County, and at the Naval Air Station in Edenton in Chowan County.[30]

## Nature of the Camps

What was the nature of these German POW camps? What did they look like? If POWs worked, what did they do? Here are some answers.

## Camp Mackall

When visited by military inspectors in late August 1944, the prisoner of war base camp at Camp Mackall, six miles north of Hoffman, had been in existence since 29 February. It had opened on the Camp Mackall military reservation with a contingent of Germans from Fort McClellan, Alabama. The camp commander, 1st Lt. Frank H. Hooper Jr., was in charge of 247 Germans: twenty-two noncommissioned officers and 225 enlisted men, a typical company-sized working branch camp. Like the American personnel in the camp, the POWs were housed in pyramidal tents. Mess halls and latrines were in wooden buildings that had screens and shutters but nonglass windows. The camp was not yet winterized.

The stockade in which the Germans lived was surrounded by a barbed-wire fence about seven feet high. It had no barbed-wire overhang. Four open-air guard towers stood at the corners of the stockade. They were manned by American soldiers with submachine guns. The majority of prisoners were used on the U.S. post to replace civilian labor decimated by the draft. A few contracts with the surrounding civilian community called for general farm work.[31]

When the POW camp at Camp Mackall was visited in September by Guy Métraux of the International Committee of the Red Cross, the camp was about the same as it had been a month before. It contained twenty-one noncommissioned officers, one member of the sanitary personnel, and 225 privates for a total of 247 German prisoners. Métraux observed that the camp had opened at the end of February 1944 and "in general, the men belong to the 'Afrika Korps.' A small group of them were captured in Normandy. The spokesman is Master Sergeant Werner Nabrotzki."[32]

Métraux noted that the prisoners lived in small tents with wooden walls up to shoulder height, like those the American army used. Each tent had five or six beds, and there were fifty-two sleeping tents. One separate barracks served as a dining hall and another contained latrines, a laundry, and showers.

Twice a week there were moving-picture presentations. Additional entertainment was provided by a POW orchestra that performed concerts regularly. A record player and radio were also available in the recreation room. Evening educational courses were described as "very successful," with subjects like English and French; elementary, intermediate, and advanced mathematics; mechanics; stenography; and accounting. Every two weeks a Catholic priest came to say Mass and a Protestant minister held services. Métraux noted that "there is quite a large group of faithful who attend services regularly."[33]

The work of the camp, according to Métraux, was primarily maintenance of the American military camp by teams of carpenters and mechanics. Additional teams of shoemakers and bakers serviced the needs of the American military. Others did sanitation work or were involved in mosquito prevention. Small groups worked on neighboring farms gathering tobacco, harvesting hay, and doing dairy work. A supplement to the International Committee of the Red Cross report noted the POWs' daily work schedule of Tuesday, 26 September 1944. The number of POWs on contract labor included thirteen working for W. N. McKenzie (no location given other than North Carolina), shaking and stacking peanuts; sixteen processing tobacco for Person-Garrett Co., Fairmont; eleven harvesting silage of corn and hay for Pinehurst; nine harvesting silage of corn and hay for W. C. Nichols, Rockingham; and twenty-three shaking and stacking peanuts for Paul Clark of Candor.[34] The Red Cross representative concluded that "this camp is very well kept and the morale of the prisoners is good. The American officers and the prisoners collaborate and the general atmosphere is pleasant. The Spokesman is respected by the prisoners and by the American authorities. Due to this fact the discipline of the camp and the quality of the work may be considered excellent."[35]

A visit by Verner Tobler of the Swiss Legation in the company of Carl Marcy of the U.S. State Department in December 1944 reflected the continuity of developments at the POW camp at Camp Mackall. There were 249 German prisoners at the camp. "These prisoners are for the most part the same prisoners who were here at the time of the last visit [by Mr. Roth of the Swiss Legation on 23 June 1944] with a few exceptions." The camp capacity was for 450 to 500 POWs, and "during the summer months about 250 prisoners were brought to Mackall for use as contract labor on nearby farms."[36]

> The physical layout of this camp is substantially the same as that described in the report made by Mr. Nelson [the State Department visitor with Mr. Roth of the Swiss Legation] after his visit of June 23, 1944. Prisoners are still housed in tents and have shown a large amount of ingenuity in making them neat and home-like. When queried recently as to whether he would like to move to wooden barracks, the spokesman voiced his satisfaction with the present arrangement. The American guard company of 55 men is housed in tents.[37]

All seemed to be well at the camp. "Mr. Tobler stated that the camp spokesman had no complaints. Mr. Tobler expressed his complete satisfaction with the camp." However, the State Department report writer did note that "During November there were four disciplinary cases involving refusals to work and refusals to obey orders. Maximum punishment was six days in the guard house."

## Camp Davis

The POW Camp at Camp Davis, a wartime Army Air Force military training center located about thirty-five miles south of Wilmington, was officially established in mid-March 1944. On 18 March 1944, 500 German POWs arrived from the camp in Aliceville, Alabama. Later they would be joined by a number of new captives from the Normandy campaign.[38] As has been noted earlier, some German POWs in the Wilmington area had already had contact with troops stationed at Camp Davis in late February. A *Durham Morning Herald* article of 28 February 1944, noted "Davis Troops Rebuked for Taunting Germans." Col. Adam E. Potts, the Camp Davis commander, "severely rebuked troops of his command for jeering at German prisoners, which are interned on the Carolina Beach Road." According to the report, Potts "pointed out to the soldiers at Davis that it is a violation of the Geneva Convention to taunt prisoners of war."[39]

A June 1944 report of an International Committee of the Red Cross visit stated that while the POW camp at Camp Davis, under the command of Capt. John R. Galbraith, had a capacity for 750 POWs, there were only 479 there. Three hundred and one were from the army (57 noncoms, 244 enlisted men), 1 was a navy enlisted man, and 177 were air corps POWs, of whom 31 were noncoms and 146 enlisted men. On 6 June, twenty troublemakers were sent to the "Nazi camp" at Alva, Oklahoma. Work for the remaining POWs was done on the American post and on several large farms in the vicinity of the camp.[40]

The Camp Davis POW camp soon became the base camp for a "permanent" branch camp at Wilmington. The POW camp at Camp Davis and its work camp in Wilmington consisted of a total of about 520 POWs. At Camp Davis there were 380 Germans; the only noncommissioned officer among them was 1st Sgt. Fritz Thieme. The German POWs occupied barracks like those used by American soldiers. There were twelve sleeping barracks, each containing about twenty-five beds. Other buildings existed for latrines, showers, a hospital building, and two kitchen-dining halls. Under the command of Capt. John R. Gailbraith, the POWs at Camp Davis performed maintenance duties—some in the shoe shop, others in automobile repair shops, and still others in the officers' club and laundry. The 140 Germans at the branch camp in Wilmington were divided into work teams of ten to twenty men and worked in the dairies, on tobacco farms, and at a nearby airfield (Bluethenthal Field). At night they were housed back at their small side camp in two-story sleeping barracks, each floor containing about thirty-five beds.[41]

When Verner Tobler of the Swiss Legation and Carl Marcy of the U.S. State Department visited the POW camp at Camp Davis in December 1944, it looked as thought the POW camp, along with Camp Davis itself, was going to be closed. The POW camp, which had a capacity for 750 men, was down to 371. The POW camp commander was now only a lieutenant, 1st Lt. M. Kolek. Most of the prisoner labor was by then done only on the post, where salvage, camp maintenance, and crating and packing were the order of the day. The prisoners were sorry to hear that their camp would probably be closed and expressed the hope, as did their American commander, that the Germans could be kept together when they were transferred to another camp. "The Camp Commander suggested that the men be kept together if possible since they have been carefully worked over and most of the trouble makers have been eliminated."[42]

Despite the Camp Davis POWs' fears, their camp did not close in the winter of 1944–1945. Work reports continued to be generated by the POW camp into September 1945. A June 1945 visit by a member of the International Committee of the Red Cross indicated that the POW camp was still functioning, but as a side camp of Camp Butner rather than as a base camp of its own. The POW camp at Davis was under 1st Lt. H. L. Burchill, assisted by his executive officer, 2nd Lt. W. W. Green. By June 1945, the number of Germans at Davis had risen to 811. Seventy-six of them performed POW camp maintenance duties and 601 were involved in Camp Davis post details: 46 with the quartermaster, 130 with the post engineers, 370 with Air Corps maintenance, 5 in ordnance, 33 at the post hospital, 12 in gardening, and 5 in general maintenance. An additional 78 were engaged under external contract in pulpwood and logging work.[43]

## Camp Sutton

The POWs at Camp Sutton in Monroe, under camp commander Capt. James B. Potter, lived and worked under similar conditions to those found at Camp Mackall and Camp Davis.[44] Originally 700 prisoners were transferred from Aliceville to Camp Sutton on 26 March 1944. Later, 300 were moved to other camps. That left 57 noncommissioned officers and 385 men living in a tent camp (that had formerly been occupied by American troops) at Sutton in the summer of 1944. Of these men, 222 worked in the American camp. Seventy-seven worked on maintenance in warehouses while the others functioned as tailors, mechanics, kitchen helpers, plumbers, and unskilled laborers. Another ninety-five prisoners were cutting trees for pulpwood production and eleven were cutting trees for lumber. The forest work tasks, performed under civilian contracts, were considered so strenuous that a rotation system was established between the groups working within the camp and those in the woods so that the latter would not be especially over-worked.[45]

## Expansion of the North Carolina POW Camps

The pattern of early POW camp expansion in North Carolina in the spring of 1944 was obvious. The camps at Mackall, Davis, and Sutton were located within military installations and the principle work of the POWs was done on the U.S. bases, where they performed tasks normally done by civilian employees. Civilian-based forestry and farming work was secondary but substantial.

The POW camps at Fort Bragg and Camp Butner, which opened in May 1944 and later became the base camps for all of the prisoner of war camps in North Carolina, followed the pattern though on a somewhat larger scale. A relatively small POW camp at Fort Bragg with less than 1,000 men opened on 10 May. What would ultimately be a much larger one at Camp Butner opened on 30 May with a similar number of Germans.

## Fort Bragg

The POW camp at Fort Bragg started under camp commander Maj. Morgan F. Simmons with 250 men from the camp at Crossville, Tennessee, and on 12 May 1944 an additional 250 Germans arrived from the camp at Aliceville, Alabama.[46] During a visit to the camp in early December, Verner Tobler of the Swiss Legation noted that the camp had received additional Germans and the number of detainees had reached a total of 848. But the camp, which had a capacity of 2,000 prisoners, was still not full. Only one of two available compounds was occupied.[47] The Germans were quartered in an enclosed part of the American camp, which included twenty-seven two-story barracks, ten mess halls and kitchens, two canteens, seven administrative buildings, and ten recreation halls. The whole POW camp was surrounded by a double barbed-wire fence approximately eight feet high with a barbed-wire overhang. The Germans were watched by guards who used seven large enclosed guard towers located at the corners and at several other points around the stockade.[48] All of the prisoners initially worked in the American military camp repairing uniforms and equipment, doing carpentry work, fixing motor vehicles, and sorting scrap metal and paper. One squad worked on draining projects to prevent mosquitos.[49]

## Camp Butner

The POW camp at Camp Butner, which would become the largest in the state, was located fourteen miles northeast of Durham. Its camp commander was Col. Thomas L. Alexander. His POW camp opened for large numbers of German prisoners on 30 May 1944, when the first group arrived from Camp Jackson in South Carolina. After that, the arrival of various groups raised the number of Wehrmacht personnel at the camp. On the day of a visit by a member of the Swiss Legation on 28 June 1944, there were 889 POWs at the main camp. Some 250 had just arrived from the Normandy beachhead on 26 June.[50]

Most of the regular German troops in the camp were employed at paid labor on the military reservation, while those at a side camp at Williamston were engaged in paid civilian labor, working in agriculture, the pulp industry, and a paper mill. There were complaints from the owners of the paper mill that in their first several weeks of work, the

Germans were performing only about 17 percent of the work that ordinary civilians could do.[51]

By December 1944, the correction of earlier problems, like the poor performance at the paper mill, had encouraged the government to continue to expand the administrative responsibilities and ties of the Butner base camp by creating additional side camps besides the one at Williamston with 451 men: Ahoskie with 226, Winston-Salem with 276, New Bern with 388, Seymour Johnson with 421, and Wilmington with 494. In short, in addition to the expanding number of Wehrmacht personnel at the Butner base camp, a total of 1,267 in the regular camp and 495 in the special "United Nations" camp, there were 2,256 POWs in six branch camps for a total of 4,018 prisoners in the Butner system.[52] That system would continue to expand throughout the war. By April 1945, there would be 5,487 in the Butner system composed of eight side camps with a total of 2,925 POWs and a base camp with 2,562. Of those in the base camp, 893 would be in the special "UN" or "Special Compound for non-German Wehrmacht members who wished segregation and possible use by the Allies."[53]

As early as June 1944, the POW camp at Camp Butner had developed its own unique characteristics. Of the original 639 "Germans" at the main camp, 138 Russians, Czechs, Poles, French, and Belgians were kept in a separate compound (the "United Nations Compound") from their "German" comrades.[54] These "UN prisoners," who had been forcibly drafted into the Wehrmacht, had let American authorities know that they were sympathetic to the forces of the United Nations and hoped to fight against Germany before the war ended. Many would be repatriated to their home countries to finish the war as combatant adversaries against their former German comrades.

The uniqueness of the base camps at Fort Bragg and Camp Butner deserve their own chapters. The following chapters will deal with POW diversity, work, escapes, reorientation, and repatriation. The story of the "Nazi enemies and German friends" in North Carolina presents a microcosm of the German POW experience throughout the United States during World War II.

# 3

# THE AFRIKA KORPS
# COMES TO MONROE

The German POW program in North Carolina really began in the spring of 1944. The early experiences with U-Boat men in the spring of 1942 were brief and passing. The proliferation of POW camps in North Carolina in the spring of 1944 was part of a general expansion of the camp system nationwide in response to two factors: the growing numbers of German POWs in Allied hands in the European theater and the need for labor at American military installations and in the civilian agricultural and forestry sectors. Labor done by civilians such as carpentry, electrical work, and even food preparation and garbage collection on the major American military bases needed to be replaced because of the draft. The draft also necessitated more food, clothing, and military products for the increased number of servicemen. Finally, it decimated the labor supply of the American agricultural and forestry economies. With several hundred thousand Germans in the United States because they could not be housed in war-ravaged Europe, able bodies were at hand. German POWs, most of whom had been held earlier in central portions of the United States, were now sent even to east coast North Carolina. The German POW program in the United States swelled to 155 base camps and 550 side camps in forty-six of the forty-eight states. Of these, eighteen camps were in North Carolina. One of the early and largest new camps in the state was in Monroe. The POW camp at the temporary wartime engineer-training facility at Camp Sutton in Monroe briefly held the largest number of Germans in the state, 750 in May 1944.[1]

The purpose of the Monroe camp initially was to provide labor for the Camp Sutton Engineer Unit Training Center. Because such military base labor was also necessary at Fort Bragg in Cumberland County, 300 of the 750 Germans sent to Monroe were soon transferred to that facility. Thereafter, the number of Germans working at Camp Sutton and in neighboring agricultural and forestry businesses ranged from between 450 to 250 men.

The Camp Sutton prisoners were housed in pyramidal tents formerly occupied by American military personnel. Their camp was located on the "central eastern part of the Camp Sutton military reservation, about 2½ miles east of Monroe," about 100 feet south of the main line of the Seaboard Airline Railroad.[2] The stockade was surrounded by the standard double-graduated hog-wire fence about eight feet high with barbed-wire overhang. Wooden guard towers were located at the four corners of the stockade. They were equipped, in accordance with army regulations, with two .30-caliber machine guns, a siren, and a telephone. According to an inspection report of August 1944, the towers did not have searchlights, but the perimeter of the camp was illuminated by electric lights. During the daylight hours only the two rear towers were used because the guards at the main gate were able to observe activity at the front of the camp. The Germans, consisting of 53 non-commissioned officers and 360 enlisted men, were guarded by an American contingent of 100 men. There were four American officers: Capt. James B. Potter, two first lieutenants, and a second lieutenant. Nineteen enlisted men, including three interpreters, administered the camp. Twenty-two additional enlisted men served as stockade guards. Another fifty-five Americans were used to accompany prisoners on work details. Later on in the camp's history, when the number of POWs was reduced only slightly to one German officer, thirteen noncoms, and 365 enlisted men in October 1945, the American guard contingent was limited to only one American officer, a first lieutenant, and thirty enlisted men.[3] A reduction of guard personnel occurred throughout the United States. The army needed manpower elsewhere and realized that prisoner escapes from POW camps turned out to be statistically lower than escapes from maximum-security federal penitentiaries.[4]

The guards were quartered in pyramidal tents like those of the POWs and camped about a quarter of a mile from the POW camp itself. According to army inspectors, "None of the tents or buildings used by either the American personnel or the prisoners of war are winterized.

Material and equipment are available and plans are being made for winterizing of this camp. However, in this respect there is a great possibility that the military reservation will be itself closed. If this occurs, the prisoner of war camp will most likely be moved."[5] In fact, the POW camp survived until March 1946, seventeen months after the departure of the last American army engineering unit. The POW camp at Camp Sutton closed three months after the army turned over Camp Sutton to the War Assets Administration as surplus property on 10 December 1945.[6]

An International Committee of the Red Cross report of a visit to Camp Sutton by representative Maurice Perret on 12 July 1944 reveals some of the history and characteristics of the early camp. Perret reported that the camp was originally a branch camp of the one in Aliceville, Alabama, from which Sutton received its first 700 prisoners on 26 March. Although it was organized as a labor detachment of this older and larger Alabama camp, the POW camp at Camp Sutton became independent of Aliceville on 25 May 1944.[7]

Perret found the camp composed of tents formerly occupied by American troops. It was equipped, he noted, with two dining halls and kitchens, four toilet and shower buildings, one canteen, an infirmary, an administration building, a store, a shoemaker's shop, a recreation building, and a music building. Structures other than tents were "theatre of operation type buildings."[8] That meant temporary constructions of wood and tarpaper. At the time of Perret's visit an additional 114 tents, five toilet and shower buildings, and five kitchens were unoccupied. The scene was enhanced in Perret's estimation by the fact that prisoners had made tables and benches for their tents and had planted flower beds with seeds sent by the German Red Cross.[9]

American military visitors in August 1944 noted that "the stockade area presents a neat and well policed appearance. Some attempt has been made at landscaping, but due to the type of soil this program has not progressed. The area is well drained, but if this camp is to be kept in operation, immediate steps should be taken to halt the damaging effects of soil erosion. In a number of instances, most of the ground around the foundations of buildings has been washed away and the foundations are very weak."[10]

In June 1944, 222 of the 443 German prisoners at Camp Sutton worked in the American camp: seventy-seven did maintenance in the warehouses and the others worked as tailors, mechanics, kitchen helpers, plumbers, and unskilled laborers. An additional ninety-five POWs were engaged in cutting down trees for the civilian pulpwood industry and eleven were cutting trees for other uses. The careful reader of Perret's report can see that work in the piney woods had its dangers: Perret remarked that fifteen to twenty prisoners "suffer from inflammation of the skin due to a poisonous plant, poison ivy, which is rather widespread in the region." He also noted that "a certain number of men have boils, doubtless due to the heat. . . . In the hospital of the American camp five men were under treatment on the day of our visit: 1 hernia which had just been operated on, 1 fractured wrist, 1 elbow wound, 1 cellulitis of the armpit, and 1 abscess of the thigh."[11]

In their free time, the Camp Sutton POWs could avail themselves of a number of spiritual and recreational opportunities. "A Protestant pastor from the town of Monroe comes to hold services on Sunday; unfortunately he speaks German with difficulty. A Catholic priest, who speaks German well, comes to say mass regularly." At the time of Perret's visit, movies were available once a week, when the POWs were taken to the movie house of the Camp Sutton military camp. By August 1944, military visitors reported that "sixteen mm. movies were shown to the prisoners of war once a week. These movies were shown in an outdoor amphitheater which is entirely unsatisfactory during inclement weather. Suggestion was made to the camp commander that he utilize one of his empty wooden buildings for the showing of movies during inclement weather."[12] The camp also had a small orchestra and avid sports participants. On a sports field the prisoners played soccer and European handball. Ping-pong was also popular. The prisoners were less interested in educational programs. Though there was a library of 275 German fiction books, 450 military instructional manuals, and 27 English fiction books, "in view of the hard work and the heat," no evening educational courses were initiated.[13]

"We spoke with the spokesman without witnesses and lunched with him," Perret noted. "He did not have any complaints to formulate and declared that the prisoners were satisfied with the treatment. The morale is good." There was only one sour note in Perret's otherwise positive evaluation of the POW camp at Camp Sutton. He mentioned it under the category of "Mishap":

On the evening before our visit there was a distressing mishap: A prisoner, who was working in the woods, escaped. Guards surprised him about 3½ kilometers from the place of work; he began to run, refused to obey the orders of the soldiers who then fired and the man was killed outright. It was First Sergeant Werner Friedrich Meier. His death has been reported to the International Committee of the Red Cross by the War Department and the results of the investigation doubtless have been transmitted by the competent authorities.

Since there is no cemetery at Camp Sutton, the body was transferred to Camp Butner and in our presence it was buried with all military honors. The coffin was covered with a German flag, a wreath had been given by the prisoners and the guard of honor was composed of 12 German prisoners from Camp Butner; an American Catholic priest said Mass which was followed by a beautiful funeral oration by the spokesman of Camp Butner, Master Sergeant Fenten. Then a triple salute was fired by a group of America soldiers.[14]

The modern reader is struck by the military honors afforded the dead escapee. It must be remembered, however, that a major consideration of the American military in their handling of the German POWs was that the honor and dignity of prisoners of war be upheld. It was hoped that consideration given to German prisoners of war in America would be repaid in kind to the American prisoners held in German hands. Both countries were signatories of the Geneva Convention of 1929, the purpose of which was to protect the lives, well-being, and dignity of captured combatants. Not only did the American government house, feed, and clothe POWs in accordance with the Geneva Convention, but it recognized the duty of military men of all nations to attempt flight from confinement. It honored those who attempted to uphold that duty, even as it honored all those who died while serving in the armed forces. Werner Friedrich Meier's funeral was standard operating procedure.

In a unique deviation from the typically limited newspaper coverage of POWs, the story of Werner Friedrich Meier's fatal escape attempt was reported in a small article on the first page of the *Durham Morning Herald* on 13 July 1944. The public usually learned about POW escape attempts only if prisoners were gone long enough to be a matter of concern to the FBI. In that case, a description of the escapee was given to the press. In the case of Meier's escape attempt, the prisoner was shot by American guards before the matter became public knowledge. One can only wonder what prompted authorities to release the details that the *Morning Herald* published under the title "German Shot in Flight to be Buried at Butner."

Werner Friedrich Meier, former sergeant in the German Luftwaffe and an inmate of the Camp Sutton prisoner of war compound, was shot to death by guards yesterday in an attempted escape near Van Wyck, SC, the Public Relations officer announced tonight.

Meier was a member of a group of Germans who have been working regularly in pulpwood mills on government contracts made in accordance with regulations of the Geneva conference.

The body was sent today to Camp Butner, near Durham, for burial there in the prisoner of war cemetery.

The announcement said two guard-escort soldiers detailed as custodians of the working war prisoners intercepted him in an attempted break and called upon him to halt. The announcement said that Meier hesitated, then continued flight, and that the guard fired and killed him instantly.[15]

First Sergeant Werner Friedrich Meier had come a long way to North Carolina to die. He and the original prisoners of the Camp Sutton POW camp came to North Carolina from Aliceville, Alabama.[16] Their American odyssey had started on the battlefields of North Africa. Later arrivals would join them from the Normandy front during the fall of 1944, but like most of the early German POWs on American shores, with exception of the U-boat men captured off her coast, Camp Sutton's founders were captured in Tunisia in May 1943, when an American and British pincer action spelled the end of Rommel's Afrika Korps. In fact, 135,000 members of the Afrika Korps and related Wehrmacht units were captured in Tunisia and transported to America in the late spring and summer of 1943.[17] The experiences of two former Sutton inmates, Matthias Buschheuer of Brühl, Germany, and an anonymous POW (henceforth designated as WKG-012) are illustrative of those of many of their comrades at Camp Sutton in the early days of the POW program in North Carolina.[18]

Matthias Buschheuer was only twenty-one and a seasoned combat veteran when he was captured by the British on 9 May 1943. He had served with a field engineer unit in Russia until he was wounded, and he later serviced with the 15th Panzer Division of Rommel's Afrika Korps in Tunisia before his capture. Buschheuer and the remnants of the Wehrmacht in North Africa were transported first to the port of Casablanca and then sent by cargo ship to New York City. A voyage of twenty-four days culminated in delousing in a New York warehouse and transfer by rail to Camp Aliceville in Alabama. During the two-day train ride, Buschheuer and his fellows experienced the uniqueness of America. First, they rode in Pullman cars rather than in cattle cars, as was usual for combat troops in Germany. Second, Buschheuer and his comrades, accustomed to sparse German military rations, ate "like kings."[19]

The Aliceville camp, with six separate enclosures that held 1,000 Germans each, for a total of 6,000 POWs, was one of the major camps in the south-central United States when the German prisoner population in America jumped from a mere 2,000 in April 1943 to 34,000 in June.[20] At the Aliceville camp, Buschheuer and his fellows became accustomed to POW life in the United States during their first nine months of captivity. One of the novelties, besides plentiful food in a land hardly touched by the war, was picking cotton. In April 1943, the War Department announced that the German POW population could be used in accordance with Article 27 of the Geneva Convention to supplement the dwindling American civilian labor pool.[21] Buschheuer, though a non-commissioned officer and not required to work other than in a supervisory capacity, volunteered late in 1943 to join enlisted comrades for labor in cotton fields near Indianola, Mississippi, a branch work camp almost 200 miles from the Aliceville base camp.

WKG-012, a Bavarian lance corporal, served with a panzer grenadier regiment, part of Buschheuer's 15th Panzer Division. He was captured by the British a month before Buschheuer. Like Buschheuer, he was shipped to New York and Aliceville before coming to Camp Sutton. The two men told similar stories. After his capture in Tunisia, WKG-012 was shipped to Algeria and then sent by truck and train to Oran. There he was turned over to the Americans, who sent him to Casablanca for shipment to the United States. The Atlantic crossing in a convoy of about forty ships lasted sixteen days. During that time the Germans were confined in holds containing between fifty and two hundred men.[22] They were allowed on deck only for a half an hour each day and were fed two meals a day unless they were employed in the ship's laundry or kitchen. After arrival in New York and a Pullman train ride, WKG-012's contingent of prisoners arrived at Aliceville on 2 June 1943.

WKG-012 was particularly revolted by one memory from his captivity in North Africa and within the United States when he wrote his memoirs in January 1959, some sixteen years after his capture. The memory was that some Germans separated themselves as soon as possible from their fellow captives in order to gain better treatment from their captors. As early as their capture in North Africa, prisoners were encouraged by their captors to volunteer that they were opponents of the Nazi regime. According to WKG-012, a number of the prisoners, in his view primarily Berliners and Saxons, volunteered and were selected to serve the Allied officers as kitchen help and waiters. Parenthetically, it might be useful to note that the Bavarians may have been likely to identify Berliners and Saxons as the most likely "turncoats" for two reasons. One was that Saxons and Berliners were from central and northern industrialized Germany, where trade unionists, socialists, and communists were more common than in Bavaria. The second reason is that the dialects of Berliners and Saxons were very different from the Bavarian dialect to which WKG-012 was accustomed. Just as Americans from the South hear and are prone to negatively stereotype as "Yankees" people who speak with other American accents than their own, so too southern Germans tended and tend to stereotype Germans from other parts of the country. Whether or not all of the "traitors" that the Bavarian remembered were Berliners or Saxons, their separation from their more loyal comrades did not last long. They showed up in the main camp at Aliceville, Alabama. However, after several months in Aliceville, they were again given the opportunity to renounce the German regime. When they did, they were segregated in a deserted part of the Aliceville camp and later sent to other camps.[23]

WKG-012 did not remember encountering their ilk while at Camp Sutton. There were dangers for former members of the Wehrmacht who, like the men WKG-012 detested, broke from their peer groups. Their fate could be death at the hands of fanatical Nazis or more loyal soldiers. Their killers might pay for their deeds, but that did not help their victims. Two German POWs detained at Camp Croft, near Aiken, South Carolina, killed a fellow German on 5 April 1944. For that killing, Sergeant Erich Gauss, 81G-28784, and Private Rudolf Straub, 31G-168830, were convicted and later hanged on 14 July 1945.[24] That killing was not the first or the last throughout the American camps. A notable case of prisoners killing a comrade because of perceived disloyalty occurred at Camp Tonkawa, Oklahoma, in November 1943. That incident led to the execution of five convicted prisoners in July 1945. A beating death at Camp Hearne, Texas, in December 1943 resulted in the execution of seven prisoners in August 1945. There were other killings and/or suspicious suicides, all of which illustrated that a POW could not afford to be seen as too cooperative with the Americans.[25] The Camp Sutton POW camp spokesman, Master Sergeant Frederick Glunz, told American military inspectors in August 1944 that "he was a soldier and in this respect his foremost duty was to see that the camp was operated properly. He further explained that his job was difficult. Because of his insistence on a clean, orderly, and well-disciplined camp, he was often accused of leaning toward the American authorities. He felt that he had to carefully walk the middle road between the pro- and anti-Nazis in fulfilling his mission."[26]

WKG-012 recalled that in June 1944, he and 300 men from the Aliceville camp were sent to Camp Sutton. He noted that it was a military training facility and that the POWs were put to work in the motor pool, PX, and warehouses in the city of Monroe. A large number were assigned to work in the woods. WKG-012, who was a medic, was assigned to the POW camp infirmary. There he was under the command of an American doctor. "During my entire experience as a prisoner of war I never met a better doctor, even from the human point of view. His assistant, who was a Jew, treated the prisoners very correctly. Those who could not work were not forced to, even when now and then the Americans tried to exert a little pressure."[27]

WKG-012 seems to have had a particular memory for the role of Jews in the American military at Camp Sutton, a memory that extended beyond his positive comments regarding the doctor's assistant. He had more negative comments regarding the arrival of an American counterintelligence officer at the camp, "who naturally was a Jew." It was to the attentions of this counterintelligence man and to the whisperings of his own "dear comrades" in Camp Sutton that he attributed his later transfer to Camp Butner and its segregated Company 11, the so-called "Nazi company."[28]

WKG-012's most interesting memories related to his undoubtedly selective recollections regarding Jewish guards. His memories are in part corroborated by the memories of at least one other POW and an American civilian. WKG-012 felt that it was immediately evident to the POWs which guards were "regular" Americans and which ones were Jewish. The latter seemed always to urge their captives to greater exertions, and they were more threatening with their weapons. In one particular case, this led to a rather bizarre parade through the camp and the official removal of a Jewish guard from contact with the prisoners. One day this guard was particularly threatening with his submachine gun while supervising two German POWs outside the regular POW stockade. Irritated, one of the prisoners grabbed the American guard's gun and forced him to raise his hands. The Germans then marched the guard back to the POW stockade, through two sets of heavily guarded gates, and to the office of the American POW camp commander. There they turned the submachine gun over to the commander. The result, said WKG-012, was not punishment for the German POWs involved but the arrest of the guard and the removal of all Jewish guards from the POW camp.[29]

Such a memory seems exaggerated, but it is echoed in related stories told by an American civilian and a fellow German prisoner. A resident of Union County whose father employed German POWs to pick cotton in Unionville remembered hearing one irritated German sergeant refer to a guard as a "Jew bastard." The youth watched in amazement as the GI angrily pulled his pistol and motioned menacingly.[30] Lost to the thirteen-year-old observer was the problem the American army had in finding guards who spoke German and its frequent use of soldiers who were German-American or Jewish-German immigrants. Matthias Buschheuer, too, recalled a continued conflict between one Jewish-American soldier and his prisoners at Camp Sutton. The situation was finally ameliorated when the guard, not the Germans involved, was transferred to another camp.[31] It must have seemed wiser to the American military to remove and transfer one "trouble-making" guard than to arrange for the disciplining or segregation and removal of individual POWs. In retrospect such a decision can be understood in two ways. It was either evidence of a very judicious, Geneva Convention–oriented "fairness" toward the enemy or evidence of American anti-Semitism. America was more anti-Semitic in the mid-twentieth century than most Americans would like to remember. It is also probable that not all "Jews" treated the prisoners as "correctly" as did the physicians' assistant that WKG-012 remembered at Camp Sutton. Germans and their American captors were only slowly realizing that "enemies are human."

Other than the "Jewish-German conflict," WKG-012 was positively impressed by the treatment of POWs at Camp Sutton in regard to disciplinary matters and general work conditions. He remembered that prisoners were disciplined for organizing small scams that allowed them to break rules or avoid work. They were punished by the American authorities by being forced to spend three days on the rocky ground between the double-tiered stockade fences. There, in the open air, instead of in a building or a tent, they served their punishment time. Though their discomforts were real, WKG-012 felt that the Americans were more lenient toward the Germans than to their own soldiers. As a medic, WKG-012 accompanied the American doctor on his rounds within the American camp. There he saw for himself the punishment of an American soldier who was condemned to thirty days' hard labor breaking rocks because of theft. By comparison, three days between the wires seemed rather minimal.

The hardest working conditions for the prisoners at Camp Sutton occurred in the course of forestry work on civilian contracts outside the camp. The POWs were expected to cut, trim, and pile seventy to eighty trees of about 12–13 centimeters a day. After some practice, most POW cutting teams were able to reach that quota. But all the teams had to stay at the work site until each team reached its quota. WKG-012 could not resist noting that the Germans brought the high quotas on themselves: "As is normally the case with Germans, the prisoners worked so industriously that this attracted the attention of the farmers who knew how to use this for their own benefit."[32]

After the end of the war in Europe in May 1945, WKG-012 found himself in a group of five Camp Sutton POWs who were abruptly transferred to the large POW installation at Camp Butner. Until he reached Camp Butner, he had no idea that the transfer was undertaken as a disciplinary measure. When he arrived at "the largest [American] training camp in the southern United States," he found himself in Company 11, the so-called "special company" or, as it was commonly called, "the Nazi Camp." But other than being segregated from the inhabitants of the other two sections of the camp, the 150 members of Company 11 were not treated in any special way. According to WKG-012, the men of this group were no "fortress of Nazism" but soldiers who kept themselves free of political tendencies and thus aroused the displeasure of the German leaders of their former camps. In his view, the Americans were not the ones who selected prisoners for Company 11; he felt that fellow Germans pointed them out to the Americans. He may have been correct in his case, as will be seen shortly. He was undoubtedly correct in believing that Company 11 was no "fortress of Nazism." The problems Americans encountered with German POWs were not necessarily caused by Nazism. There were Nazis within the camps, of course. But there were also German soldiers whose loyalty to their fatherland and/or to their comrades led them to be seen as opponents of the American authorities. But there were also German camp leaders who knew how to manipulate the fears of American authorities for their own purposes and in line with their own prejudices. Such may have been the case at Camp Sutton, or so it seemed to WKG-012.

On one work exercise outside Camp Butner, WKG-012 encountered another former Camp Sutton inmate. From him he learned that the German camp leader at Sutton had warned that prisoner not to follow in the footsteps of WKG-012. Since this warning had come to his former Sutton comrade as that man was working one Sunday setting up the altar for the chaplain, WKG-012 contacted the American divisional chaplain at Camp Butner and explained this act of intimidation. Several weeks later, WKG-012 was pleased to notice his former antagonist, the Camp Sutton German leader, at work with "spade and shovel" at the regular Camp Butner POW camp. The worm had turned. The man who had denounced others and caused transfers had received a taste of his own medicine.

Personality conflicts between POWs that caused denunciations to the Americans and the transfer of "troublemakers" were not the only problems at Camp Sutton. Another problem there and on the national level was the Austrian-German identity problem. After the Allies announced the Moscow Declaration of December 1943 that stated that Austria was "the first victim" of German aggression, some prisoners whose homeland had been Austria before the spring of 1938 declared their "Austrianness." Such assertions of "otherness" naturally alienated Wehrmacht comrades and confused American military men. The Americans were uncertain about how to handle such a turn of events.

The problem surfaced at Camp Sutton. On 1 December 1944, Capt. James B. Potter, the commander of the POW camp there, wrote to the commanding general of the Fourth Service Command describing the problem at his camp and requesting ideas for a solution. The problem was a great deal of friction between the Germans and Austrians within the prisoner compound. That, he stated, seemed to have been the case in other POW camps from which new prisoners at Camp Sutton had come. In Potter's view,

> This grudge and dislike which sometimes develops into hate goes back centuries. They are two completely different kinds of people who have been known never to get along with each other. The Austrians represent the majority of Anti-Nazis on one hand, on the other they are always the minority as far as the total number of Prisoners of War within a compound is concerned. Consequently they are the butt of all oppressive actions taken by the Nazis against Anti-Nazis. The Austrians have mentioned repeatedly that they have been promised at the time of capture that they would be sent to PW Camps for Austrians alone. Such action would make them even more cooperative, if that is possible at all, and would prove to them that the decision of the Moscow conference by Hull, Eden, and Molotoff, to create an independent

Austria after the war again is more than propaganda talk. We have forty (40) Prisoners of War that come under this category.[33]

Officers at the Fourth Service Command headquarters did not know what to do either. They contacted the Prisoner of War Division of the provost marshal general's office in a message of 2 December 1944. Their answer came from Maj. Howard W. Smith Jr., of the Prisoner of War Operations Division of the Office of the Provost Marshal General. There was no agreement about a policy concerning prisoners of war of Austrian descent. Smith's advice to the commanding general of the Fourth Service Command was to send all such prisoners to Fort Campbell, Kentucky, if they really seemed to be anti-Nazis or to set up a special camp for Austrians at one of the camps in the Fourth Service Command.[34] It is not evident that either option was taken. Some self-proclaimed "Austrians" were later held in the "Allies camp" or "United Nations camp" at Camp Butner. There they produced the only POW camp newspaper in the United States expressly published for "Austrian" prisoners.[35]

While the German POWs bickered among themselves, they were also forced to work for the Americans. In December 1944, more than half of them at Camp Sutton were assigned duties on the military post. In mid-October 1944, all the American engineering units had been evacuated and the Germans were employed in dismantling the American camp and loading tent frames.[36] Because of work details, the POWs had little time to police their own quarters. Visiting army inspectors noted that sidewalks were in disrepair and the prisoners' stockade was crowded with tents. Only 151 prisoners were involved in private contract labor in December 1944, cutting pulpwood, picking cotton and corn, and cultivating nearby farms. Others were assigned to sheet-metal work at the Mecklenburg Iron Works in Charlotte.[37]

When the American military base at Camp Sutton closed, there was a question about the future of the POW camp. A YMCA representative who visited Camp Sutton in February 1945 reported that most of the prisoners had already been transferred to Camp Butner. In the spring of 1945 the Camp Sutton POW facility lost its designation as a base camp. It became a branch camp under the jurisdiction of the larger, 4,000-man POW camp at Camp Butner. Sewage, electricity, and water were contracted through the City of Monroe. Rations were drawn from the quartermaster depot at Morris Field in Charlotte, and canteen supplies were sent from Camp Butner. But the POW camp in Monroe continued to exist. While the prisoner population dropped to 272 in May 1945, it would fluctuate throughout the following year as contract employment became available: 364 men in July 1945, 283 in September, 370 in October, 327 in December, and 281 in March 1946.[38]

In April 1945, the possibility that German prisoners from Camp Sutton might be used for grading work on the grounds of Charlotte Memorial Hospital aroused the ire of a local labor union. On 4 April 1945, the *Charlotte News* proclaimed "Prisoner of War Labor Use in the County Opposed: Organized Labor Takes Firm Stand." The paper reported that J. A. Moore, president of the Charlotte Central Labor Union, "flatly refused permission for prisoner of war labor to be used in this county except for farming, and the lumbering and pulpwood industries." Moore based the union position on his concern that prisoners of war were dangerous and that there would be plenty of manpower available if local employers would pay base rates as high as elsewhere in the United States. The prevailing wages for unskilled labor was 50–60 cents an hour. Those rates, Moore said, would persuade native labor to stay home instead of finding jobs elsewhere.[39]

If unionized labor wanted to keep Camp Sutton's POWs away from some jobs, the army and local farmers were glad to have them. A June 1945 report noted that 145 POWs were employed at the Charlotte Quartermaster Depot as mechanics, loaders, and maintenance workers, ninety-two in the pulpwood industry, thirty-two in the logging industry, and thirteen in agriculture. Food preparation, clerical, and maintenance work within the POW compound and U.S. army camp maintenance involved fifty-five others.[40] Local farmers, with the encouragement of state agricultural agents, looked to Camp Sutton's POWs for supplementary labor and found able workers. They were young fellows in their twenties, "nice boys," recalled one farmer, who added that the Germans brought along their own lunches and were not accompanied by a guard. One former farm agent commented, "The German sergeants worked them hard, harder than civilians would have worked."[41]

The POWs at Camp Sutton were also remembered vividly by paperboys and farm boys who were fascinated by the exotic Germans. A former paperboy remembers seeing trains transporting German POWs stopped in the Monroe station before going on to Camp Sutton. American guards warned spectators to stay clear of the "dangerous Nazis." But the same paperboy later delivered newspapers to the German camp and was invited to join the prisoners for a "bite to eat" in their mess hall. Another resident of Monroe recalled how he and a friend spoke to Germans through the camp fence and exchanged a pack of cigarettes for an English-German dictionary. The next day the cigarettes were long gone, but the Germans requested and got the dictionary back from the boys.[42] The German POWs at Camp Sutton, like their counterparts throughout North Carolina, added spice to the life of local residents and contributed inexpensive labor to the American military and the civilian pulpwood, forestry, and agricultural sectors when the Afrika Korps came to Monroe.

# 4

# NORTH CAROLINA'S TWO BASE CAMPS

## Fort Bragg and Camp Butner

### Fort Bragg: First North Carolina Camp and Second Largest

The temporary POW camp for captured German U-boat men that existed at Fort Bragg in the spring and summer of 1942 was shut down in early 1943. The first "permanent" German POW camp at Fort Bragg was not established until 10 May 1944. On that day, 250 German POWs from Crossville, Tennessee, and 250 from Aliceville, Alabama, arrived at the new and expanded POW facility at Fort Bragg. This POW camp and the one that would be created at Camp Butner would become the two largest POW camps in North Carolina. They would also be the two base camps and administrative centers for all the other camps in the state. The POW camp at Fort Bragg, like the many POW camps located on military bases throughout America, was easily overlooked by North Carolina residents. It was situated within the confines of one of America's largest army training centers. Fort Bragg, which occupied 235,000 acres, was one of the large permanent army training centers established during World War I. Within this vast complex, the POW camp was a tiny area, located at the south-central edge of the base. Fort Bragg was rather rural. It lay ten miles southwest of Fayetteville, a small southern town with a normal population of 17,000 that rose during World War II to about 40,000.[1]

The camp spokesman for the Germans in the spring of 1944 was Oberfähnrich [Senior Officer Candidate] Erick Blaser. On the American side, the overall Fort Bragg post commander was Brig. Gen. John C. Kennedy. The POW camp commander was Maj. M. F. Simmons. His executive officer was Capt. Thomas A. McFarlan. The American medical officer, in the absence of a German doctor, was Capt. T. W. Long.[2]

An International Committee of the Red Cross visitor in June 1944 described the countryside in which the POW camp was located as "slightly rolling with very sandy soil covered with pine forests" and noted that the prisoner camp had no trees and thin vegetation. The POW camp within the regular American camp was enclosed and put under guard. Its buildings consisted of twenty-seven two-story barracks. Each sleeping room had thirty beds. The entire POW camp had ten mess halls and kitchens, two canteens, seven administrative buildings, ten recreation halls, a barrack for visitors, two workshops, an infirmary, two laundries, one assembly hall, and one prison. All of the prisoners were working in the American military camp repairing uniforms and military equipment, doing mechanical and carpentry work, repairing cars, and sorting scrap metal and old papers. There was also a squad working on a drainage project to prevent mosquitoes and a group of eighteen men worked nights in a tailor shop.[3]

A report of a 21 June 1944 visit by Dr. R. W. Roth of the Swiss consulate, as a representative of the Protecting Power, furnished more details. Though the POW camp had a capacity for 2,000, it had only 500 German prisoners at the time: 84 noncoms and 416 enlisted men. Guarding them was an American guard company of 125 enlisted men and five officers.[4] Each POW barracks contained six washstands, four shower baths, five stools, and one long urinal. A separate building for each company contained forty washtubs for washing clothes. The POWs had laid out two regulation-size soccer fields and enjoyed twice-weekly movies shown in a large recreation hall. As there was no German chaplain, religious services were conducted in English by the Protestant and Catholic American camp chaplains. Many of the Germans preferred to attend services held twice a month by a civilian Lutheran minister, Reverend Roland H. G. Weng, who knew some German. Eldon Nelson of the Department of State, who wrote a report of the Swiss visit, concluded that "the camp appears to be well administered and one gets the impression that the POWs will be fairly but firmly dealt with. While it is regretted that the educational and cultural life of this camp is at present not functioning, it is hoped that after the summer these activities will be developed."[5]

More details emerge from a provost marshal general's office inspection report of the camp based on a visit at the beginning of September 1944. Within three months, the POW population had tripled to more than 1,600 men. The POW camp was described as divided into two compounds, though only the western compound was in use. It held 154 noncommissioned officers and 1,452 enlisted men at the time of the visit. The eastern compound had previously been used for purposes of segregation. The whole stockaded area that housed the German camp was surrounded by a double barbed-wire eight-foot fence with a barbed-wire overhang. There were seven large enclosed guard towers, each containing a searchlight, a siren, a telephone, and a machine gun. The two guard towers adjacent to the unused eastern compound were not manned, but the other five towers were manned twenty-four hours a day by guards armed with submachine guns.[6]

The standing orders for American guard personnel were shared with the September visitors. They detailed the standing operating procedures of the camp. There were the Orders for Tower Guards, dated 7 June 1944: "Guards will shoot any prisoner who climbs, cuts or in any way tampers with the fence, unless other methods of seizing the prisoner or prisoners are practicable. Before shooting a prisoner, the tower guard will call 'Halt' three times in a tone loud enough to be heard by the prisoners." Another set of orders pertained to chasers, guards who accompanied prisoners on work details. Among the rules was one that stated that "chasers will not allow any communications, oral or written, to pass between persons and prisoners while on work projects. Chasers will obtain names of all persons who take part in an attempt to pass messages and submit a full report to this Headquarters. Chasers will keep unauthorized persons a reasonable distance away from prisoners."

There is also an 18 May 1944 memorandum on the subject of "Instructions in Case of Escape":

1. In the event a Prisoner of War escapes from the Compound or a work detail, the sentry or chaser will *IMMEDIATELY NOTIFY* the following in the order shown below:

   a. 1. The Officer of the Day (PW Camp)

      2. Military Police Radio. Phone 26205

   b. The Officer of the Day will advise the Commanding Officer, the Executive Officer or the Adjutant, who in turn will notify:

      1. The Provost Marshal, Ft. Bragg, N.C. Office phone 28164; Quarters 25161

      2. The Agent in Charge, Federal Bureau of Investigation, Edward Schiedt, 914 Johnson Bldg., Charlotte, N.C. Phone 34127

      3. Agent Quirk, Federal Bureau of Investigation, Fayetteville, N.C. Dial 9-3878, Residence phone Dial 9-3914 or call Agent Slate, Office phone Dial 9-3878; Residence phone Dial 9-2998.

      4. State Highway Patrol, Lt. Moore, 9-3950.

      5. Police Dept., Fayetteville, N.C. 9-4111.

2. The Officer of the Day will immediately make a check of all prisoners to ascertain the name of the escaped prisoner or prisoners.

3. Descriptive data, including pictures and fingerprints will be forwarded to the Agent in Charge, Federal Bureau of Investigation, Charlotte, N.C., by the quickest available means for reproduction and distribution.

4. The Provost Marshal General will be notified by the quickest available means, giving Name and Serial no. of the escaped prisoner or prisoners.[7]

Standard operating procedures remained, but changes did occur in the camp by December 1944. A report written by Carl Marcy of the Department of State, who accompanied Verner Tobler of the Swiss Legation on his visit to the prisoner of war camp at Fort Bragg on 9 December 1944, noted minor but significant changes that had recently occurred at the camp.[8] One was that two German medical officers had been transferred to the camp, where they were housed in the dispensary and thus were available twenty-four hours a day. Though under the supervision of Capt. T. W. Long, the American medical officer, they were chiefly responsible for their German countrymen. Another change by early December was that there had been two German POW deaths: Wilhelm Burghardt died of an automobile accident and Wilhelm Blum died from a brain abscess. There would soon be more deaths at the North Carolina camps. When the POW story was over, there were nineteen graves in North Carolina.

Meanwhile, there were changes for the living as well. The State Department representative noted the educational activities of the POWs: "The prisoners have organized a number of classes. A schedule of classes is now being prepared by Lt. Fogarty, an American officer, which will stress subject matter dealing with the U.S. and its institutions." The mention of Lieutenant Fogarty and classes on the United States and its institutions is a clue that a secretive American reorientation program was starting to be initiated. Fogarty was the "assistant executive officer" of the camp. This title was the purposely vague designation given to members of the provost marshal general's Special Projects Division. The task of this unit was to try to convert "Nazis," or at least loyal German soldiers, into America's postwar German friends.

It is useful to remember that members of communities like the one at the POW camp at Fort Bragg in December 1944, which consisted of 3 officers, 76 noncommissioned officers, and 769 enlisted men, do not always get along well each other. The report of the December 1944 visit noted that there had been "four disciplinary cases. Several cases brought a disciplinary confinement of 30 days, one involving a theft, another involving disobedience of orders, and another involving an assault."[9]

But cooperative working POWs could become a problem for assistant executive officers, too. There were 583 Germans working on the Fort Bragg post. Post authorities wanted to keep them working, but the assistant executive officers wanted time to reorient them. Therein lay a problem. The report of the December 1944 Swiss visit noted: "The commanding officer reported that his experience with the labor of the prisoners has been satisfactory. They have established a good reputation about the Post for labor. This appears to be attributable largely to the skill of the Camp Commander in having the prisoners selected for the work for which they are individually suited and see that there is plenty of work for them." It was obvious that Maj. M. F. Simmons liked his working POWs and had every intention of keeping them working. If Special Projects people from the provost marshal general's office planned to upset this smooth working relationship through segregative transfers or educational programs, the American commanding officer had other plans.

But the conflict of interest between two groups of American military authorities was only the tip of the iceberg of a problem that would face American reorientation programs. What seemed in February 1945 like a happy and well-ordered camp to Edouard Patte, a YMCA visitor, had the earmarks of a German-run compound at odds with American officers' hopes to undermine Wehrmacht loyalty and transform Wehrmacht internees into America-loving Germans. Patte, always upbeat when confronted with happy prisoners, noted of the German camp at Fort Bragg that it was a "beautifully located and kept camp, with fine modern buildings, well ventilated and heated." The prisoner population was "55% Africa Korps, 45% from France, working almost all on the Post, and some on pulpwood contracts." Patte was also pleased to comment that the quarters for the prisoners were well-built permanent barracks with showers and toilets. Prisoners also had access to two dayrooms with small clubrooms, "very attractive and well equipped." There was a "splendid theater, with stage, screen and two projectors" and "one beautiful canteen with paintings of 'The life of the Afrika-Korps soldier.'" Patte exulted that the canteen depictions included German, Italian, and North African scenes as well as pictures of prison camp life in America, and, finally, a scene of the captives' happy return to Germany. Patte also noted that there was an excellent camp orchestra, a theatrical group, and a "well planned program for every evening from 6 P.M. to 10:30 with classes in English, French, Spanish, German, shorthand, accountancy, bookkeeping, physics, [and] mathematics." In short, the YMCA visitor concluded the POW camp at Fort Bragg was "a good, well-organized camp."[10]

What was wrong with this picture? Nothing was wrong from the perspective of the YMCA visitor or the German leadership within the camp. The Germans were well housed, well organized, and happily running their own educational programs. But those educational programs were not fostering the study of America's history, culture, and democracy, as the provost marshal general's office Special Projects Division hoped. Instead, the Germans were pursuing the same studies they would have had in a military camp within Germany: subjects such as languages, shorthand, accounting, physics, and mathematics. Yes, they had nice buildings for their housing and recreational use. But the Germans also had decorated them to celebrate their fatherland, their military experiences, and their future triumphal return to Germany. The pictures in the German canteen were designed not to democratize the Wehrmacht but to reinforce its coherence, pride, and "Germanness." Nor was any of that particularly surprising in a camp with so many denizens (over half) who were members of the Afrika Korps, a unit that prided itself on its soldierly qualities and loyalty to the fatherland. Though 45 percent of the camp was made up of newcomers from the French campaign, men who were much older and much younger than the camp's original POWS and had been in captivity a shorter period of time, these men had seen the beginning of Germany's slide toward losing the war. Even so, the optimism and coherence of the earlier captives were still prominent and even dominant at Fort Bragg. The men of the Afrika Korps still thought that their capture had been a fluke, that Germany would still win the war. To them, any sign of acceptance of the victory of American culture, democracy, or military might was wholly unacceptable.

From the perspective of the Special Projects Division of the provost marshal general's office, German militarists at best, and "Nazis" at worst still were dominant within the German compounds. Worse, the American camp commander seemed both unaware of the problem and reluctant to interfere with the well-honed German organization and discipline within the camp that seemed to contribute so much to the work efficiency and general discipline of his German charges. At Fort Bragg, as at many camps within the United States, a disciplined, work-efficient "Nazi" camp seemed preferable to an undisciplined, inefficient democratic one. This was certainly the view of an older prisoner from Baden who was captured in March 1945 in the Ruhr area. When he was sent to Fort Bragg, he experienced the tensions between the Afrika Korps men and the newer and often older arrivals from the European Theater. His view was that the Americans never bothered to notice the tensions between the two groups of prisoners, a lack of awareness that hindered American reeducation efforts.[11] The old prisoner had a telling insight, and the Special Projects Division would try hard to change the situation, particularly as the war neared an end in Europe. More will be said of these efforts at Fort Bragg, Camp Mackall, and especially at Camp Butner in Chapter 8. But now it is appropriate to examine the other major and, in fact, largest base POW camp in North Carolina, the one at Camp Butner.

## Camp Butner: North Carolina's Largest and Most Diverse Camp

The POW Camp at Camp Butner, which was administering 5,487 German prisoners of war by April 1945, became the largest POW facility in the Tar Heel State. It had a base camp of 2,562 and eight side camps with 2,925 men and housed the most diverse POW population in America.[12] Because of these factors, Camp Butner can be viewed as a microcosm of all of the German POW camps in America.

The POW camp at Camp Butner, which was activated on 7 September 1943, started out as an internment camp for Italian prisoners of war. The camp commander was Col. Thomas L. Alexander, a man who would continue in that role when the camp later housed German POWs. Assisting Alexander as executive officer was Maj. Venison G. Pullium. On the staff was Lt. Burton Spear, who was designated as camp welfare officer.[13] Spear would later function as the camp intelligence officer when German POWs replaced the Italians in 1944.

The Italian POW camp was described by a State Department visitor as located about fourteen miles northeast of Durham on the military reservation of Camp Butner. The countryside was "slightly rolling or undulating ground, which is surrounded by a second growth forest of hard wood and pine. The camp is in the midst of a general farming area engaged in the cultivation of tobacco, some peanuts and corn." A portion of Camp Butner, which had been built in late 1942, was later converted into the prisoner of war camp, some of the buildings for which were still under construction at the time of the first official visit from representatives of the Swiss Legation and the State Department in October 1943. The construction was "standard theater of operation hutments," each of which housed approximately fifty men. "The infirmary and guard house are heated by hot air system. The remainder of the camp is heated by stoves burning coal." The three compounds of the camp, which in all had a capacity of 2,950 men, were located in a rectangular area "about 1140' long and about 870' wide. Water for the camp's hot- and cold-water showers and flush toilets was supplied from a large lake that was the water supply for the city of Durham, and the camp had an underground sewage disposal system.

American soldiers and local citizens in the areas around Camp Butner were already being introduced to "the enemy among us" because the camp administration had employed the prisoners, both to keep them occupied and "because of local agricultural labor shortages." They were put to work building roads, clearing land, conserving soil, and farming. In October 1943, at the time of the visit from the Swiss Legation, there were three smaller branch camps of Camp Butner's Italian prisoners, who were living in tents and helping with the North Carolina peanut harvest: 495 at Tarboro, 500 at Windsor, and 500 at Scotland Neck. Plans were also under way to utilize an old Civilian Conservation Corps camp and employ prisoners in cutting pulpwood.[14] As would later be the case with the German POWs, all prisoners received $3 worth of POW canteen coupons each month. Those working within the POW camp received no additional pay, but those employed externally, some 1,900 in October 1943, received an additional eighty cents a day for their efforts.

The State Department men commented favorably on the personnel of the three guard companies, which were staffed with eight officers who were responsible for their 2,897 Italian charges (1 officer and 2,896 enlisted men) and the thirteen officers in the general camp administration. "The guard personnel at this camp give the impression of being much better trained than at some other camps. . . . The camp is especially well ordered; the prisoners themselves obviously respect the camp commander and the camp administration."[15]

However, the State Department visitors mentioned one problem with the setting of the camp. Because the POW camp used only about one-third of the huts originally built for U.S. army personnel, American army units were located nearby. The main traffic of the camp, both military and civilian, passed the POW camp, and it was necessary to discipline the American soldiers who had been annoying the prisoners. Fortunately a new road was opened that diverted traffic away from the front of the POW camp. The camp commander suggested that the whole area, part of which had been vacated by the army, should be converted to a POW camp so that the camp would be removed three or four miles from any other U.S. military activity.[16] Article 2 of the Geneva Convention stated that prisoners must "at all times be humanely treated and protected, particularly against acts of violence, insults and public curiosity."[17]

By May 1944, the Italian POWs at Camp Butner had been transferred. In June 1944, instead of holding 2,897 Italian POWs, Camp Butner was administering 1,124 German POWs. The first group of Germans arrived on 30 May from Camp Jackson, South Carolina. On 26 June, they were joined by another group who had just arrived from the Normandy beachhead. The 1,224 Germans were held in two separate compounds within the Camp Butner camp and at one side camp at Williamston, which held 335 men engaged in agriculture and the pulpwood and paper industries. One officer, 56 noncommissioned officers, and 582 enlisted men were at the main camp before the arrival of the 250 newcomers from the Normandy invasion. Of the original inmates of the main camp, 128 were kept in a separate compound because they were what their erstwhile German comrades called "Überlaufer" [turncoats].[18] That is to say that they were Russians, Czechs, Poles, Frenchmen, and Belgians who had served in the German army but who expressed a desire to join the Allies in the fight against Nazism. These men of the "special compound" were of particular interest to their fellow POWs, to the American government, and to other official camp visitors. Edouard Patte, a representative of the YMCA who visited the Camp Butner POW camp in November 1944, was especially intrigued:

Owing to special conditions, the compounds have been entirely separated, so that there is no contact whatsoever between the 100% Germans and the non-Nazis or non-Germans of Camp Butner. It is indeed an amazing experience for a YMCA Secretary to find a good number of Belgian, French, Dutch, Czech, Polish, Russian and Mongolian prisoners in an American camp. But where the experience becomes even more surprising is, when you visit the dormitories and mess halls of these prisoners, to see well known billboards in display with "Buy that Invasion Bond," powerful and several portraits of General de Gaulle and Churchill, and in an array of colors, the Polish White Eagle, the Croix de Lorraine and the U.S. Stars and Stripes.[19]

In June 1944, 503 of the Germans at the main camp were engaged in paid labor on the military reservation. The 335 at Williamston worked in the private sector. That work, as of June 1944, was considered not entirely satisfactory. In the words of a State Department visitor, "Some men who were working on pulp wood cutting on the day we arrived were only doing about six-tenths of the quantity of work that had been set up for them to do, although prior to that time they had shown that they were able to do the full amount of work." Also, there were problems in the paper mill where three shifts of POWs were working. "The paper mill authorities had compiled statistical figures showing what the average civilian did [in] that kind of work in 1942, what the average man did in 1943, what the Italian prisoners of war had done, and what these German prisoners of war had done during the first two weeks of their work. The amount of work performed on the day of the visit was way below the amount any one else had done on this job and the paper mill authorities estimated that these POWs were performing about 17% of the work that an ordinary civilian would do." The American camp commander estimated that because the mill was located at a considerable distance from the side camp and the mill paid for transportation and supervisory costs, "the paper mill was actually losing money on the contract." But the State Department report writer expressed his belief that the camp commander, Col. T. L. Alexander, "appears to be a very able individual and no doubt he will be able to cope with these POWs who are malingering. At one time 500 POWs had been put on bread and water for two days for refusing to work."[20]

Colonel Alexander had to deal with problems the American military created for him as well. Since Camp Butner had become a German prisoner of war camp there had been a decrease in the strength and caliber of the guards. This was due to a national policy designed to send qualified soldiers overseas while limiting guard contingents at home and assigning POW guard duty to "limited service men," those who because of age or infirmity were deemed unfit for foreign duty. In contrast to the three guard companies and eight officers who had guarded the 2,897

Italians, only 125 men and six officers guarded the 1,224 Germans. Furthermore, "as general service men are transferred out, limited service men are used as replacements and according to the Camp Commander some of these replacements are not of the quality suitable for this kind of work. This is creating a considerable problem for the Camp Commander here."[21]

Colonel Alexander would continue to have his work cut out for him as the number of German prisoners at the base camp and the branch work camps under Camp Butner multiplied during the fall of 1944 in response to military and civilian needs in North Carolina. By early December 1944, a State Department man accompanying Verner Tobler of the Swiss Legation found 4,018 Germans under Alexander's purview. This number included 1,713 at the base camp. Of these, 495 were in the Upper Compound, which was "used for the detention of German prisoners of war who have indicated their sympathy for the Allied cause. For the most part these prisoners are Poles and Czechs." A total of 1,218 were in the Lower and Center Compound, and there was "a separate compound for a small group of non-commissioned officers. At present, this compound has less than 100 prisoners." This separate compound (which Fritz Teichmann was transferred to in early 1945), was later unofficially called the "Nazi Camp."[22]

By the fall of 1944, Alexander and his Camp Butner POW camp also administered six side camps: Williamston with 451 POWs, Ahoskie with 226, Winston-Salem with 276, and three camps that had been transferred to Camp Butner from Fort Bragg as of 11 November 1944: New Bern with 388 POWs, Seymour Johnson with 421, and Wilmington with 494. The purpose of the side camps was to provide labor for farmers, the pulpwood industry, and the tobacco industry. According to Carl Marcy of the State Department, who accompanied a Swiss Legation visitor in December 1944, "There is apparently more demand for prisoners' labor than the Camp Commander was able to supply at the present."[23]

By the spring of 1945, Colonel Alexander was supervising a total of 5,487 Germans: 2,562 in the compounds of the main camp and 2,925 more in eight side camps. To the earlier side camps under Butner—Ahoskie, New Bern, Seymour Johnson, Williamston, Wilmington, and Winston-Salem—were added Camp Davis with 562 men and Monroe

(Camp Sutton) with 274. Both of these camps, originally established as independent base camps, were relegated to the status of side camps under Camp Butner. "The camp commander stated that about 500 more prisoners were to be sent to Camp Davis in a short time, and that about 1,000 additional prisoners would be assigned to Camp Butner in the near future. He stated that there was a demand for prisoner of war labor in this area and that several thousand additional prisoners of war could be accommodated in the base and side camps after the proposed increment noted above had been received." Serving as guards for these prisoners were twenty-five American officers and 750 enlisted men stationed at Camp Butner and its side camps: two officers and between forty-three and seventy-six enlisted men at each of the side camps.[24]

A June 1945 visit to Butner and its side camps by Dr. Werner Bubb of the International Committee of the Red Cross and Mr. J. L. Toohey of the State Department revealed that Colonel Alexander's responsibilities had continued to grow. Despite the fact that the war in Europe had ended, America's war in the Pacific continued. So too did the labor shortages and need for POW labor in the American civilian agricultural sector. The main camp at Butner rose to 3,174 prisoners, and the ten side camps held an additional 3,920. To the eight side camps under Camp Butner's earlier purview were added new side camps at Asheville, with 260 POWs, and Whiteville, with 237.[25]

In early summer 1945, Dr. Werner Bubb inspected Camp Butner for the International Committee of the Red Cross. His description of the POW camp was very positive, despite his negative remarks regarding what was considered insufficient food. But that was a phenomenon throughout the POW camp system within the United States during the late spring and early summer of 1945.[26] "The country is slightly hilly; it resembles a park; the location of this camp is altogether healthful. . . . As before, the prisoners are lodged in one-story wooden barracks of the usual type, the capacity of each of which comes to about 50 men. All the quarters are in a good state of repair; normally they are always filled. There is sufficient heat and ventilation. The beds are of iron, double-decked, and provided with the customary bed linen; the prisoners have at their disposal small clothes closets which they have made themselves; a sufficient number of benches and tables have been placed in the center of the camp. Each company of the camp (about 300 men) has at its disposal 6 sleeping barracks, one barrack for lavatories, and one for a kitchen."[27]

According to Dr. Bubb, about one-quarter of the prisoners at the main camp worked in the woods: "Each man must cut down and pile 160 cubic feet of wood to be used in the manufacture of paper. Such an output required great physical exertion, if one has in mind the humid heat of the summer months and the indispensable preliminary clearing of the ground. The work lasts on the average from ten to twelve hours and includes the trip back and forth." Half of the prisoners worked in the Camp Butner storerooms and in the kitchens of the Camp Butner General Hospital. The final one-quarter worked on various local farms.[28]

Dr. Bubb mentioned that the compounds at the prisoner of war camp held distinctly different sorts of prisoners: "Compound B or nationalities camp" and "Compound C or 11th company" (the "Nazi Compound").

Compound B, the nationalities camp, which was represented by its spokesman Lance Corporal Franz Antl, 4WG-20487, contained 782 men. There were 332 Czechs, 150 Poles, 147 Dutch, 117 French, 34 Austrians, 11 Luxembourgers, and 1 Lithuanian in June 1945. The Russians and Mongolians YMCA representative Edouard Patte mentioned in his report of his visit in November 1944 had been transferred to other camps or repatriated to their fate at the hands of the Soviet government.[29] The reason all of these non-German nationals were held in a compound apart from their fellow POWs was that "the men asked to be transferred, after having declared themselves to be in accord with their respective national governments (governments in exile). Each nationality group has its own spokesman, whose role is however strictly internal; he fulfills rather the functions of an interpreter. Each nationality group is likewise in constant touch with the representatives of their countries in Washington, who visit them regularly. . . . The Spokesman for this Compound declared that occupants of this Compound were frequently repatriated." The camp commander was reluctant to give a nationality breakdown in June 1945, merely saying that "practically all non-German prisoners except Arabs were transferred."[30]

The story of the odyssey of one of the "Allied" prisoners is worth relating because it is illustrative.[31] Pierre Mertz had lived near Metz. His father was a miner in Merlebach in Alsace-Lorraine. This long-disputed region on the French-German border had bilingual inhabitants who found themselves serving in either the French or German army, depending on the contemporary peace treaty or military occupation. At the outbreak of World War II, Pierre Mertz was a soldier in the French army but was taken prisoner by the Germans on 10 May 1940. He was sent to a prisoner of war camp near Breslau. Six months later he was freed as a German national who was a citizen of a German-occupied area. He was subsequently mobilized into the Wehrmacht on 25 June 1943 and sent to East Prussia, then later to the area near Anzio, Italy. But because people from Lorraine were not fully trusted and the Germans feared they would desert, the men from Lorraine were separated from each other and integrated into "more German" units. Such precautions proved necessary but not adequate. One night while at an advanced listening post, Mertz heard Americans about 100 meters away. He chose not to report this to his officers, and the next morning at about six o'clock, he and his unit were prisoners of the Americans.

Taken to Anzio, Mertz and thirty of his fellow Lorrainers asked to be turned over to the French. Instead, they found themselves on a Liberty ship full of Germans heading for Oran. In a temporary POW camp in Oran, conflicts arose between the Lorrainers and their fellow prisoners; several of Mertz's buddies were beaten up. When that happened, the Americans took these unique prisoners out of the general camp and put them in with the Italian prisoners. Then, like the other German prisoners, the Lorrainers were taken directly to a boat headed for New York. After debarking in New York, Mertz and company were put on a train headed for Chicago and then on to a POW camp in Colorado Springs. Conflicts continued. Loyal Germans controlled the camp and threatened Mertz and his comrades from Lorraine, calling them deserters. After an incident in the kitchen of the camp in which one of the men from Lorraine menaced the German adjutant with a kitchen knife, the Americans put the group from Lorraine in the camp prison. They, not the loyal Germans, were considered to be the troublemakers. When Mertz and his friends protested their treatment and showed their rejection of their Wehrmacht affiliation by burning their German uniforms, the Americans punished them with a restricted diet of bread and water. They were informed by their captors that "the German uniform was considered as American property!"[32]

After about three weeks, the dissident Lorrainers were put on a train to Fort Campbell, Kentucky, supposedly an anti-Nazi camp. All kinds of people were there: Poles, Austrians, and Belgians. The first thing that Mertz and his friends did was to write to the French military mission in Washington. Governmental strings were pulled, and the Alsacians and Lorrainers in the camp were assembled and permitted to volunteer to rejoin the French army. Pierre Mertz's decision to rejoin the French led to his transfer to the special "Allied camp" in Camp Butner, North Carolina.

At that separate camp within the POW enclosures at Camp Butner, Mertz and his fellows were not forced to work, but they could receive $24 a month for working rather than the standard $3 dollars per month if they did not work. Mertz volunteered and enjoyed working as a custodian in an office in which there were about forty female typists. "We had a colonel who had been in the war in France in 1918, he spoke French well and he adopted me and treated me as a son."[33]

According to Mertz, "Every thing that took place in the camp was truly very astonishing."[34] The Germans complained that the "Allied prisoners" did not have their clothing marked with a PW, so the separated prisoners marked their clothing with PWs out of fear. Nevertheless there were clashes. One occurred when some Hollanders accidentally entered the German side of the camp as they were returning from a sports field. After a small riot, the Hollanders decided to retaliate that night, and they crossed the wire to attack the Germans. "For the first time one could see armed Americans enter our camp."[35]

On 15 August 1944, a colonel from the French military mission visited the Allied camp at Camp Butner and urged Mertz and his fellows to sign up with the French army. But he told them that "I can promise nothing, that depends on the good will of the Americans." That goodwill was realized on 9 November when Mertz and the other volunteers were taken to Norfolk, Virginia, where they were visited by the son of General Charles de Gaulle, Philippe de Gaulle, who was in the air force and training in a base in the region. Finally, on 11 November, the volunteers for the French army embarked on a cruiser. Also on the boat was a battalion of marksmen from Martinique and an Alsacian from Mexico. "What surprised and shocked us was that we were continually guarded." That continued until they reached Naples. From there they were sent to Oran. There, in North Africa, members of the French Foreign Legion recruited them. Mertz was sent to the 8th Zouave Regiment at Tlemcen in northwestern Algeria.

Mertz's war did not end in North Africa. His unit fought in Europe in the campaign for Alsace right up to Lindau and the armistice. After demobilization at the end of the war, he returned home to find that his wife and daughter had been killed in an air raid on Metz.[36] Thus concluded one Camp Butner "Allied Camp" inhabitant's odyssey: captured as a French soldier in 1940, serving as a German Panzer grenadier in 1943, and finally serving as a French Zouave in 1944.

In contrast to Compound B (the "Special Compound" or "Allied Compound") at Camp Butner stood Compound C or the 11th Company, the "Nazi camp." That portion of the camp was different from "Compound A or main camp" as well. The differences between the regular camp and the "Nazi" one attracted the attention of Dr. Bubb of the International Committee of the Red Cross when he visited in June 1945. At that time the 11th Company, or "Nazi camp," held 266 German POWs, including ninety-four noncommissioned officers. The C Compound's spokesman was regimental Sgt. Maj. Erwin Herbst, 81G-271224. The "81G" in his POW serial number indicated that Herbst was a German, because of the "G," but also that he had been captured in North Africa, because of the "81."[37] The "Africans" seemed to have risen to leadership here, as in most camps in America. Dr. Bubb described Compound C, the "Nazi camp":

Opened in the course of September 1944, this part of the camp, which had only held 50 prisoners to begin with, has since then seen its total strength constantly on the increase. According to the statements of the Camp Commander, this part of the camp houses those of the prisoners considered to be National Socialists; one encounters likewise among them those undisciplined elements which the detaining power regards with suspicion from the political point of view. The Spokesman denies these statements; in his estimation there have been few prisoners in this camp who are members of the Nazi Party. Most of the men did not know why they were transferred to the 11th company; they request to be readmitted to the main camp.[38]

Fritz Teichmann, the wily Nuremberger, musician, and former Luftwaffe member we encountered earlier, still claims he never really knew why he was transferred to the special section of Camp Butner. However, he did not consider his transfer a real punishment: "We were isolated. No contact to anybody of the other compounds was allowed. The whole atmosphere of the 'ill-famed Komp.11' was so good that nobody ever wanted to be retransferred."[39]

According to Dr. Bubb, "The arrangements and installations of the three parts of the camp do not differ much; the same is true in regard to living conditions and treatment, fortunately identical, owing to the fact that no attention is paid to what part of the camp the men are assigned."[40] Though there had been no motion picture shows in Company 11 for several months because they had been discontinued for disciplinary reasons, there was talk of resuming them when Dr. Bubb visited. The men of the segregated company could take courses and borrow books from the main camp library, and they had even formed an orchestra. Fritz Teichmann, in fact, was in charge of the music for a concert based on the operetta by Johann Strauss, *The Gypsy Baron*, presented by and for the 11th Company.[41]

Differences between the compounds increased with time. Between June 1945 and April 1946, when Guy S. Métraux of the International Committee of the Red Cross visited the POW camp at Camp Butner on the eve of its dissolution, the political differences between and within the camp compounds became more and more visible. The end of the war in Europe both facilitated and provoked political discussions. These discussions emerged naturally between the different elements within the Wehrmacht prisoner population. They were also encouraged by American authorities as part of a reorientation program that was to prepare the prisoners for a productive and participatory life in a defeated, reconstructed, and Allied-controlled postwar Germany. The American reorientation program encouraged political discussions through POW camp newspapers. It was in these newspapers, manipulated by American authorities, that emerging differences within the German POW camps became most evident. This phenomenon is illustrated in the three Camp Butner POW camp newspapers that began to make their appearance in the various compounds in June 1945, the *Lagerfackel* [The Camp Torch], which appeared between June 1945 and March 1946 in the main compound; the *European*, which was published in the nationalities compound between July 1945 and March 1946; and a special "Austrian" newspaper, *Mitteilungsblatt für österreichischen Kriegsgefangenen im Camp Butner* [Information Sheet for Austrian Prisoners of War in Camp Butner], which appeared for several controversial editions in late 1945 and early 1946.[42] The distinctive nature of each of these camp papers and their relationship to the American reorientation program will be the focus of Chapter 8.

# 5

# BRANCH CAMPS

After the establishment of the first "permanent" North Carolina German POW camps at Camp Mackall, Camp Davis, Camp Sutton, Fort Bragg, and Camp Butner in the winter and spring of 1944, thirteen other camps appeared in North Carolina from the summer of 1944 to the spring of 1946. These additional thirteen camps, like their predecessors, were developed to serve the needs of American military installations but also to provide labor for North Carolina agricultural and pulpwood interests. These camps proliferated in waves: a second wave of camps at Wilmington and Williamston in the spring of 1944; a third wave of branch camps of Fort Bragg at New Bern, Scotland Neck, and Seymour Johnson and branch camps of Camp Butner at Ahoskie and Winston-Salem in the summer of 1944; and finally a fourth wave consisting of branch camps of Camp Butner at Hendersonville, Swannanoa, Whiteville, Greensboro, Edenton, and Roanoke Rapids in the summer of 1945. Each camp increased the number of German POWs living and working in the state. Each new camp also increased the number of Tar Heel citizens who experienced the presence of "Nazis" next door. To the surprise of residents on both sides of the barbed-wire POW enclosures, many wartime enemies became lifelong friends.

## Second Wave: Wilmington and Williamston

### Wilmington

The POW camp in Wilmington was a branch camp of several base camps during its existence from the winter of 1944 to March 1946. The work reports from the Wilmington camp read like a tour of the German POW base camps of Georgia and North Carolina. They bear witness to the continuity of work needs—military and civilian—in the Wilmington area and of the army's changing administrative units based on regional labor needs. The Wilmington camp started out as a branch camp of Camp Gordon, Georgia, making its first labor report on 13 June 1944. As the camp system moved into North Carolina, the Wilmington camp was shifted to the control of the newly opened base camp at nearby Camp Davis as of 15 August 1944. By the end of September, the new POW base camp at the much larger military installation at Fort Bragg had taken over as the base camp for Wilmington. Finally, the army's tentativeness regarding the continuing existence of a POW facility at Fort Bragg led the Wilmington camp to be transferred to the administrative control of Camp Butner as of 11 November 1944.[1] It remained under Camp Butner through its last labor report of 31 March 1946.[2]

Arguably, the POW camp at Wilmington, which started out as a branch camp of Camp Gordon, Georgia, was the first "permanent" German POW camp in North Carolina.[3] It should be so counted because the temporary facility for German U-boat men at Fort Bragg in 1942 was closed that year and was not reopened for Germans again until the spring of 1944. The Wilmington camp became the first "permanent" camp because it opened in February 1944 as a branch camp of Camp Gordon and continued as a branch camp of Camp Davis and later Camp Butner until it closed in March 1946.

There were 140 Germans at the work camp in Wilmington in September 1944 when it was visited by Guy Métraux of the International Committee of the Red Cross. They were all enlisted men except for their spokesman, Rudolf Haynk, a noncommissioned officer. The camp was still a branch camp of nearby Camp Davis, which had opened in March. The Wilmington camp was designed as a work camp. Its detainees were divided into teams of ten to twenty men who were employed in dairies, tobacco farms, and at a nearby airfield, Bluethenthal Field. As early as September 1944, some of these men complained to the visiting International Red Cross representative that they are obliged to work nine hours a day when other prisoners in the region worked only eight hours.[4] It was obvious that they assumed that Americans should and would treat them "fairly." This assumption was based upon false premises; the American army and their civilian employers would demand more rather than less labor from German prisoners as their time in America increased.

First labor reports from the Wilmington camp indicated that the work was split between agricultural and forestry work. These reports covered two-week periods; individual prisoners (man-days) were involved in various types of labor during the reporting period of what amounted to two six-day work weeks. There were 1,165 man-days designated as agricultural and 1,522 listed as forestry and logging, all private contract work, according to a 13 June 1944 labor report signed by 2nd Lt. James T. Hayes, the administrative officer of the camp. The number of POWs involved in each activity during the twelve work days of each period was thus about ninety-seven POWs involved in agricultural work and 126 in forestry and logging. Later reports indicated an "emergency detail to harvest peanuts" in Scotland Neck in September 1944. Work details were also sent to the Bluethenthal Airfield, a training site for combat crews and fighter gunners in Wilmington. Private contract work was done for the New Hanover Mutual Exchange in Wilmington, Southern Box and Lumber in Wilmington, and the Whiteville Tobacco Board of Trade. POWs also helped prepare graves at the National Cemetery in Wilmington and worked on mosquito control for the Wilmington Department of Health.[5]

Verner Tobler of the Swiss Legation had several comments about the Wilmington camp after his visit to Camp Butner and its branch camps in December 1944. Prisoners told the Swiss that "the discipline was severe and that some guards had kicked prisoners. Another complaint was that some prisoners placed on bread and water had received only three slices of bread per day in violation of army regulations. Before the Swiss representative left camp, the Commanding officer [Col. Thomas L. Alexander of Camp Butner] had taken steps to lessen the severity of the discipline at Wilmington and indicated that he would look into the matter personally."[6]

If logging and pulpwood harvesting were demanding for the Wilmington POWs and discipline often severe, there were compensations to being in Wilmington. Though originally in a tent camp, the Germans were moved in October 1944 into new and more comfortable lodgings.

Their housing impressed official visitors as "very fine and very comfortable." The prisoners were in two-story sleeping barracks, each floor containing about thirty-five beds. Each sleeping barracks had a shower, a latrine, and a small laundry. One barracks served as a refectory and kitchen and another as a recreation room, chapel, and canteen. Another large building was to be used for administrative offices. Most significantly, perhaps, "all these buildings have central heating and running hot and cold water at all times." It was no wonder that the commander of Camp Davis, who was in charge of the Wilmington camp until it was transferred to Butner's administration, suggested that the Red Cross delegation visit the work detachment of Wilmington. He was very anxious for the International Committee of the Red Cross to see these new barracks. Tobler's report concluded that "this small camp makes a very good impression. The morale of the men is good and as soon as they are moved into the new camp which we have visited they will have quarters providing all modern comforts."[7]

The POWs at the Wilmington camp did not suffer from a lack of recreational opportunities. There was a moving-picture presentation once a week and they had a small popular orchestra of five or six instruments that gave occasional concerts. "As in most of these camps the prisoners like football, handball and faustball [a form of German volleyball] very much. Until they are transferred to a new camp they will go to the town stadium every Sunday afternoon."[8]

When the Wilmington camp was visited again by a representative of the International Committee of the Red Cross, Dr. Werner Bubb, in June 1945, the camp had been a side camp of Camp Butner since 11 November 1944.[9] The housing and food available were again praised. However, there seemed to be new problems facing the commanding officer, 1st Lt. R. H. Hazel, and his executive officer, 2nd Lt. R. E. Isaacson.[10]

Dr. Bubb described the housing in very positive terms. It was "in a former WAC installation (with some added buildings) which originally was a Marine hospital. It has steam heat of its own but city water, lights, and sewage." Likewise, he singled out the food supplies for praise: "This camp had the best food observed under the regulations in force at the time of the visit. It has large gardens of its own with which it supplies fresh vegetables to several other side camps. In addition, it gets many extra soup bones from the nearby airfield where it draws rations and canteen supplies." It must be remembered that in June 1945, German POWs throughout the United States were experiencing a "hunger time." Restrictions in calorie consumption, restrictions in the variety of meats and vegetables available to POWs, and increased work hours and quotas were put in place by an American government smarting under public criticism of "coddled" POWs. Popular revulsion against the discovery of German concentration camps at the end of the war in Europe led to a period of several months in the summer of 1945 when the German POWs in North Carolina and nationally would pay for the crimes of the Nazi government. (Those developments will be the topic of a later chapter that deals with postwar American reactions to the POW programs.)

Despite the relatively better food situation that existed for the Wilmington POWs in the summer of 1945, all was not well in the camp. Of course, there were the standard problems associated with a work camp where 181 POWs were doing airfield maintenance, 128 were doing farm work, 38 were logging, 92 were harvesting pulpwood, 10 were manufacturing fertilizer, 39 were working on the post, and 35 were doing chores within the POW camp on the day of the International Committee of the Red Cross visit. Dr. Bubb found that 17 were sick and 21 were resting when he visited.[11] "Most of the sick and hospitalized cases are said to come from accidents in the woods such as fingers being chopped off. The camp commander attributes this to carelessness on the part of the prisoners since they stay on details permanently and should be experienced. The only death the camp has had occurred in April from a gas gangrene case arising from an injury received in jumping off a truck." Though "no escapes had been made from the camp according to the commanding officer . . . prisoners are the most sullen observed on this trip."[12]

The Wilmington POWs "claim to be and act as though they are treated like criminals." Some of this was due to a combination of postwar malaise and new American work policies. "Some of the low morale is said to arise from the fact that the Service Command recently directed that non-commissioned officers would not work unless they signed certificates of having volunteered to perform other than supervisory work." This was a major change that, at least at Wilmington, led noncommissioned officers who had previously been working as supervisors to suddenly become "a very bad influence on the work details." Unhappy noncom workers made for unhappy other ranks as well.

The Americans seemed to go overboard to punish the Germans. Anyone reluctant to work was seen as malingering. "A strong complaint was made by the International Committee of the Red Cross representative in regard to the disciplinary arrangements of the two men in the guardhouse. . . . One was said by the commanding officer to be an expert malingerer. The German doctor, however, had said that this man has a bad heart and cannot perform heavy labor. The Red Cross representative who is a doctor of medicine examined the man and said that he could not be put on hard labor without endangering his life."[13]

Additional complaints were recorded by J. L. Toohey of the State Department, who accompanied Dr. Bubb and compiled the report. One was that many work details claimed that contractors carried too many men and not enough water on their trucks. The result was that POWs were forced by thirst to drink creek water and become ill. The camp commander, Lieutenant Hazel, on the other hand, said that "the epidemic of dysentery was caused by some spoiled beets which inadvertently had been served." A further complaint was made about "the new work unit of 1½ cords per day being too much in this coastal jungle area. The commanding officer replied that local Negroes cut from 4 to 5 cords per day a piece." In the summer of 1945, angry Americans, victors over a vicious Nazi regime, were in no mood to "coddle" German POWs in America.

## Williamston

The first prisoners to arrive in Williamston were 500 Italians in 1943. Soon, conflicts between northern and southern Italians led to the need to segregate the two groups, and the whole contingent was removed to Camp Butner.[14] The larger camp had room to segregate and/or confine troublemakers; the smaller work camp at Williamston did not. The Italians were a part of a group of 2,897 prisoners who were under the command of Camp Butner and were sent out to temporary tent camps in groups of about 500 to help with local agricultural or forestry projects in 1943. In addition, 500 men were sent to each of the temporary side camps to help with peanut harvests at Tarboro, Windsor, and Scotland Neck in the fall of 1943.[15]

When the German POWs arrived by passenger train at Williamston in the spring of 1944, they came from camps in Tennessee. Warned that these men were from Rommel's Afrika Korps, Williamston locals who watched their arrival were struck by the contrasts between expectations and actuality: rather than rough, hostile enemies, many of the North Carolinians saw young, frail, friendly boys.[16]

The Germans had been brought in to do work, and the Americans found work for them to do: in a local slaughterhouse, in a basket factory, in a fertilizer plant, and in lumber mills. Private contracts were made with the Williamston Package Manufacturing Company, Planters Fertilizer Company and Standard Fertilizer Company, Southern Box and Lumber Company, Farmville-Woodward Lumber Company, Rowland Lumber Company, Moss Planning Mill Company, and the Farmers Peanut and Cotton Company. The POWs also did work for the military at Bluethenthal Field in Wilmington and the naval air station in Edenton. But much of the work was on farms suckering and harvesting tobacco, cutting wood, and ditching or stacking peanuts. During 1944, the Germans at the Williamston camp worked for 181 farmers and harvested 71,245 stacks of peanuts.[17]

Emil Greuter of the Swiss Legation visited the Williamston camp on 27 April 1945 during his tour of Camp Butner and its branch camps. His State Department minder, Louis S. N. Phillipp, who reported on the visit described it as "located in the village of the same name, which lies 43 miles south of Ahoskie." His impressions of the camp were very positive, even though the POWs were still quartered in winterized tents, unlike their more pampered comrades in Wilmington, who lived in centrally heated barracks. The Williamston POWs made the most of their situation and "decorated their tents and planted grass and flowers along the company streets." They also had their own chapel, dispensary, bakery, mess hall, canteen, and recreation hall. "This latter building had been constructed of wood which had been cut, sawed and finished by the work of the prisoners."[18] When they worked for farmers, the POWs would ask for scrub pine trees, which they hauled back and used to construct their buildings. They cut the pine into boards using an old Model A Ford engine and a small saw and proudly constructed their recreation hall, a building of some 110 by 30 feet. They painted murals on its inside walls and built a stage for their theatrical productions.[19]

Good work by the Germans encouraged appreciative farmers to disregard government regulations about not fraternizing with the POWs. They enjoyed fellowship over soft drinks during drink breaks and at least on one occasion a farmer lent a small boat to some prisoners so that they might go fishing. He covered for the Germans by making their guards think that he had accompanied them.[20] The Germans reciprocated by sharing improvised gifts with special American friends. Onward and Verona Robertson of Williamston received and cherished a pair of wooden medallions that a prisoner patterned after the Indian on the Buffalo nickel. Another prisoner gave Mr. Robertson a painting of a desert scene that the German remembered from North Africa. One departing German even gave Robertson a pair of hobnailed boots that he had been wearing when he was captured in North Africa.[21]

When the Williamston side camp was visited on 5 April 1946 by Guy Métraux of the International Committee of the Red Cross, it was already scheduled for deactivation on 15 April. The number of prisoners detained had fallen to 9 noncommissioned officers and 114 privates. They were guarded by a slim American contingent of one officer and thirteen enlisted men. The American camp commander was Capt. Vincent A. Vehar and the German camp spokesman was Obergefreiter [Corporal] Gotthold Horny. Work details were still being undertaken by assigned prisoners: 28 worked on farms, 50 worked in the fertilizer factory, 9 worked in the slaughterhouse, 15 worked on camp overhead, and 8 worked on other details. An average of twenty-five POWs attended the Catholic services that were held on Sundays by a civilian priest. About thirty attended evangelical services conducted by a fellow POW from Camp Butner. "Discipline is very good," wrote Louis S. N. Phillipp of the State Department. However, he complained, "The food averages 3000 calories, which is not sufficient." Promises to improve the calorie count for workers had not yet been instituted.[22]

## Third Wave: Bragg's Branches: New Bern, Scotland Neck, Seymour Johnson

### New Bern

The POW camp at New Bern was one of three North Carolina work camps that opened in the summer of 1944 under the administration of the recently activated base camp at Fort Bragg. The camp at New Bern, along with a temporary one at Scotland Neck and a more permanent branch camp at Seymour Johnson Airfield in Goldsboro, were part of the general expansion of work camps that came to the Tar Heel State in the summer of 1944. The camp at New Bern was activated on 3 August 1944 when an advance detail of fifty POWs arrived. The remainder of their comrades came two days later on 5 August. Under the direction of Capt. Ira C. Ballard, the camp commander, the Germans were engaged almost exclusively in private work contracts. Of course, a small number of them were needed for camp maintenance and supply, mosquito control, and mess duty. As of 11 November 1944, the New Bern camp and the other Fort Bragg branch camps at Seymour Johnson and Wilmington were transferred to the administrative control of Camp Butner, under whose wing they would function through 31 March 1946.[23] By early December 1944, New Bern held 388 POWs.[24] The POWs performed labor for farmers and for the pulpwood industry. A 15 December 1944 labor report noted that "normally farmers will use from 130–150 prisoners per day," but inclement weather had reduced these numbers in early December. During the same two-week period in December, 240 POWs had cut an average of one cord per man per day.[25]

When the camp was visited by Emil Greuter of the Swiss Legation on 27 April 1945, as part of his inspection of Camp Butner and its side camps, Louis S. N. Phillipp of the State Department noted that the camp was located about two miles west of the village of New Bern and about sixty-four miles south of Williamston. "The enclosure is located in a fine grove of pines on the bank of the Neuse River." The prisoners were housed in CCC-type barracks and had mess halls, a recreation hall, a dispensary, and a canteen. Their spokesman was Feldwebel [Sergeant] Schroeder. The visitors noted that the prisoners were working in a fertilizer factory, a sawmill, and a pulpwood-cutting operation.[26] An August 1945 labor report added that at one point thirty-two POWs were put to work at the United States National Cemetery in New Bern.[27]

When Dr. Bubb of the International Committee of the Red Cross visited the New Bern camp in June 1945, it was commanded by 1st Lt. George S. Middleton. His executive officer was 2nd Lt. Nathan T. Gottlieb. The camp had 307 prisoners. "About thirty percent of the prisoners work on logging projects, twenty percent in saw mills, ten percent meat packing and other food processing, twenty percent farming, three percent in the fertilizer works, seven percent in scattered miscellaneous industrial plants, and ten percent overhead." Rations were drawn from the Seymour Johnson Air Base and seemed to the visitors to be, like those at the POW camp at Seymour Johnson itself, "more adequate" than at most branch camps. So too were the canteen supplies that came from both Seymour Johnson and from Camp Butner. On the other hand, maintenance work for the camp was arranged through Fort Bragg and was "very slow because of the distance there." Discipline and morale were reported as being good. J. L. Toohey, the State Department representative who accompanied Dr. Bubb reported that "there was one escape in April. The man was known to be a psycho-neurotic and wandered away into a very dense coastal jungle in which his body cannot be found because of the dense growth."[28] Paul Schmidt's remains were found in a swampy area near New Bern more than two years later, on 27 November 1946.[29]

The New Bern camp was still functioning as a branch camp of Camp Butner in April 1946. At that time there were only six Butner branch camps. Though the war in Europe had ended nearly a year before, the continuing need for POW labor meant that branch camps of Butner at Roanoke Rapids, Williamston, Ahoskie, Moore General Hospital, Wilmington, and New Bern remained open. The American camp commander at New Bern was Capt. George S. Middleton and Sieghert Mascher was the German acting camp spokesman for a camp that had only 106 men: twenty-two noncommissioned officers and eighty-four privates. Louis Phillipp of the State Department accompanied Guy Métraux of the International Committee of the Red Cross on a visit on 5 April 1946. Phillipp noted there were a large number of Austrians in the camp. But work, not nationality, was the key for the U.S. government. The division of labor included: pulpwood 25 men; overhead 11 men; slaughterhouse 15 men; and farming 40 men. Other POWs remained idle because of the U.S. military authorities' controversy over a contract with one of the private employers of POW labor.

Food rations were obtained from Seymour-Johnson Field. They were reported to be "good and sufficient, and average about 3700 calories at a cost of 50–55 cents per man." The POWs' hunger for spiritual comfort was also cared for. Catholic services were held on Sundays by a civilian priest, with about thirty in attendance. Evangelical services were conducted by a POW stationed at New Bern, who also serviced four other camps. The average Protestant attendance was only fifteen POWs. "This is a fine camp and everything appears to be in order," the State Department visitor concluded.[30]

## Scotland Neck

The temporary branch camp of Fort Bragg, and later of Camp Butner, was set up at Scotland Neck to provide help in the peanut harvests. It went through two brief and distinct periods of existence: 30 September 1944 to 19 October 1944 and again 30 September 1945 to 10 November 1945. In the fall of 1944, about 500 German POWs were detailed to assist with the peanut harvest under the wary eye of 1st Lt. Albert H. Rich. One of this officer's first hurdles was to deal with the refusal of some Germans to work. The reason they refused is not clear from the army labor records. But in September a total of 91 man-days were lost because these POWs were confined to the guardhouse for their refusal to work. Privates were not the only troublemakers for Lieutenant Rich. Twenty man-days were lost due to a noncommissioned officer's refusal to work on 20 September. By 17 October 1944, POW contracts had been terminated, and the camp was seasonally deactivated on 19 October. At that time 400 men were transferred from Scotland Neck to Wilmington and New Bern. A further 100 were transferred from Scotland Neck to Fort Bragg on 19 October, while 99 more worked with the post engineer at Scotland Neck to tear down the camp.[31]

A temporary branch camp at Scotland Neck was set up again in October 1945 under 1st Lt. Harry L. Burchill to provide workers for the annual peanut harvest. The prisoners were used principally to shake and stack peanuts on contract work. The last labor report was filed on

10 November 1945, and no German POWs were assigned to the camp as of 11 November 1945.

## Seymour Johnson

The POW camp located at Seymour Johnson Field in Goldsboro was set up as a branch camp of the larger camp at Fort Bragg and began sending in labor reports in mid-October 1944. It was under the command of Capt. Henry D. Lee.[32] Within a month, in November 1944, the continuing labor reports listed Camp Butner as the base camp. The camp was officially transferred to Camp Butner from Fort Bragg as of 11 November.[33] In December 1944 there were 421 German POWs at the camp.[34] Camp Butner would continue as its base camp through the last labor reports in mid-March 1946. 1st Lt. F. F. Becker II, later Captain Becker, would be the commanding officer for the remaining existence of the camp.[35]

A State Department report that came out of a 9 June 1945 visit by an International Committee of the Red Cross delegate noted that this side camp of Camp Butner was located on Seymour Johnson Air Field and that its buildings and utilities were part of the air base. While there were many unused barracks in the POW area that could have been used to house more than the 382 prisoners located there, the air post would not allow any more POWs unless they were used on the air base. "Relations between the two installations [Seymour Johnson Air Field and the POW camp] seem to be somewhat tense because of conflicting directives from the two separate channels," the State Department representative noted. Under the command of 1st Lieutenant Becker and his executive officer, Warrant Officer J. F. Buffaloe, a guard company of forty-four American enlisted men and three medical corpsmen supervised the prisoners. The prisoners worked chiefly around the post. Some 243 of the 382 prisoners worked in the laundry, repair shops, butcher shop, and messes of the post; 31 were carried as stockade overhead; and an additional 104 worked for local paper companies.

As at numerous POW camps throughout the nation in the summer of 1945, menu restrictions and calorie cutbacks were something that International Committee of the Red Cross visitors looked for and came to expect. Happily, the POWs at Seymour Johnson Field were relatively fortunate in that regard. "Although the same menu is used as at Butner and throughout the 4th Service Command, the diet seems to be better than in the base camp." Perhaps the Army Air Corps supply personnel at Seymour Johnson Field were more generous in the amount of food they allowed. Otherwise it is difficult to say why using the same menu there could be much variation among the camps. Though discipline among the POWs seemed lax to the International Committee of the Red Cross visitors, German morale was good and the POWs were well satisfied with their diet.[36] Perhaps diet was the key.

The last labor report from the POW camp at Seymour Johnson Field was dated 15 March 1946. It noted, "This camp deactivated 15 March 1946. Employment of Prisoners of War ceased 13 March 1946." The report was signed "F. F. Becker, Capt. CMP."[37]

## Butner's Branches: Ahoskie and Winston-Salem

### Ahoskie

The POW branch camp of Camp Butner at Ahoskie was activated on 26 August 1944. Its first labor report was from the period 26–31 August. It was signed by 2nd Lt. James L. Nipper, the camp commander.[38] When the Ahoskie camp opened, it held only 226 POWs and was the smallest of the six Butner side camps at the time: Ahoskie had 226, Winston-Salem had 276, New Bern had 383, Seymour Johnson had 421, Williamston had 451, and Wilmington had 494.[39] Housing facilities at Ahoskie, as at Williamston, consisted of winterized tents. The purpose of the camp was chiefly to supply labor for the nearby lumber, pulpwood, and peanut industries, and the camp had contracts with firms like J. F. Beam & Sons Lumber, Chesapeake Lumber, Harrelsville Lumber, and Morris Lumber; Williams Pulpwood and Johnson Pulpwood; and the Columbian Peanut Company, the Bertie Peanut Company, and the Hertford County Farm Bureau.[40]

1st Lt. Jack H. Hagerty was the commanding office at Ahoskie in April 1945.[41] When Emil Greuter of the Swiss Legation visited the Ahoskie camp on 26 April, his State Department guide, Louis Phillipp described the camp as "located on the edge of the village of the same name about 130 miles northeast of Camp Butner." The prisoners were still housed in winterized tents, "which the prisoners have decorated and in some cases lined with wallboard." Phillipp, noted that the prisoners had a large recreation tent (20 × 50) that had a piano and a pool table. They also enjoyed a small athletic field. Tents for showers and latrines had a cement floor and automatic flush toilets. The camp also had a "well stocked canteen tent."[42] The report was obviously submitted before the diet restrictions of the summer of 1945 and the accompanying restrictions on items available at POW canteens.

An inspection report of Camp Butner and its branch camps between 17 and 23 October 1945 indicated that there were fifteen branch camps. One of these was Detachment #1, located in Ahoskie. That branch camp had two German officers, eight noncommissioned officers and 374 German enlisted men. They were guarded by one American officer and twenty-nine enlisted men. Though farm contracts at the Ahoskie branch camp stated that fourteen hours was the normal work day, POWs were working only eight to nine hours.[43] The extended hours were a product of the American reactions to revelations about the existence of the concentration camps in the spring and summer of 1945. By the fall of 1945 most of the earlier restrictions had been reconsidered and retracted. Pragmatic concern for POW welfare began to come into conflict with private contracts that had been signed based on earlier interest in getting the most out of America's "guilty" captives.

When visited by the International Committee of the Red Cross on 4 April 1946, 1st Lt. James L. Nipper was the camp commander. The German spokesman for the 110 prisoners (one noncommissioned officer and 109 privates) was Obergefreiter [Corporal] Ferdinand Hain. The International Committee of the Red Cross delegate considered the installation "a very good camp." He was still concerned, however, that the food was insufficient. A promise of better rations was made to him. It is not known whether appropriate changes were made before the camp closed. The Red Cross representative was told that the camp was to close about 1 June 1946.[44] It should be remembered that the war in Europe had been over for more than a year and the war with Japan had been over for nine months. The American government had seen the need to end America's dependence on POW labor and return that labor to a Germany that needed its own rehabilitation. By July 1946 the last large numbers of German POWs were leaving American shores. Some of those in the North Carolina branch camps, like the one at Ahoskie, were among the last to return to Europe.

## Winston-Salem

On 24 October 1944, 210 POWs were transferred from Camp Butner to a new compound in Winston-Salem. An additional twenty-four arrived on 26 October. The first labor report from the new camp, submitted 31 October 1944 by 1st Lt. A. A. Wilson, the commanding officer, indicated that most of the labor was in private contract agricultural work.[45] This allocation of labor would hold true in April 1945. A Swiss Legation visit to Camp Butner and its branch camps indicated that of the 273 POWs at the camp, 211 were working for private companies and of these 129 were involved in agriculture, 52 in pulpwood and logging, and 30 in the chemical industry.[46] A large number of the first contingent of Germans at the Winston-Salem camp worked at R. J. Reynolds Tobacco Company. This first group, made up of young enlisted men, went to work at #2 Leaf House at the beginning of the Burley tobacco season in 1944.[47]

In December 1944, the branch camp of Camp Butner at Winston-Salem held 276 Germans. Verner Tobler, who visited Camp Butner at that time, commented favorably on the overall administration of the Camp Butner POW system and its commanding officer, Colonel Alexander, but registered some concerns about the side camps at Wilmington and Winston-Salem. His concern regarding Winston-Salem was that "barracks accommodations . . . were alleged to be rather poor with 40 prisoners being held in a basement. Three prisoners at this camp had gone on strike because of allegedly unhealthful conditions and one prisoner had been struck by a guard. The Commanding Officer [at Camp Butner] said that he would investigate this charge."[48] A labor report of 10 December indicates that the camp commander transferred thirty-two POWs back to Camp Butner. Though no specifics were mentioned, the report also stated that thirty-nine man-days of labor had been lost because of disciplinary action.[49] The branch camp officer had no time, men, or space for uncooperative prisoners. They were returned to the base camp that had the manpower and space to deal with such people.

When visited by the International Committee of the Red Cross in June 1945, the Winston-Salem camp was still located in the old National Guard armory at the edge of the Winston-Salem business district on Patterson Avenue.[50] Alterations from its former usage were minimal. The Red Cross visitors found the POW installation "an excellent camp in spite of the present overcrowding." The American commanding officer was still Lt. A. A. Wilson, assisted by his executive officer, Lt. L. W. Schloss. At the time there were 266 POWs, including one German medical officer. The forty-eight members of the American enlisted men of the guard detail supervised twenty-one POWs who did camp overhead work, 155 who worked in farming details, 50 who worked in pulpwood harvesting, and 25 who performed air base maintenance at Greensboro. Their supplies and rations were drawn from the Greensboro Air Field. POW camp maintenance was done by both Camp Butner and the Greensboro Air Field. Plans called for the airfield administration to construct new buildings for a company of 400 POWs that would be assigned during July.[51] The new men would all be officers and they would radically change the complexion of the Winston-Salem branch camp.

An October 1945 inspection report indicates that there were 371 officers, one noncommissioned officer and 253 enlisted men at the Winston-Salem camp. They were guarded by two American officers and fifty American enlisted men.[52] The reason for the large number of German officers at the camp in the late summer and fall of 1945 was that on 4 August 1945, 375 German officers were transferred from Camp Como, Mississippi, to the Winston-Salem camp.[53] The officers volunteered for labor despite their Geneva Convention exemption. (The convention allowed for the labor of enlisted men, the supervision of such work by noncommissioned officer, and the exemption of all officers from labor.) One of new officer prisoners from Camp Como was Lt. Werner Lobback, a man who later returned to visit North Carolina in May of 2004.[54]

New quarters were built for the increased number of Germans. Shed #112, a metal-sheathed storage building at the corner of Reynolds Boulevard and Indiana Avenue, was converted into quarters. Bunks were installed, as were toilet and kitchen facilities. The area was surrounded by barbed wire.[55] The June 1945 International Committee of the Red

Cross report noted that "the camp has had only one escape, which occurred last year, and the man was promptly recaptured. One man was in the guard house for malingering at the time of the visit. Discipline and morale seemed good."[56] It would become even better with addition of the large number of cooperative officer volunteers.

The Winston-Salem branch camp was deactivated on 26 February 1946.[57] Lieutenant Lobback and his Wehrmacht officer colleagues were sent to Camp Butner, Winston-Salem's base camp, and from there to New York in April for shipment back to Europe. The Winston-Salem branch, like many of the branch camps devoted to labor in the American civilian economy, was among the last to be phased out of existence.

## Fourth Wave in the Summer of 1945: Hendersonville, Swannanoa, Whiteville, Greensboro, Edenton, and Roanoke Rapids

### Hendersonville

The POW camp at Hendersonville was a seasonal agricultural camp and had two relatively brief periods of existence: July to September 1944 and again July into October 1945.

The first incarnation of the camp was as a temporary branch camp of Camp Forrest, Tennessee. The camp was activated on 4 July 1944, but immediately there were problems. One was rain. The other was that one of the German leaders, Master Sgt. Alfred Fehrens, 4W-20052, was cited as the "direct cause of one hundred P.S. [prisoners] not working on Monday 9 July 1944." Capt. Willie C. Boyce, the camp commander, requested that the trouble-making master sergeant be removed from the work camp and shipped to the large base camp at Camp Forrest in Tennessee.[58] Apparently no other major difficulties were encountered during the remaining harvest days. The camp's agricultural work was finally completed and the camp was broken up by its 263 POWs on 20 and 21 September 1944. The Germans were then moved to another camp in Oneonta, Alabama.[59]

The second appearance of a POW camp in Hendersonville came as part of the fourth wave of camps in the Tar Heel State in the summer of 1945. The war in Europe was over, but the war with Japan continued and American labor shortages continued, too. POWs were still seen as a partial solution to the problem. Temporary branch camps were a phenomenon as the American government sought to deal with seasonal agricultural labor shortages. The seasonal Hendersonville branch camp was to be a temporary one; it existed from 15 July to 12 October 1945. This time the camp was under the administration of Camp Butner. Its commanding officer was 1st Lt. James L. Nipper.[60] When their labor was completed, his POW charges were sent to other camps.

## Swannanoa

The POW camp at Moore General Hospital in Swannanoa was opened as a branch camp of Camp Butner on 16 May 1945.[61] During its year of existence it provided labor for the military service command in and around the hospital. It functioned as Field Company 10 under the administration of Camp Butner from the end of May 1945 until 15 April 1946. In the last two weeks of its existence it was under the administration of the POW camp at Fort Jackson, South Carolina, as Company 28. Through the 15 October 1945 labor report, the commander of the camp was Capt. Vincent A. Vehar. The labor reports for 15 November 1945 through 15 February 1946 were signed by 1st Lt. Nathan T. Gottlieb. Finally, from 28 February 1946–30 April 1946 labor reports were signed by 1st Lt. James T. Hayes.[62]

The camp was visited on 7 April 1946, in the waning days of its existence, by Guy S. Métraux of the International Committee of the Red Cross. No previous YMCA or International Committee of the Red Cross visit had taken place. The camp was described as "located in the grounds of Moore General Hospital near the village of Swannanoa, North Carolina, about 13 miles east of Asheville . . . on Highway 70. The camp buildings are former CCC barracks. The capacity of the camp is 250 prisoners of war." However, as of 7 April 1946 there were only 109 men: thirty noncommissioned officers and seventy-nine privates. The Germans slept twenty-seven or twenty-eight men in each barracks. They were guarded by an army contingent of only one officer and six enlisted men. The war in Europe had ended, POW escapes in America had proven to be limited, and seven American soldiers seemed enough to guard the 109 Germans who were chiefly waiting patiently to be returned to their homes. "The camp commander reported that discipline is 'excellent' . . . [and] the guardhouse is used as a ping pong room. No collective punishments were reported."[63]

The camp spokesman, Unterofficer [Corporal] Heinrich Bopp, "reported the food to be 'very good.'" Rations, clothing, and canteen supplies were received from Moore General Hospital. The prisoners worked for the post engineer and for the post quartermaster and in the hospital messes and wards (chiefly tuberculosis wards). "Protective clothing and devices are furnished prisoners of war and civilian employees in the TB wards. The work varies from 8–12 hours daily, but not over 72 hours per week in messes or 60 hours per week in wards."

Recreational facilities were available for outdoor sports such as faustball, tennis, and soccer, while indoor recreation included ping-pong and chess. Movies were shown two or three times weekly. There was a radio in one of the barracks, and records were exchanged with Camp Butner. Study courses had been disrupted by prisoner transfers in preparation for return to Europe. Nevertheless two English courses continued as well as a discussion group.

Part of the reorientation program included government support for the Germans' religious activities. Americans still believed that the Germans who prayed together would be likely to be good postwar citizens together. The International Committee of the Red Cross and YMCA visitors supported the spiritual growth of the prisoners for somewhat more altruistic reasons. Their reports always mention the religious activities of the camps they visited. The International Committee of the Red Cross report of the visit to the Swannanoa camp mentioned that a local German-speaking evangelical minister preached to about fifteen POWs every Sunday and an army chaplain held Catholic services that were attended by an average of 20–25 prisoners. The State Department visitor, who wrote up his observations of the visit and those of the visiting International Committee of the Red Cross representative, noted that the camp had a "predominantly Catholic group (Austrians and S[outh] Germans)." He also concluded that "the general impression of the IRC Delegate was that the morale is good, discipline good, and the camp very satisfactory."[64] Like the other work camps in North Carolina and throughout the United States, the one at Swannanoa was set to close in the waning days of April 1946.

## Whiteville

The branch camp of Camp Butner at Whiteville, Detachment #9, had a relatively short existence. It opened on 12 May 1945. Judging from its labor reports of November 1945, which were signed by 1st Lt. James T. Hayes, most of its men were involved in private contract work with the pulpwood and lumber industry.[65] An 11 June 1945 visit by Dr. Bubb of the International Committee of the Red Cross and Mr. J. L. Toohey of the State Department furnishes a few more details. There were 235 POWs in the camp. The American commanding officer was 1st Lt. J. T. Hayes and his executive officer was 2nd Lt. J. G. Murray. Of the working Germans they guarded, sixty-nine worked on pulp contracts and 123 in logging. In addition fourteen prisoners served as camp overhead.[66] Initially expected quotas in pulpwood production were not met. A labor report for the end of May 1945 noted that in the previous two weeks only 0.55 cords of pulpwood were cut per assigned man each workday. The hope was that at least one cord would be cut per man. The reporting officer felt it necessary to explain that the hoped-for quotas were not met because the POWs were still involved in a 30-day schooling process.[67] The "schooling" must have worked. At the end of August 1945, Lieutenant Murray reported that the average cords cut had risen to 1.257 cords cut per man.[68]

Though the Whiteville camp was a side camp of Camp Butner, Fort Bragg furnished the canteen supplies, food, and engineering maintenance. Electricity and water came from the town of Whiteville. But none of that helped the already-unhealthy German soldiers, many of whom were sick. A State Department visitor on 14 June 1945 noted that "the average so far has been five per day on quarters and 2 per day in the regional hospital at Fort Bragg. Most of the hospital cases have been either malaria or appendicitis. These prisoners have been in America only about two months and seem to have considerable trouble with recurrent malaria."[69]

During September 1945, POWs at the Whiteville camp supplemented its pulpwood work with work in the peanut harvest. On 30 September 1945, 1st Lt. James T. Hayes, the camp commander, reported that the pulpwood average was 1.250 cords per man and that prisoners who worked in the peanut harvest "have maintained the quota of 25 stacks [per man-day] after [a] two day training period."[70]

The last labor report from the Whiteville POW detachment was dated 30 November 1945.[71]

## Greensboro

The POW camp at Greensboro was activated as Detachment #14 of Camp Butner in August 1945 and existed into mid-March 1946. The war in Europe had been over since May 1945. Throughout the existence of the new camp, its labor reports were signed by 1st Lt. Charles M. Pace, commanding officer. The work of the POWs centered on the activities of the Army Air Force base at Greensboro. A March 1946 labor report noted that in the prior two weeks, 1,966 man-days involved work for the Army Air Force. In comparison, 336 days were spent on POW camp maintenance. Later, things changed slightly: one-third of the POWs were involved in contract work that was equally divided between agricultural work and work in a fertilizer plant—a March 1946 two-week labor report shows that 489 man-days were spent on contract work in agriculture and 412 man-days were devoted to contracts with the fertilizer industry.[72] It was ultimately the work in American agriculture that kept the German POWs employed the longest, and it was with reluctance that American farmers saw the return of these laborers to Europe in the spring of 1946.

## Edenton

The POW branch camp at Edenton was created to supply labor for the naval air station at Edenton. It also provided local farmers with agricultural assistance. Labor reports were generated by the camp from 15 August 1945 to 15 March 1946. The American commanding officer who certified the labor reports was 1st Lt. Joseph B. Borel. An indication of the allocation of the POW labor can be found in the fact that the two-week labor report of 15 March 1945 indicated that labor was divided between POW camp overhead work and work for the navy: 96 man-days for POW camp overhead and 841 man-days for the navy. In this last report Lieutenant Borel also noted that "this is the last report to be submitted from this Camp—Camp inactivated 15 March 1946."[73]

## Roanoke Rapids

The Roanoke Rapids camp was founded as Detachment #12 of the base camp of Camp Butner on 4 August 1945. Its purpose, like the purpose of the Whiteville camp, which was established in May, was to serve the interests of the American logging and pulpwood industries. 1st Lt. Robert S. Leach, the detachment commander, was concerned by the fact that few of his POWs fulfilled their quotas and sought to excuse it in his labor reports by referring to the "inexperience" of his charges and their lack of sufficient tools. In fact, the camp served well enough that it was not inactivated until the end of March 1946.[74]

When it was visited on 3 April 1946 by a delegate of the International Committee of the Red Cross, the facility held 205 POWs: 7 noncommissioned officers and 198 privates. Its German spokesman was Gefreiter [private first class] Erwin Weber. The location of the camp was half a mile southeast of Roanoke Rapids, where the Germans were housed in winterized tents, six men to a tent. There were tents also for offices, a dayroom, latrines, and showers. A wooden building was used as a mess hall. The focus of the camp labor was working in pulpwood and lumbering. "The task required the prisoners to do the following amount of work: Pulpwood—240 cubic feet per man" and "Saw Mill Logs—2000 feet per man." Work groups consisted of twenty-seven to thirty-one men each.[75]

Unterarzt [Dr.] Erwin Strohr, who was not officially recognized by the Americans as a doctor because he had the abilities but not adequate documentation to prove his status to American officials, held daily sick call. Patients requiring hospitalization were taken to Camp Butner. Catholic religious services were held weekly by a civilian priest and Protestant services were conducted by "protected personnel" twice a month. These wearers of the distinguishing "PP" letters stenciled on their POW clothing were credentialed religious or medical men of the German armed forces who were allowed freedom to interact with German and American personnel without normal American military supervision. The International Committee of the Red Cross delegate who visited the camp shortly before it closed said that it was a "very good camp."[76]

This survey of the existence and purposes of the North Carolina branch camps provides some insight into the minimal information that the American government maintained and has preserved regarding these "temporary" work camps. What is most eye-catching is the fact that these North Carolina camps emerged late in the war because of the belated dispersal of America's captives throughout most of the continental United States. The purpose of the North Carolina branch camps, as with all branch camps throughout the United States, was to service the labor needs of American military installations but also to be available to supplement the hard-pressed labor supply for the agriculture and pulpwood industries. Five of the North Carolina branch camps did not come into existence until the summer of 1945. By then the war was over in Europe. American authorities delayed the return of their German captives for two reasons: to limit their potentially negative impact on an already malnourished and politically unstable occupied Germany and to provide labor for American agriculture and the pulpwood industry. In January 1946, President Truman bowed to agricultural interests and announced a 60-day delay in the repatriation of POWs involved in "critical segments of the economy."[77] Major movements of prisoners back to Europe were to have taken place monthly from December 1945 through April 1946. Smaller movements continued, but by the end of May there were still 37,391 German POWs in America. On 23 July 1946, the army announced the departure of the last Germans from America.[78] The camps in North Carolina had closed by the end of April 1946. They had provided the state with many willing but also a number of unwilling workers. Both stories are the subject of the next chapter.

Camp Sutton, Christmas pamphlet, 1945, front cover. Courtesy of Malcom Privette, Gainesville, Florida.

Camp Sutton, Christmas pamphlet, 1945, back cover. Courtesy of Malcom Privette, Gainesville, Florida.

Crew of the *U-352*. Courtesy of the North Carolina Office of Archives and History, Raleigh, North Carolina.

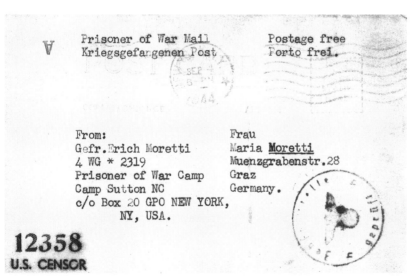

Postcard Erich Moretti sent from Camp Sutton. Courtesy of Erich Moretti.

Erich Moretti (*center*) in group postcard picture from Camp Sutton. Courtesy of Eric Moretti.

Erich Moretti in Graz, Austria, in June 2004. Courtesy of Erich Moretti.

Fritz Teichmann leading a choir in Germany, 1941. Courtesy of Fritz Teichmann.

Matthias Buschheuer, cook at Camp Sutton. Courtesy of Matthias Buschheuer.

Max Reiter as a seventeen-year-old Waffen-SS man. Courtesy of Max Reiter.

Mr. Hunt with wife and daughter. Courtesy of Max Reiter.

Max Reiter (*right*) with a fellow POW at Camp Butner. Courtesy of Max Reiter.

Lt. Werner Lobback as a soldier in the Wehrmacht. Courtesy of Werner Lobback.

Werner Lobback (*left*) with Sion Harrington, during his visit to the North Carolina Office of Archives and History in June 2004. Courtesy of the North Carolina Office of Archives and History, Raleigh, North Carolina.

Picture of landscape painting of Camp Butner POW camp, painted by POW E. Kamler in 1945. Courtesy of North Carolina Museum of History, Raleigh, North Carolina, #2000.71.1.

Picking cotton in Monroe. Courtesy of National Archives, 208-AA-309K-8.

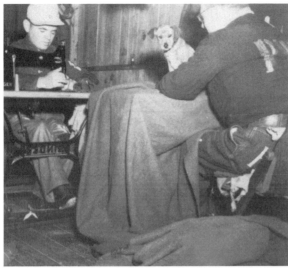

Camp Sutton POWs working in textile repair shop. Courtesy of Edith Long, Indian Trail, North Carolina.

Camp Sutton POWs repairing trucks. Courtesy of Edith Long, Indian Trail, North Carolina.

Camp Sutton POW in the camp's art studio. Courtesy of Edith Long, Indian Trail, North Carolina.

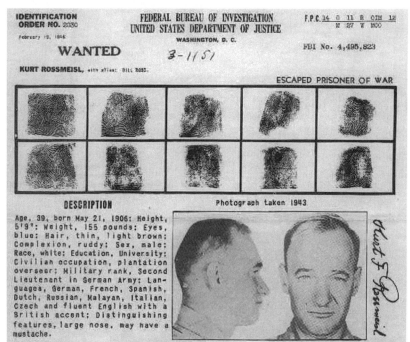

FBI Wanted poster for Kurt Rossmeisl. Courtesy of Robert Billinger.

# 6

# UNCLE SAM'S WILLING AND UNWILLING WORKERS

Uncle Sam needed workers to replace American civilians who were drafted into the armed forces and military maintenance forces that were to be shipped overseas. Another source of manpower had to be tapped to replace servicemen and civilians employed on home front military installations and civilians in the farming, lumbering, and pulpwood industries. By 1943, prisoners of war were an available resource. They were soon replacing American employees on military bases and in the agricultural economy.[1]

The first large groups of POW laborers that American servicemen and farmers encountered in North Carolina and throughout the United States were not Germans but Italians, and the first contingent of POWs at the American military reservation at Camp Butner were 2,897 Italians. They were visited there by delegates of the Swiss Legation on 11 13 October 1943. The Swiss reported that the camp administration had provided as much work as possible not only to keep the POWs busy but also because of local agricultural labor shortages. At the time of the visit, the Italians were engaged in some seventy work projects, which included building roads, conserving soil, clearing land, and farming. Contingents of 500 men each were quartered in tent camps in Tarboro, Windsor, and Scotland Neck. The prisoners in each of these camps were engaged in the seasonal agricultural work of picking the peanut crop. Plans were under way to utilize a Civilian Conservation Corps camp for another contingent of prisoners that was to be assigned to pulpwood cutting.[2]

One reason for the proliferation of POW camps throughout the United States during World War II was the increasing number of POWs who needed lodging far from North African and European battle-grounds. A second reason was the overstressed economies of Britain and her dominions. They needed prisoners in their hands to be sent to the less-stressed United States. A third reason was America's need for wartime laborers.

In North Carolina, as in most of the forty-six states that held Italian or German POWs during World War II, the work of POWs was primarily done on American military reservations. An Army Service Forces directive of 14 August 1943 specified three work priorities for POWs. First was "essential work for the maintenance and operation of military installations." Second was contract labor certified as necessary by the War Manpower Commission or War Foods Administration for private employers. The third priority was "useful but nonessential work on or connected to military reservations."[3] The jobs performed by the POWs were standard American military camp maintenance: carpentry, electrical work, plumbing, dining hall services, and garbage collection. The original POW camps were within large American military reservations, such as those at Camp Mackall, Camp Davis, Camp Sutton, Fort Bragg, and Camp Butner. There were jobs to be done in these locations, security was high, and contact with the American public was minimal. As the war progressed, the combination of labor shortages in the agricultural and forestry sectors and the low number of POW escape attempts encouraged American administrators to take the calculated risk necessary to set up branch camps throughout the United States. These new camps proliferated everywhere that military bases or the civilian agricultural and pulpwood industries had labor shortages. North Carolina was one of the new areas where POW branch camps proliferated in the winter and spring of 1944.

Some idea of the relationship between the desire of agricultural interests for labor and the expansion of the POW camp system appears in Table 6.1. The statistics were sent on 3 August 1944 to farm labor officers in the peanut-growing states of the Fourth Service Command by Capt. Richard E. Smith, the assistant chief of the Labor Branch of the Fourth Service Command. Smith wrote that the chart was distributed "in order to keep the records straight and to promote good-will among the Extension Offices of all the states concerned."[4]

Table 6.1. Camps with POWs Available for Peanut Harvest in Southeastern United States, August 1944, by State

| State | Number of Camps | Number of POWs | Acres in peanuts | POWs per Acre |
|---|---|---|---|---|
| Alabama | 8 | 2,225 | 500,000 | 1/266 |
| Florida | 1 | 300 | 55,000 | 1/183 |
| Georgia | 15 | 4,700 | 1,450,000 | 1/309 |
| South Carolina | 4 | 1,000 | 60,000 | 1/60 |
| North Carolina | 3 | 1,500 | 230,000 | 1/166 |

"Notes: Column three, the number of POWs is the total number in the camps and not all available for peanut harvest. Regulations state 10% will be held for administrative and overhead within the POW compound . . . thus variations from chart. This chart is drawn up for the *peanut harvest* only."
*Source of chart numbers and "notes" above*: Capt. Richard E. Smith, Asst. Chief, Labor Branch, Fourth Service Command, to all farm labor officers in the peanut-growing states, 3 August 1944, RG 389, Entry 467C, Box 1574.

Additional insights about the labor needs on military reservations and within the civilian economy of North Carolina can be gathered by consulting POW labor statistics for Camp Butner and its side camps in February of 1945. Although the following tables are merely a snapshot in time of a labor supply whose allocation and numbers were seasonal, they give an indication of the kind of labor needs in North Carolina that were supplied by individual POW camps. What is obvious from the charts is the very high proportion of prisoners used within military installations and their auxiliary enterprises within North Carolina, especially at Camp Butner, Seymour Johnson Air Field, Camp Davis Air Field, and the Camp Sutton engineer training facility in Monroe. One also notes the large number of POWs employed by privately owned companies engaged in pulpwood and logging. The American pulpwood industry was particularly hard hit by labor shortages during the war. Supplying POW labor for that industry became a high priority for the War Labor Board. By 1945, "one-third of all pulpwood in the South and in Appalachia was cut by POWs. The pulpwood and lumber industries used a total of 165,743 man/months of POW labor from June 1944 to August 1945, and yet the lumbermen apparently had difficulty obtaining as many prisoners as they wanted from the government."[5] Note

Table 6.2. Work, Kind and Number of Men Engaged [at Camp Butner and Butner Branch Camps, April 1945]

| Camp | POWs Working on Camp Overhead | Post Details | POWs Working for Private Companies | Total POWs Working | Total POWs |
|---|---|---|---|---|---|
| Butner (base camp) | 238 | 1,342* | 419 | 1,999 | 2,696 |
| Ahoskie | 21 | 14 | 167 | 202 | 210 |
| Winston-Salem | 26 | 25 | 211 | 262 | 273 |
| Seymour Johnson | 32 | 189 | 96 | 317 | 342 |
| New Bern | 33 | 27 | 223 | 283 | 310 |
| Wilmington | 44 | 124 | 279 | 447 | 532 |
| Williamston | 36 | 39 | 289 | 364 | 395 |
| Davis | 47 | 464 | 26 | 537 | 562 |
| Monroe (Camp Sutton) | 27 | 207 | 22 | 256 | 274 |

*One hundred and seventy-six prisoners working in the general hospital and 294 in the convalescent hospitals in Camp Butner.

*Source:* Louis S. N. Phillip, Report of visit by Emil Greuter of the Legation of Switzerland and Louis S. N. Phillipp, Department of State, to the prisoner of war camp at Camp Butner, North Carolina, 26–27 April 1945, RG 59, Entry 1353, Lot 58D7, Box 23.

Table 6.3 Types of Work Performed for Privately Owned Companies by POWs at Camp Butner and Side Camps, April 1945

| Camp | Pulpwood Logging | Chemical Industry | Agriculture | Food Processing Industry | Other |
|---|---|---|---|---|---|
| Butner (base camp) | 218 | 33 | 50 | 8 | 110[a] |
| Ahoskie | 127 | — | 4 | 21 | 15 |
| Winston-Salem | 52 | 30 | 129 | — | — |
| Seymour-Johnson | 37 | 24 | — | — | 35 |
| New Bern | 121 | — | 7 | 20 | 75 |
| Wilmington | 55 | 149 | 75 | — | — |
| Williamston | 106 | 118 | — | 8 | 57[b] |
| Davis | 26 | — | — | — | — |
| Monroe (Camp Sutton) | 22 | — | — | — | — |

[a]One hundred and ten prisoners employed as mess attendants at Duke University and the University of North Carolina (Chapel Hill).
[b]Forty prisoners working for the navy.

*Source:* "Work, Kind and Number of Men Engaged," Report by Louis Phillipp of visit by Emil Greuter of the Legation of Switzerland and Louis S. N. Phillipp, Department of State, to the prisoner of war camp at Camp Butner, North Carolina, 26–27 April 1945, RG 59, Entry 1353, Lot 58D7, Box 23.

especially the high proportions of POWs at New Bern, Wilmington, and Monroe involved in these industries. Note, too, that the needs of the chemical industry, primarily fertilizer plants, were obvious at both Wilmington and Williamston.

German POWs did not always receive involuntary labor forced upon them by a foreign enemy well. While many Americans remember smiling and efficient German POW workers, there is also sufficient evidence to suggest that there were problems to be confronted as well. A report of an early December 1944 visit by a member of the Swiss Legation to Camp Butner noted that "some difficulty has been experienced in getting the prisoners to work. The Camp Commander, however, by a firm policy, segregation of trouble makers, and a careful selection of prisoners on the basis of their qualifications has now achieved a high degree of efficiency."[6]

One former German POW stationed in Winston-Salem remembers that he and a number of his fellows worked at the Winston cigarette plant on machines, bringing in the tobacco, and piling up boxes. "It was rather strenuous, but one was well-treated."[7] Another German who worked at Winston-Salem remembered the working conditions at the cigarette plant. He noted that the Germans worked along with blacks on an assembly line. "With a 'typically German reflex' the POWs wanted to do better than the Blacks so they set off 'like horses at a race.' . . . Working on an assembly line for the first time was amusing with its foolish cadences." After five days of doing the same movement for ten hours a day, the Germans were completely exhausted. They all went to see their camp commander to request other work.[8]

In late June 1944, Dr. R.W. Roth of the Swiss legation visited the Camp Butner's side camp at Williamston. His State Department minders noted that the Germans had complained about being required to work at a fertilizer plan. On the day of the visit, no German POWs were employed in the fertilizer plant. Since the season was slack at that time anyway, the POWs were taken out on the day they complained in writing. American authorities decided to see what the visiting Swiss representative thought. After inspecting the plant, the Swiss visitor concluded that considerable dust came from the mixing of the elements required to make fertilizer. However, he felt that if the POWs were given protective masks when they were working in the mixing and unloading, the job might not be considered injurious to their health.[9]

Of course, the willingness of the German POWs to work and the degree of satisfaction they found in it was directly proportionate to the kinds of work required. Work in a fertilizer plant, like the rigorous and often-dangerous work of logging and timbering in the forests of North Carolina, was less popular than work on the military posts in kitchens, canteens, and repair shops. An inspector of the Camp Sutton POW camp in July 1944 noted: "A rotation system has been established between the groups working in the camp and those working in the woods because the latter have a more arduous work."[10]

Work in the piney woods was indeed arduous and could be dangerous. Certainly some POWs considered it so. A July 1945 article in *Der Aufbruch*, a Fort Bragg POW newspaper, claimed that

> when we Germans hear the word "Forest" we think of the beauty of our homeland. . . . This is a forest of a different color. A thicket of thorns blocks the way to the trees. You have to hack your way in just to get to the trees. The thorns cut your hands. You're in a hurry since there's a lot of wood in a cord. When you fell the tree it doesn't always fall as you had hoped. You hack and saw . . . the saw sticks. You put in a wedge . . . you oil the saw but these ameliorate the work only for the shortest time.[11]

From a Red Cross report on a June 1945 visit to the POW camp in Wilmington came word of similar complaints:

> 200 POWs are detailed to pulpwood felling and cutting. . . . As in other camps the quota is 160 cu. ft. per man per day. The spokesman [for the POWs] complained that increasingly they can't make the quota because they have to cut their way into the trees before cutting the required wood and because of the well-nigh intolerable heat and humidity.[12]

Forestry work could and did lead to POW deaths. On 8 July 1945, Fort Bragg's *Der Aufbruch* noted the death of Sergeant Willi Schaeffer: "On the 20th of June at 3:00 P.M. an accident took place which proved fatal. Sergeant Willi Schaeffer of the 6th company was struck by a falling limb." He was killed instantly, and his funeral was held at the military cemetery at Camp Butner.[13]

American military administrators often tried to increase the productivity of POWs by making concessions to their concerns and interests. A Red Cross visit to Camp Davis in September 1944 revealed that with regard to the POWs employed in the maintenance of the military camp:

> American officers have been very careful to see that the prisoners are employed only in activities which are familiar to them and this line of conduct has produced excellent results. Some prisoners work in the shoe shop; others in the automobile and ambulance repair shop. Others are employed in the officer's club and in the laundry. We have spoken to several prisoners and all not only expressed their satisfaction but also their pleasure in doing the work which was assigned to them.[14]

But despite the efforts of the American POW camp personnel to encourage the Germans to work, labor reports from the North Carolina camps reported a variety of instances when POWs tested the American authorities on the labor issue.

This was especially the case in the spring through the fall of 1944, the early months after the arrival of POWs to North Carolina. The testing took the form of strikes or labor stoppages, which in most cases brought punishments or transfers of the Germans involved. For example, a former Camp Davis POW remembered that there were plans for a strike on Good Friday 1944 because that day was a national holiday in Germany. "The Americans wanted none of that so left us standing in the open for half a day. But when the American administration decided to take away the sports equipment, then the main critics were stilled and since then there were no more strikes. Thus sports were more important than Vaterland!"[15]

When the Germans did not budge, their leaders were transferred to other camps. That was the case in early July 1944, when prisoners at the Hendersonville work camp did not work the required time because of the uncooperative spirit of one of their leaders, Master Sergeant Fehrens. Because he was an obstacle to the American work program, he was transferred from the work camp to the larger base camp at Camp Forrest, Tennessee.[16]

Work stoppages could lead to other punishments. Such was the case at the temporary peanut-harvesting camp at Scotland Neck in late September 1944. A labor report from the camp noted that ninety-one man-days had been lost due to confinement of prisoners in the company guardhouse because of their refusal to work. Twenty more man-days were lost when a noncommissioned officer refused to work on 20 September 1944.[17] Confinement in a guardhouse and reduced rations were also the lot of a group of German POWs from Camp Butner who refused to work at a Durham tobacco plant in late October 1944. Fifteen POWs who refused to work at the Imperial Tobacco Company's night detail in Durham were promptly marched the fifteen miles back to Camp Butner. There, at 3:45 a.m. on 26 October, they were tried and sentenced to fourteen days on bread and water in the compound stockade and sixteen days of hard labor.[18]

Sometimes the "unwilling workers" among the Germans caused problems for reasons that went beyond shirking or the possibility of hindering the American war effort. The conflicts could be personal, racial, or a mixture of both. The conflicts between Jewish-American guards and POWs at Camp Sutton have been mentioned. An apparently cross-racial incident at Camp Butner intrigued contemporaries and has attracted and puzzled historians. A report filed by Lt. Burton Spear, the intelligence officer at Camp Butner, with the commanding general of the Fourth Service Command read as follows:

> As per telephone conservation between Colonel Alexander, Commanding Officer, this Prisoner of War Camp, and Colonel Cockrell, your headquarters, on 29 January, the following report is submitted:
>
> On 10 January 1945 at 1645 during an argument between a Negro civilian who worked on the post and Prisoner of War ROTHKEGEL, Adolf, 81G 225548, the Prisoner was struck and knocked down by the Negro civilian. The civilian's name is JAKE BATTLE, and according to reports from those witnessing the incident, the ill feeling had been brewing for some time. Both prisoner and civilian were employed at the coal yard on the post and have been

working on the same detail for several months. The civilian, JAKE BATTLE, was taken before the U.S. Commissioner at Raleigh, N.C. at 1000, 12 January 1945. The civilian was given a $7.50 fine which was suspended with a promise from the civilian for future good behavior. The Prisoner of War protested the decision of the Commissioner because he stated that if such an incident should occur in Germany, the civilian would be given at least thirty (30) days confinement.

The Negro civilian was considered as the instigator of the trouble and has since been transferred to another place of work. The Prisoner of War was retained on the same detail and to date his work has proven very satisfactory. No complications have arisen from this incident.[19]

The incident was also reported in the local press under the title "Negro Knocks Out Hitler 'Superman.'" The story adds few additional details, but it does present an interesting slant to the incident that is worth considering because of the commonly held view that southerners were more respectful of Aryan Germans than of their African-American countrymen. This story presents a different perspective:

> The Negro, Jake Battle, 50, of Henderson went on trial because he "slapped down" one of Hitler's so-called "supermen" who refused to work under the Negro's supervision.
>
> Battle, who was in charge of a group of German prisoners of war working on the reservation, entered a plea of guilty to hitting Adolph Rothkegel. Battle told Mrs. Garton that he had been ordered to report any German prisoner who refused to work. Rothkegel refused to work, so Battle reported him to the proper authorities.
>
> Still Rothkegel refused to work. He and Battle argued, and Rothkegel, who speaks very little English, cursed Battle—in plain English.
>
> So Battle knocked the German down.
>
> After Mrs. Garton passed judgment in the case, Rothkegel asked the interpreter what had been done with Battle. When informed that Battle had received a suspended fine, Rothkegel told the interpreter to tell Mrs. Garton that "if such a thing had happened

in Germany, the defendant would have gotten 30 days in jail with no questions asked."[20]

The reports of both Lieutenant Spear and the local newspaper are of interest because they suggest by implication the differing attitudes of the military and the local civilian population toward the German POWs. The military report focused on the issue of smooth working relations, even at the expense of disrespect shown by a German to an African American. The local newspaper, however, took the opposite view. Instead of presenting a favorable interpretation of the actions of a white man, albeit an enemy national, the paper presented a sympathetic view of a local civilian, a black. In contrast, the assaulted German is portrayed pejoratively as a "Hitler superman."

Another interesting aspect of this incident is its apparent rarity in the contemporary and historical literature. In the memories of many former German POWs in America as well as in the German historical literature on the subject, the German POWs and their black American fellow workers were friends rather than antagonists. In a recent book by Matthias Reiss, *Die Schwarzen waren unsere Freunde*, the Butner incident is presented as an anomaly. The title is taken from the comments of a former German POW who described the second-class status of both POWs and American blacks and the resulting cooperation and friendships between the two alienated groups: "The blacks were our friends."[21]

Certainly that was the experience of Fritz Teichmann, who traded soap powder with his black fellow workers for the American cash that he hoped would eventually buy him a false American passport and escape.[22] The friendship between German POWs and American blacks was also commented on by a former member of the Hermann Göring Division, who was captured in Tunisia in 1943 and later spent time in Aliceville, Camp Davis, and the POW camp in New Bern. He remembered that every day buses came to the New Bern camp to take German POWs to work at the Chesterfield plant in Greenville. He also remembered that "the Americans were not happy that we made friends with the Blacks, but at the end of the day they were *unsere Schicksalsgenossen* [our companions in fate]."[23]

Similar feelings of goodwill between the Germans and African-American soldiers were experienced and remembered by a prisoner who was held at Fort Bragg after his capture in the Ruhr in the spring of 1945. He remembered that the black soldiers who drove the Germans who collected post garbage showed tolerant and sympathetic smiles when the POWs "rescued" cigarette butts or baking fat from the garbage in order to bring such treats back into the prisoner camp. He noted that "the Black soldiers seemed to have a special empathy for the prisoners from Germany. They seemed to secretly see them as fellow-sufferers." On the other hand, the Germans realized that the racial stereotypes that they brought along from Nazi Germany contrasted with the reality of their experiences with these American blacks. The Germans sometimes gave little souvenir gifts to black soldiers of things they still had from before their capture: German coins, portions of correspondence, a mirror. Such small tokens were much appreciated. "There were never conflicts between the members of these so very different races, and the Germans, who were counted as so impatient by other peoples, became good friends of the Blacks."[24]

German prisoners of war showed their defiance of what they considered "unfair" working conditions or payments in North Carolina during the winter and spring of 1945. These incidents help to explain the late war and early postwar reactions of North Carolinians and other Americans to what was thought to be official "coddling" of the POWs at a time when revelations regarding Nazi concentration camp and POW camp atrocities became public knowledge during the waning days of the European war. One of the problems the American military encountered when handling German POWs was that rather than becoming more docile during their confinement in American camps, the Germans picked up their own ideas about the American "fairness" and "freedoms" and began to assert "their rights." Sometimes that meant work stoppages to get the attention of the Americans. Almost always the attention that was gotten from the American military was negative: it led to the enforcement of discipline, especially work discipline, at the Germans' expense. In a memorandum for the Director of the Prisoner of War Operations Division of the Provost Marshal General's Office, Maj. Howard W. Smith Jr., the chief of the camp operations branch reported a strike at the prisoner of war camp at Camp Butner on 1 February 1945:

> Lt. Spear, Prisoner of War Camp, Camp Butner, North Carolina, reported a short-lived strike at the camp on 1 February 1945. According to Lt. Spear, one prisoner in a special compound for pro-Nazis protested that he had not been paid on schedule and as a result he and 44 other prisoners in the compound refused to go to work after the noon meal on 1 February 1945. The strike spread to the entire work group of 200 prisoners, all of whom refused to get out of their bunks when commanded to report for work. Lt. Spear stated that the two leaders of the group were removed and are being held for court-martial for refusing to obey official orders. Tear gas grenades were thrown into the barracks where the remainder of the 200 men were in bed. They promptly came out and went to work.[25]

Reports of such incidents at prisoner of war camps continued through the spring of 1945. One of five incidents mentioned in a 23 March 1945 report took place when 504 German POWs went on strike at Wilmington to protest the confinement of twenty-six men who "refused to work properly at their job in a fertilizer factory on the night of 21 March 1945. A subsequent report stated that the strike ended on the night of 22 March 1945 after the prisoners had had one day on bread and water."[26] 1st Lt. R. H. Hazel, the commanding officer of the POW camp in Wilmington, listed the names of the POWs who were confined to the camp guardhouse on 23 March 1945 for three hours because of their refusal to work.[27]

Information gathered by the German camp spokesman at Camp Butner in March and April 1945 and sent through 1st Lt. Burton Spear, the intelligence officer at Camp Butner, to the Swiss Legation (with copies to the Office of the Provost Marshal General in Washington) in preparation for a Swiss visit to Camp Butner and its side camps provides insights into the disciplinary actions taken within the POW camp system in the Tar Heel State.[28] Most of the disciplinary actions, like that at the Wilmington camp, related to prisoner insubordination. This was usually related to reluctance to work or intent to avoid it altogether through absence or escape. The American military reaction was administrative punishments that ranged from forfeiture of pay and/or the $3 monthly allowance in camp coupons that was given to even nonworking prisoners to confinement and bread-and-water diets for two weeks. Formal court-martials potentially could bring sentences of confinement and hard labor for multiple years.

Offences that occurred and were punished at Camp Butner and its side camps in March and April 1945 included a court martial at Camp Butner of a German sergeant under Article 64 of the Articles of War.[29] It pertained to insubordination toward a noncommissioned officer. The accused had refused to pass along an order to German prisoners of war under his leadership that they were to get out in the company street. The prisoner's sentence was "to forfeit all pay and allowances due or to become due and to be confined at hard labor at such place as the reviewing authority may direct for ten (10) years."

Lesser punishments doled out during March and April of 1945 within the Butner system included thirty days' confinement to the guardhouse at Camp Butner for a prisoner who absented himself from his assignment without proper authority. In another work-related situation, on 10 April, a prisoner at Williamston was given fifteen days' hard labor without pay for attempting to slow down a work detail. Another was given seven days' hard labor without pay for "falsifying records."

From Winston-Salem came reports of six disciplinary actions during March 1945. Most were cases of refusing to work, loafing, or disobeying orders, and none carried a penalty of more than fourteen days on bread and water and the withholding of about $10 in pay. One of the lesser punishments was the withholding of $3 pay from a prisoner who was described as loafing and bothering others during a night shift at R. J. Reynolds. In one case a prisoner who hid the weight from a scale, presumably in a tobacco plant, was accused by a fellow prisoner and as a result struck that prisoner, "causing contusion of left eye." The punishment was ten days' bread and water and the withholding of $7 of pay.

The Seymour Johnson Field camp reported fifteen disciplinary punishments in March 1945. Most were related to charges of being late for formation and resulted in only a day and a half of confinement and a restricted diet. There were only four cases of refusal to work, which netted the delinquents two days' confinement and restricted diet, and a couple of cases of "misconduct," which resulted in five days' confinement and a restricted diet. The only exception to the limited sentences concerned Pvt. Wilhelm Jendricke. His failed escape attempt on 12 March 1945 led to his transfer to Camp Butner for disciplinary action. For "absenting himself from work detail without permission," Jendricke received thirty days' prison, fourteen days' restricted diet, and "all pay & 2/3 allowance withheld."[30] At Ahoskie, one prisoner was charged with possession of enough American money to affect an escape and another of lying in order to conceal the funds of the first. Both men were put on a 30-day restricted diet and had two-thirds of their monthly allowances withheld.

In April, 1st Lt. Harry L. Burchill, commanding officer at Camp Davis, reported that there had been only one disciplinary punishment during the month of March 1945. For "behavior in a disrespectful and insubordinate manner towards an American Non-Commissioned Officer, who was then in the execution of his office," a sentence of confinement "not to exceed fourteen days on a restricted diet of bread and water" was begun on 10 March 1945. At Camp Sutton in Monroe, only one prisoner received disciplinary punishment in late March and April 1945. He was "confined at hard labor, without pay, for a period of seven (7) days," between 11 April and 18 April 1945. The charge was not specified in the report by the executive officer, Lt. Jack H. Smith.[31]

The report of disciplinary punishments for March 1945 from Camp Butner was exceedingly long compared to the lists from the branch camps. Eighty-five POWs were listed by name for disciplinary action in March 1945. The large number is not surprising, of course. In March 1945, Butner had 2,562 prisoners in its four compounds: Lower Compound, Middle Compound, Company 11, and Special (nationalities) Compound. By comparison, its eight side camps housed a total of 2,925 POWs, but five of those camps had about 300 men each. The largest side camps of Camp Davis and Wilmington had only 562 and 532 POWs, respectively.[32] The severity of the sentences handed out at the Camp Butner camp included up to thirty days of prison with fourteen days of restricted diet and the withholding of all pay and two-thirds of allowances. The offenses that earned such punishment included "refusal to work, insolence & repeated insubordination," "absenting himself from work detail without permission" (in the case of Wilhelm Jendricke, who escaped for ten hours from the Seymour Johnson camp and was returned to Camp Butner for punishment), "refusal to obey a direct order of American Officer," "insubordination and possession of contraband," "threatening another prisoner with knife," and "refusal to mark clothing properly, insolent and insubordination." One German at Camp Butner was engaged in "illegal passing of notes." Another prisoner received five days on a restricted diet because of "drunk and disorderly conduct." On the other hand, some punishments were as low as half pay withheld. In the latter category were such offenses as "missing from appointed place of work for 2 hours," "failure to salute American Officer, refusal to obey order," to "taking fruit intended for PW's from which he attempted to make wine," and "late for work detail."[33]

At the end of March 1945 there seemed to be a rash of "refusal to work" incidents at Camp Butner that resulted in punishments of "14 days prison, restricted diet and all pay and 2/3 allowance withheld."

Two work-related incidents that occurred in North Carolina camps were mentioned in a 14 May 1945 memorandum from the Office of the Provost Marshal General that reported incidents at five camps across the nation. The two North Carolina incidents occurred at New Bern and at Fort Bragg. At Fort Bragg,

On 23 April 1945, 14 POWs working on the Mosquito Control Project refused to work because of weather. Civilian labor was working at the time. Immediate action was taken and administrative pressure applied. The prisoners were placed on bread and water and signified their willingness to return to work 25 April 1945. On the afternoon of 23 April 1945, 68 prisoners employed in the Ordnance Maintenance Branch refused to work after 1700 hours. Military personnel and civilian employees were working until 2000 hours in order to cut down a back log. The prisoners were placed on bread and water and at 1300 hours, 24 April 1945, at their own request, were returned to the project and worked the same number of hours as civilian employees, i.e. 0800 to 2000 hours.[34]

From the report indicated above, it seems that the Germans refused to work or staged strikes when they felt they were being treated "unfairly." American personnel, still trying to win a war in Europe and in

Asia, were less interested in "fairness" than in discipline and productivity. Bread and water or even teargas seemed appropriate disciplinary or coercive measures against recalcitrant prisoners of war.

From the perspective of the American army, there was a fine line between disciplinary disobedience that slowed work projects and sabotage. One report used the word *sabotage* in connection with an event at New Bern:

> A report has been received from the Chief, Domestic & CI Branch, Intelligence Division, ASF, concerning sabotage committed at the Dixie Chemical Company, New Bern, North Carolina. Three German prisoners of war stationed at Prisoner of War Branch Camp, New Bern, North Carolina, who had been employed in the plant in question, are suspected of having thrown a broken shovel and a brick into a fertilizer machine at 1130 hours, 23 April 1945. An estimate of damage as yet has not been made to this office.[35]

Nevertheless, the overall impression of the contributions of German POWs to North Carolina's work force was very positive. On 24 November 1945, a newspaper article entitled "POW's to be Taken from NC Industries," reported comments by the state director of the War Manpower Commission, Dr. J. S. Dorton:

> After performing nearly 2,000,000 man days of labor in North Carolina agriculture and rural industries prisoners of war will be withdrawn from Tar Heel farms and plants by the end of this year. . . . The employment of POW labor reached a peak in the State last month, when 5,100 prisoners were employed in agriculture and industry. At one time during the war, Dr. Dorton said, there were applications on the file for at least 12,000 prisoners. War prisoners first were used in the State in the late Spring of 1943.[36]

As things worked out, the German POWs in North Carolina camps were not withdrawn from the state at the end of year in 1945. The demands of the American agricultural and pulpwood industries delayed the repatriation of large numbers of them into late spring of 1946. Their contributions to the maintenance of American military installations to state agricultural and pulpwood production continued. So too did their combination of willingness and unwillingness to work. For their American captors, as for the German POWs, World War II was over after September 1945 but the POW program in America was still in session. So too was the lure of freedom that led some POWs to attempt to escape from their work camps. Of the twenty-nine escape attempts that occurred in North Carolina camps, almost half occurred between September 1945 and the end of January 1946.

# 7

# ESCAPES

Mention of escapes from prisoner of war camps conjures up images of desperate and daring young men willing to risk life and limb in pursuit of national or individual honor. Often the motivations for escape were more prosaic: escape from alienated comrades or escape from boredom. Sixty years after events it is difficult to determine the motivations of particular escapees. Helmut Haeberlein, the first escapee from a North Carolina camp, explained his motivation in a note for the commanding officer of the camp at Wilmington. Others left few hints of their thought processes. Most North Carolinians, unaware of the POW presence in their state, learned little about POW escapes.

Details of escapes are rare. During the war in Europe, the U.S. government attempted to give the POW program a low profile. It wanted to avoid frightened civilians and an intrusive press. In addition, the army had an interest in upholding the sections of the Geneva Convention that protected prisoners from "insults and public curiosity." It also wanted public relations policies that would secure the most efficient use of POW labor and maintain a favorable public attitude toward the POW program. Only a few carefully screened and positive articles about the German POW program appeared in newspapers before early 1945.[1] An occasional description of an escaped prisoner was released to the regional press by the army or the FBI, but otherwise the public was told little about its government's German guests. Because of the limited press coverage of POW escapes, sources of information for the historian are contained chiefly in FBI files and the more readily accessible contemporary International Committee of the Red Cross, Swiss Legation, or army inspection reports. Because these reports concerned camp conditions, little was said about escapees or escapes except in the

Table 7.1. Escapes from North Carolina POW camps, July 1944 to January 1946

| | | |
|---|---|---|
| July 1944 | Camp Davis | Helmut Haeberlein |
| | Camp Sutton | Werner Friedrich Meier |
| September 1944 | Camp Butner | (Karl) Helmut Hiesberger |
| | Camp Butner | Samuel Lechner |
| | Camp Butner | Gerhard Borack |
| March 1945 | Seymour Johnson Field | Wilhelm Jendricke |
| April 1945 | Fort Bragg | Alfred Moster |
| | New Bern | Paul Schmidt |
| | Camp Butner | Gerd Roempke |
| | Camp Butner | Rudolf Streinz |
| May 1945 | Camp Butner | Richard Doll |
| June 1945 | Camp Butner | Guenther Radam |
| | Camp Butner | Rudolf Wenzel |
| | Camp Butner | Joseph Schnobel |
| | Camp Butner | Wolf-Sasha Kaubisch |
| August 1945 | Camp Butner | Kurt Rossmeisl |
| September 1945 | Camp Butner | Gerd Roempke |
| | Camp Butner | Claus Hoyer |
| | Camp Butner | Johann Lunger |
| | Camp Butner | Wilhelm Gordsen |
| | Camp Butner | Helmut Zenker |
| October 1945 | Seymour Johnson | Hermann Nerlich |
| | Seymour Johnson | Hans Georg Schewe |
| November 1945 | Camp Butner | Rudolf Wenzel |
| | Camp Butner | Gerd Roempke |
| December 1945 | Camp Butner | Friedrich Tiel |
| | Camp Butner | Eugen Buber |
| | Camp Butner | Franz Friedau |
| January 1946 | Camp Butner | Guido Graffield |

Source: Escaped Prisoners of War, RG 389, Entry 461, Box 2598 and/or *Durham Morning Herald*.

most general terms. Details were of little interest to these agencies. The most revealing and interesting information on POW escapes is found in stories picked up by the local press from farmers, rural sheriff's deputies, or city policemen who had contact with escapees before military guards or FBI men arrived on the scene. Government agents tried to limit public knowledge of their concerns regarding POWs. Armed with dry-as-dust minimalist military lists of escapees, their bases, and their dates of flight and capture, one can find a few juicy stories that filtered into the regional press. FBI reports concerning prisoners who eluded early army recapture provide additional insights.

The available archival and printed sources reveal that there were at least twenty-nine escape attempts by German POWs during their stay in the Tar Heel State. Considering that there were about 10,000 German POWs in North Carolina during the war, the rate of escapes was about 0.29 percent. In Florida the escape rate was about 0.33 percent; the overall national rate was about 0.36 percent. These rates compared very favorably, according to the army, with an escape rate from maximum security federal penitentiaries of 0.44 percent.[2] More escapes may have been attempted, but they were thwarted early enough that they were not recorded in official records or the press. Of these twenty-nine escape attempts, four resulted in deaths. At least two of these were accidental. Three escapes were undertaken by the same individual. One escape was successful enough to last for almost three months. One escape ended only when the escapee turned himself in to the FBI in 1959.

At the end of June 1944, after nearly six months of having large numbers of German POWs in the state, there had been no escapes from Camp Butner and its branch camps. However, there had been an attempted escape from the branch camp at Williamston on the day of the visit by a representative of the Swiss Legation.[3] The International Committee of the Red Cross report did not mention the prisoner's name or the details of the escape attempt. Shortly afterward, though, an escape from the Camp Davis POW compound quickly attracted the intense and sustained interest of the FBI. It was the first and most mysterious of the escapes that occurred in the North Carolina camps.

On 4 July 1944, at 9:43 a.m., Agent Edward Scheidt of the FBI office in Charlotte sent a teletype to FBI director J. Edgar Hoover and to the regional offices in Norfolk, Richmond, Savannah, and Atlanta. The urgent memo shared information received from Capt. J. R. Galbraith of the POW camp at Camp Davis, Wilmington, North Carolina. Helmut Haeberlein, a German prisoner of war, had escaped from the camp stockade sometime during the night of 3–4 July 1944. The Charlotte office had information that the escapee had told several Americans working on a garbage detail in the POW stockade of his plans. He told them that he planned to conceal himself in a garbage can and proceed to New York City, where he had relatives living in Brooklyn. The Charlotte office of the FBI described the escapee as age 30, 5'6" tall, and 142 pounds with gray-brown eyes, a fair complexion, brown hair, and a mole on his back. He spoke English with a noticeable German accent. The teletype concluded, "Information of escape has been released over police radio and arrangements being made for immediate newspaper releases and radio announcements in vicinity of Wilmington, NC. Charlotte office preparing for state wide publication and announcement [regarding] subject's escape."[4]

At 6:29 p.m., a supplementary teletype message to Hoover and the regional offices added more information concerning the possible time of the escape, a description of the clothing that the escapee might be wearing, and the progress of the search at that point. The escape was believed to have taken place between 5:15 p.m. and 11:30 p.m. on the night of July 3. It was possible that Haeberlein was dressed in a khaki shirt and pants and an army garrison cap with a red ribbon because these items were missing from the camp laundry, "which was visited by [the] subject shortly before [his] disappearance." It was noted that the escapee had been born in Leipzig on 1 February 1913, had a high school education and technical training, and was "reported to be able to drive [a] car." The army had established an extensive roadblock system around Camp Davis for fifteen miles around the camp that was supplemented by roving patrols and state patrol and local police agencies were cooperating in the search. Extensive newspaper and radio publicity in North Carolina had not yet resulted in the development of any information on the escapee's whereabouts. As a result, the Charlotte office of the FBI requested that the FBI offices in Savannah, Richmond, and Norfolk issue local newspaper and radio releases in addition to alerting appropriate state police authorities.

On 14 July 1944, copies of a "wanted" circular for Helmut Haeberlein were ordered for distribution to the FBI field divisions in Charlotte, Richmond, Norfolk, Huntington, Louisville, Knoxville, Memphis, Savannah, Atlanta, and Birmingham. The poster, with a photo of Haeberlein that had been taken in August 1943, described him as a corporal in the Germany army. It provided his physical description and said that his former occupation was "hosiery weaver." It noted that he spoke German, French, and Spanish. The FBI collected other information about the escapee that it did not publish on the wanted poster. Haeberlein's basic personnel record noted that his internment number was 4WG-3952 and that his first internment in the United States had been in Aliceville, Alabama, on 13 August 1943. The "4WG" indicated that he was among the first 3,952 prisoners to be registered in the Fourth Service Command. His internment at Aliceville on 13 August 1943 meant that he was among the first several thousand German prisoners who arrived in the United States. They were all captives who were taken in North Africa in the spring of 1943, when Rommel's Afrika Korps and its supporting units surrendered to encircling English and American forces.

While Haeberlein was being sought, another former German inmate from the Aliceville camp became the second North Carolina escapee and the first to be shot while attempting to escape. Werner Friedrich Meier's story was told in Chapter 3. Meier's escape is mentioned again here because the FBI checked for a possible connection between the two North Carolina escapes. An 11 July 1944 teletype from Agent Scheidt in Charlotte to the FBI director noted that originally information had been received that indicated that Meier had intended to contact Haeberlein. However, further investigation had led to the conclusion that that information was unfounded. A search of the effects found on Meier, who was shot and killed by guards during his escape from a Camp Sutton working party near Van Wyck, South Carolina, revealed no clues that Meier had intended to contact the Camp Davis escapee.

The FBI was interested in trying to understand the motives and thought of its quarry. An office memorandum from the Charlotte office to the FBI director on 14 July 1945 bears quotation in full:

> Since it appears unusual, I thought the Bureau would be interested in the following note which was turned in to Captain Gallbright [sic] of the prisoner of war camp at Camp Davis, North Carolina, by one of the German prisoners of war. This note, according to the prisoner of war, was found in his personal effects where it had been left by the above subject [Helmut Haeberlein].
>
> Mon Capitaine,
> According to the great philosopher Spinoza every man has to seek happiness. Having not found it in this camp of war prisoners, I must go some where else. As you are not supposed to give me a furlough, though, I am taking it myself. Once, one of your fellows told me "If you would live two weeks in the U.S.A. as a free man, you never would want to return home.'" Now I am going to

try it and take way [*sic*] in search of happiness and freedom, which will cause you some troubles. I beg you to excuse and forgive me, after a certain lapse of time, if your authorities don't catch me before, I will return myself. Herewith I give you my parole, as a soldier, that I will not commit any act of sabotage, espionage, propaganda against the U.S.A. or any act of violence.

Yours truly, Helmut Haeberlein

"It matters not how straight the gate,

How charged with punishment the scroll

I am master of my fate

I am Captain of my soul."

(Henley)[5]

The FBI was dealing with an intrepid romantic who was out to discover America. How he escaped and where he might be heading were the questions that concerned his pursuers. A detailed report of 22 July 1944 from the FBI's Charlotte office reviewed existing information regarding Haeberlein and the ongoing investigation concerning his escape:

> Through the medium of an American translator, prisoners living in subject's barracks and serving on the laundry detail were questioned. . . . Haeberlein was last seen at 5 o'clock [on 3 July 1944] at roll call. He was not seen at dinner immediately after roll call. At 10:30 p.m. on July 3, 1944, at which time prisoners are to be in bed, the subject's bed was empty. The subject was said to have been an individual who did not mix with the other men and who as a result was not well liked. He is said to have been a studious individual. The prisoners further claimed that his escape was a surprise to them and they did not know the means used or his destination.[6]

Frank M. Phillips, the civilian night superintendent of the Camp Davis laundry, where Haeberlein was well known and was sometimes used by Phillips as a translator, noted that Haeberlein had asked him how far it was to Norfolk, Virginia, and Wilmington, North Carolina, and the population of both places. Another time he inquired about the distance to Jacksonville, North Carolina. "Once in his conversation with

Phillips, Haeberlein mentioned that he did not like Hitler, [and] that he [Haeberlein] was going to live in Argentina, South America after the war."[7]

Capt. James E. Lewis Jr., acting director of the Security and Intelligence Division at Camp Davis, informed the FBI office in Charlotte that Helmut Haeberlein had approached two American prisoners in the stockade at Camp Davis who were assigned on a garbage detail within the POW area with the offer of a reward if they would help him escape. The German's plan was to conceal himself in a garbage can until free of the area. He told the American pair that he had relatives living in New York on Hart Street in Brooklyn. The relatives would furnish him with funds and transportation for travel to Mexico. An FBI investigator checked into this information and found that the American prisoners had been confronted with Haeberlein's plan about the first of May. They had reported the matter to their captain, R. T. McEvoy, who was the stockade officer at Camp Davis. When that officer showed them photos of various German POWs, they were able to identify Haeberlein as the one who had talked to them about escape. The problem was that there was no evidence of Haeberlein ever receiving any mail from American relatives. Furthermore, it was ascertained that a garbage truck had not been in the compound after 5 p.m. on 3 July, when Haeberlein was last seen. A check of Camp Davis, the Wilmington Police Department, the New Hanover sheriff's office, the State Highway Patrol, and the local Carolina Beach and Wrightsville Beach police revealed that no automobiles had been reported stolen on the 3rd or 4th of July. An FBI search for possible relatives of Haeberlein in the New York area initially proved unsuccessful.

The Charlotte FBI office informed Hoover by teletype on 27 July that "an individual possibly identical with subject [Helmut Karl Haeberlein] . . . was reported to have been seen by several citizens in the vicinity of Lumberton and Fayetteville, NC, on July twenty-fourth. . . . Investigation continuing and local newspapers and radios in the vicinity of above cities notified." Then on 31 July came reports from the FBI's Richmond office that it was investigating numerous reports from individuals in the Richmond area who claimed to have seen an individual who looked like Haeberlein. By early August, the FBI was also investigating the possibility that Haeberlein might try to contact a relative who was a night baker at a hotel in Swampscott, Massachusetts, or a cousin who lived in Andover. The FBI also canvassed over 100 families on Hart Street in Brooklyn, showing them pictures of Haeberlein. Results of all the investigations proved negative. Haeberlein seemed never to have made contacts with the people the FBI interviewed.

On 3 October 1944, a body later identified through fingerprints as that of Helmut Haeberlein was found in the Hudson River off Pier D of Jersey City. The subject was pronounced dead by a coroner and removed to the Hudson County morgue in Hoboken, New Jersey. No evidence of foul play was found. Among the possessions found with the body were a German passport dated 9 January 1938 bearing the name of Karl Helmut Haeberlein that listed journeys to France, Switzerland, and Spain. There was also a safe conduct certificate for travel through Spain dated June 1940.

Among other items found were his military dog tag and numerous photos and letters in German and Romanian, all of which were in no condition to be examined due to immersion. "When found body was clothed in khaki pants, khaki shirt underneath white shirt, black sox, brown filigree shoes. Due to present condition, body cannot be fingerprinted until afternoon of October five. Body viewed by agent this office and tentatively identified as Haeberlein."[8] The investigation was continuing.

On 7 October, J. Edgar Hoover sent a memorandum to Charles Malcolmson, the FBI's director of public relations, that he later "might wish to make . . . available to the press." The memorandum read:

> The Department of Justice announced today that the FBI has identified a body recovered from the Hudson River at Jersey City, New Jersey, as that of Helmut Haeberlein, 31, escaped German prisoner of war.
>
> Director J. Edgar Hoover of the Federal Bureau of Investigation said the body was found October 3, 1944, by the Jersey City Police Department, which has cooperated in work to identify the man. There was no evidence of foul play. The identification, at first tentative, was established positively today through fingerprints.

Haeberlein escaped from a camp at Wilmington, North Carolina, during the night of July 3, 1944. He left a letter for the commanding officer in which he apologized for escaping.

"According to the great philosopher Spinoza, every man has to seek happiness," Haeberlein also wrote. "Having not found it in this camp of war prisoners, I must go somewhere else."

He added that he had been told that two weeks in the United States as a free man would make him "never want to return home." He said he wanted to test that claim, promised he would not do anything to hurt the United States while he was at liberty, and said he would return voluntarily if not caught.

Haeberlein was a corporal in the German army and was a weaver prior to the war.[9]

The Associated Press distributed the Hoover memorandum with very minor modifications. Haeberlein's comments and references to Spinoza appeared in the *Sunday Star-News* of Wilmington on Sunday morning, 8 October. The title on the first page of that local paper proclaimed: "Escaped German Prisoner Drowns: Body of Corp. Haeberlein, Who Fled Camp Davis Stockade, Found."[10]

An extensive case report by Edmond J. Kennedy of the Newark FBI office dated 15 October 1944 revealed the full story of the discovery of Haeberlein's body on 3 October. The emergency squad had received a call from a police patrolman that the body of an unidentified man had been found floating in the Hudson River off Pier D. The body was removed from the water, pronounced dead by a police surgeon, and taken to the Hoffman morgue in Hoboken, New Jersey. A total of seventy-five effects of various sorts were found in Haeberlein's possession when his body was recovered by the Jersey City Police Department.[11] Though the number of recovered items seems large, the long list enumerated in the FBI report reveals that most of the items were small paper products. These documents and keepsakes such as a passport, a German driver's license, an address book, photos, postcards, postage stamps, and newspaper clippings, along with a pocket knife, ring, watch, and keys, offer many clues to Haeberlein's life during the war years.

In addition to the German passport, which revealed Haeberlein's travel in Spain and Portugal, other documents revealed that he had registered for military service with the German Consul at Barcelona on 20 September 1939. A form letter dated at Berlin on 1 July 1940 addressed to Helmut Haeberlein at Valencia, Spain, advised him to report to Quartermasters Corps #570 in Berlin on 2 July 1940.

Also found were his birth certificate, indicating he was born on 3 February 1913 in Leipzig. There were several letters addressed to Soldat Helmut Haeberlein from a Romanian while he was stationed in Romania. There was an unused bus ticket good for one passage from Laurel, Maryland, to Baltimore, dated at Laurel, 6 July 1944, and a purchase receipt from Hechts Reliable Stores, Baltimore, Maryland, dated 10 July 1944. Also there was a purchase receipt from Gimbel Brothers, New York City, 17 July 1944.

There were several newspaper clippings. One had a dateline of Mexico City, 22 July, and was entitled "Sees Free German Rule." It dealt with a speech given by Paul Merker, general secretary of the Free German Latin American Committee. The speech predicted that the Free German Group in Moscow would constitute itself as a German anti-Fascist government in East Prussian territory. Another newspaper clipping datelined Washington, D.C., 7 May, was entitled "U.S. Now Has 183,618 War Prisoners."

There were photographs as well. Among them were three Coney Island photos of Haeberlein in civilian clothes sitting in a painted boat with the name *Mayflower*; six full-faced and two right-profile passport-sized photographs of Haeberlein in civilian clothes; and one photograph of the right profile of Haeberlein in his German uniform. There were several other photos of Haeberlein in uniform set in a tropical background. There were also eighteen photos of various young women.

In addition to these items there was a social security card in the name of John Earl Howk, a portion of a U.S. Army Motor Vehicle Permit issued to J. W. Howk, and an identification card for John E. Howk with the Atlantic Coast Railroad and an Auburn, Alabama, Polytechnic Institute ID, all of which bore a photo of Haeberlein. There was also a green and black fountain pen, a gold ring with the initials "H. H.," a double-bladed knife, seven dollar bills, one quarter, and three nickels

FBI visits to the dental office on 116th Street, New York, where "John Howk" had had a dental appointment for 28 August 1944, did not reveal much. The dentist was unable to describe his patient or recognize photographs of Haeberlein. The dental secretary was also unable to say whether or not Haeberlein was the man who had visited the office.[12]

Follow-up investigation in the New York area after the discovery of Haeberlein's body proved inconclusive. Photos taken of the body were shown to residents of Hart Street in Brooklyn without positive results. Residents in the area of 116th Street in Manhattan, the address given for "John E. Howk" on the dental appointment card, were no more helpful. Investigation of the New York area businesses listed in an address book found on Haeberlein's body brought similar negative results. The New York FBI report of 11 December 1944 concluded: "Inasmuch as all logical investigation to ascertain the activities of the subject in this field division has been conducted, no further investigation is being made in this matter by this office."[13]

A 9 April 1945 report from the Charlotte office noted that the possessions found on Haeberlein's body had been returned to the POW camp at Camp Davis in December 1944. "Inasmuch as the subject's whereabouts has been ascertained and inasmuch as there are no leads outstanding which would lead to the securing of information concerning subject's activities during the period of time elapsing between his escape and the finding of his body, this case is being closed."[14]

How the escape occurred and what the escapee did in the three months before his death are mysteries. The story of the escape of Helmut Haeberlein remains to this day a subject best suited for novelists. The information the American military was able to share with the German government through the Swiss government and the International Committee of the Red Cross was very limited. The assistant director of the Prisoner of War Division, Col. A. M. Tollefson, wrote to the Swiss Legation in Washington, D.C., informing it of "the death by drowning, of Prisoner of War Corporal Karl Helmut Haberlein [sic], 4WG-3952, on 3 October 1944." The report noted where the body had been found in the Hudson River and promised that a report of any ongoing investigation would be passed on to the Swiss. The report gave Haeberlein's date of birth and said that his listed next of kin had an address in Saxony.[15] A final report of 13 March 1945 from Maj. Stephen

M. Farrand of the Prisoner of War Division of the provost marshal general's office to the Special War Problems Division of the Department of State for communication to the International Committee of the Red Cross repeated the earlier details. The only information added was that "cause of death was drowning by immersion in salt water."[16]

There were at least two other probable drowning deaths of North Carolina escapees: Paul Schmidt, who escaped from the branch camp at New Bern on 12 April 1945, and Rudolf Streinz, who escaped from the base camp at Camp Butner on 15 April 1945. The fate of these men remained uncertain for a long time. As late as June 1946 the director of the Prisoner of War Operations Division was trying to get some final closure information on these two men, who were among a total of five from the Fourth Service Command who had "escaped from camps in the Fourth Service Command and are still at large."[17] The response from that command's office in Atlanta indicated the belief that both men had drowned soon after escaping: "Their bodies were never recovered; however, the Federal Bureau of Investigation continues investigation."[18] The Red Cross and State Department representatives who visited New Bern were led to believe that Paul Schmidt was known to be a psychoneurotic who wandered off into the coastal jungle where his body could not be found.[19] Schmidt escaped on 18 July 1944. His remains were not found until 27 November 1946. Newspaper reports of the capture of Rudolf Streinz's fellow escapee, Gerd Roempke, reveal that Roempke and American authorities believed that Streinz had drowned while trying to escape by swimming with Roempke across Lake Michie.[20]

Another violent death occurred during an escape attempt from a North Carolina camp when 1st Sgt. Werner Friedrich Meier was shot to death while trying to escape on 11 July 1944. His was the only shooting death that took place in North Carolina.[21]

Most escape attempts received minimal newspaper coverage. What coverage there was consisted chiefly of cursory FBI descriptions of the escapees. These descriptions are instructive because they clash with stereotypes of German "supermen" that existed among the American public during the war and have tended to continue to color popular images of the German POWs.[22] The most striking fact is the height of escapees: they were usually between 5'7" and 5'11". "Nazi supermen" were about as tall as the average American of the 1940s. A typical newspaper description of escaped German POWs in North Carolina reads like this:

> Streinz is five feet, seven inches tall, weighs 169 pounds, has brown eyes, brown hair, and a ruddy complexion. He was a baker by profession before entering the German Army where he served as a corporal in the Signal Corps. As far as it is known, he speaks only German.
>
> Roempke is five feet, 10 inches tall, weighs 135 pounds, has blue eyes, blond hair, and was an automobile mechanic by trade. He speaks English very well. He was a lance corporal in the infantry of the German Army.
>
> Anyone having information in regard to these men are urged to call the FBI office in Charlotte collect.[23]

When local authorities apprehended escapees before they could be corralled by the FBI or military authorities, North Carolina newspapermen could garner a few more details about the case. This happened when an international trio of escapees from Camp Butner were apprehended by local authorities in Durham in September 1944. The wording of the newspaper story and its details capture the flavor of wartime America's experiences with German POWs. It also reveals some of the complexities of the POW program that bear explanation. These include the multiple ethnicity and political allegiances of the "German" POWs:

> Three escaped prisoners of war from the Camp Butner stockade were captured by Durham policemen early yesterday before they had even "officially" escaped.
>
> An Austrian, a Pole and a Lithuanian were apprehended by Patrolmen R. W. Mills and F. L. Wilkins near Club Boulevard and Roxboro Road.
>
> Officers said Butner officials had not discovered the escape of the three Axis soldiers when notified by Durham authorities that the prisoners had been recaptured.
>
> The men told arresting officers they walked away from Butner at 9 o'clock Friday night and made about 16 miles through unfamiliar country before they were captured about 3:30 a.m.

The 20-year-old-prisoners were Baroick Gerhard [*sic*; Gerhard Borack], Lithuanian, Samuel Lichner, Polish, and Ernst Hiesberger, Austrian.

The officers had been called to 2505 Cascadille Street to investigate a Peeping Tom report. At Club Boulevard and Roxboro Street, they saw three men dressed in mixed fatigue and G.I. clothing. Mills and Wilkins, armed with sawed-off shotguns, challenged the men who surrendered.

Hiesberger told the officers he was on his way to California to fight the Japanese. He said that he was studying to be a missionary before being drafted into the German army. The other two had no definite destination in mind.

One of the prisoners carried letters from a Camp Butner woman employee, officers said. A picture of the woman was also found.

They were wearing new shoes and carried large quantities of cigarettes, candy, and some money. They were lodged in the City Jail in separate cells.

The men told police they were well fed and well treated at Butner. Asked about working conditions, they replied "No work hard."

Butner authorities placed the men back in custody later yesterday. A reward of $50 is paid for the capture of an escaped war prisoner.[24]

The Lithuanian, Polish, and Austrian nationality of these men indicates that they were either volunteers or draftees from territories subject to German control. One of the things that bewildered American military men in the early days after the D-Day invasion was the presence of large numbers of Eastern Europeans among their Wehrmacht captives. Some of these men did not even speak German. It was difficult to tell if their captives were even pro-German let alone pro-Nazi. There were Austrians such as Ernst Hiesberger, who described himself as "on his way to California to fight the Japanese."[25] By 1944 a small but increasing number of Austrians identified themselves as Austrians rather than as Germans. They wished that Hitler had not been born an Austrian and that Nazi Germany had not incorporated Austria into Greater Germany. Some of them, like Hiesberger, were willing to show their animosity toward Germany and her Axis allies by volunteering to fight against an enemy of America and her allies, Japan. Such complexities of national and political allegiance were registered but were little understood by the American military and the American public.

Simpler stories that fit into existing stereotypes probably attracted more attention and were more memorable. Writers for a local paper such as the *Durham Morning Herald* were especially attracted to the flair and verve of one German escapee from Camp Butner, Gerd Roempke. He escaped three times from April to November 1945. Durham news writers had a field day with Roempke's case because each time he was apprehended it was by local officers. Because of this, interactions between locals and the German could be recorded before the would-be escapee was whisked away into the official anonymity of the large prisoner of war camp at Camp Butner. The military and the FBI had little interest in giving the German POWs a forum for propaganda. Nor did they wish the American public to worry about the presence of German POWs in their midst. The image they strove for was an unobtrusive presence of "Uncle Sam's willing workers." Newspaper articles about escaped German POWs created the potential for frightened and/or indignant citizens. But an escaped "Nazi," "superman," and "jaunty Jerry" made for marvelous human interest stories for local newspapers.

Gerd Roempke, 5WG-921, first escaped from Camp Butner on 15 April 1945. He would flee again on 11 September, and again on 31 October 1945. From the reports of his first escape and capture, the 21-year-old Roempke became a fascinating figure to the reporters of the *Durham Morning Herald*. The survivor of a swimming escape across Lake Michie that took the life of his fellow escapee, Rudolf Streinz, Roempke was characterized by his apparent self-confidence and arrogance: "Swimming and talking at the same time ('It's easy for me,' the Nazi bragged), Roempke said that he turned to see how Rudolf was doing, and failed to find the man in sight." Roempke fitted and also played to the *Morning Herald* reporter's preconceptions: "When one of the officers who scoured the bank of the stream asked how he escaped from Camp Butner's prisoner of war stockade, the blond-haired 'superman' grinned and shrugged his shoulders."[26]

When Roempke escaped again in September 1945, he was reintroduced to the readers of the *Durham Morning Herald* as a familiar figure:

"The jaunty Jerry, who was a corporal in the German infantry and a mechanic in civilian life was wearing a complete olive drab fatigue uniform with the letters 'PW' at the time of his escape. Roempke is the same English-speaking, blond-haired Kraut who with Rudolf Streinz, 22-year-old fellow prisoner, last April made an impromptu dash from the reservation."[27] He was not caught for almost two weeks.[28]

Roempke's third flight from Butner, his fourth in American camps, according to the *Durham Morning Herald*, occurred on 31 October and lasted until 22 November.[29] "Gerde [*sic*] Roempke, 22-year-old slender blond-haired German prisoner who has already staged three AWOL treks from POW stockades has done it again, it was reported yesterday by the FBI."[30] Somehow the *Herald* seems to have missed his recapture along with that of his fellow escapee, Rudolf Wenzel, on 22 November 1945.[31] Perhaps for the first time Roempke was arrested by other than local law enforcement officers and the newspaper did not get the opportunity for its usual story.

What happened to escapees like Roempke when they were recaptured? It was their soldierly duty to attempt escape, and according to the Geneva Convention, POWs were not to be unduly penalized for attempting to do that duty[32] According to Article 45 of the Geneva Convention, prisoners were subject to all regulations and laws as members of the detaining army. Much was left up to the discretion of camp commanders, but one option authorized by Article 59 of the convention allowed the prisoner to be confined for up to thirty days, fourteen of them on a restricted diet.[33] Such was the case with Wilhelm Jendricke, 31G-514193, after his attempt to escape from the Butner's branch camp Seymour Johnson Field in Goldsboro on 12 March 1945. Jendricke was apprehended in downtown Goldsboro within eight hours and then transferred to the POW prisoner stockade at the base camp at Camp Butner. There he was given the appropriate disciplinary punishment. A disciplinary punishment list for March 1945 noted that for "absenting himself from work detail without permission," Jendricke was given "30 days prison, 14 days restricted diet, all pay and 2/3 allowance withheld."[34]

One of the most interesting escapees from a North Carolina POW camp was Kurt Rossmeisl, a former member of Rommel's crack 10th Panzer Division, who disappeared from Camp Butner on 4 August 1945.

He did not resurface until he turned himself in to the FBI in Cincinnati on 10 May 1959. By then the 52-year-old arthritis sufferer was lonely and tired of looking over his shoulder. He had been on the run for fourteen years after his years in Camp Butner. Originally, he had caught a train to Chicago and lived there under the name *Frank Ellis*, melting into the work force as a punch press operator, bartender, and elevator operator. He even joined a Moose lodge.[35]

The reason Rossmeisl was so successful in staying undercover so long is suggested in the original FBI description that appeared along with his picture in the *Durham Morning Herald* shortly after his escape:

> Local FBI agents last night released a full description of German 2nd Lt. Kurt Rossmeisl who one week ago escaped from Camp Butner's Prisoner of War compound. Rossmeisl, who was captured in Tunisia, once worked in the East Indies as a plantation overseer. He speaks excellent English with a pronounced British accent. He also speaks fluent Italian, Russian, and Spanish. He is believed to be wearing G.I. khaki trousers and shirt, and an overseas cap. He is five feet, seven inches in height and weighs 155 pounds. His eyes are blue, his complexion ruddy and he has thin sandy hair and a large nose. Anyone possessing information concerning this man is urged to immediately contact the FBI through the Durham Police Department.[36]

Rossmeisl was of average height, multilingual, and obviously adept at blending into a variety of cultures.

Though the Rossmeisl story seems to have ended in 1959, his means and method of escape from Camp Butner are still in dispute. Arnold Krammer, who published his well-received *Nazi Prisoners of War* in 1979, says that "Kurt Rossmeisl simply pushed a wheelbarrow past several guards during a wood-gathering detail on August 4, 1945, and caught a train for Chicago."[37] Max Reiter, a former Waffen-SS man who knew Rossmeisl in Camp Butner, wrote to this author on 3 December 2002 suggesting that Krammer got the story wrong. According to Reiter,

> On 4 August 1945 Kurt packed his things together, said his good-byes to his fellow prisoners and marched to the camp gate. In front stood a car, into which Kurt climbed while the guards looked

the other way. Only a quarter hour later did the sirens go off and the both guards cried, "A POW has escaped!" We all laughed! Kurt surely told his story differently than it was so as not to bring difficulties to his helpers.[38]

Certainly one of the longer escapes, though not as impressive as Rossmeisl's marathon, was one by Guido Graffield, 81G-225544. He escaped from Camp Butner on 6 January 1946 and returned voluntarily and in style on 25 March 1946, almost three months later. His arrival back at Camp Butner made quite a story for the *Durham Morning Herald*. It reveals what wartime North Carolinians could have learned about its German POW guests. Their reactions must have been a mixture of amusement, pride, and indignation at the attitude and activities of a German POW who wanted nothing better than to enjoy the freedoms of being in America, both during and after his captivity:

> Second Lt. Guido Graffield of the German army, a 30-year-old Camp Butner prisoner of war, who went AWOL last Jan 6 in prisoner garb, yesterday returned to the military reservation by taxi.
>
> Sporting a complete new civilian outfit, plus fresh shave and hair cut, the English-speaking Nazi officer, flippantly remarked that he had paid $8 for the 17-mile cab ride from Durham.
>
> He was wearing a brown homburg style hat, a brown striped suit, flowered cravat, yellow muffler and handsomely shined shoes.

The $14 he was pocketing was confiscated and the hard-to-get suit of clothes was exchanged for the old familiar type of garment he was wearing at the time he sauntered from captivity.

> Graffield declined to comment as to where he had been living during his period of freedom, or just what he had been doing.

He did explain that while he was a free man he adopted Christian Science as his religion, and he had "learned more in three months than during the three years in a POW camp."

> Along with his book on religion, the German carried a book by Plato, a study he remarked that was most interesting.
>
> Graffield, who had faked going to the Butner General Hospital

during an illness, while he was working at an officers' club house, and made his successful break, said that the reason he came back voluntarily was because he thought it would help him to return to the United States after he is sent to Germany.

Under the rules of the Geneva Conference, a prisoner of war does not have to reveal other than his name, rank, and serial number.

He cannot be punished, only being placed in a penal place deemed safe from future attempts to escape.[39]

When the POW program came to an end in North Carolina, there had been twenty-nine escape attempts, only one of which lasted longer than three months. Most lasted a matter of days. There were 2,222 German POW escapes nationally from 1942 through 1946 in a population of 378,000 German POWs.[40] Obviously, as in the United States as a whole, German POWs in the North Carolina camps had little inducement or occasion to undertake fruitless escapes from camps that were generally safe and relatively comfortable. That did not mean, however, that the Germans were happy to be far from home. The Americans were not successful in persuading all of their prisoners to behave as their captors wished—as docile workers and reformed future allies. That was not, however, for lack of effort on the part of the American government to reorient their "Nazi" visitors.

# 8

# REORIENTATION PROGRAMS AT CAMP BUTNER, CAMP MACKALL, AND FORT BRAGG

## The Special Projects Branch at Camp Butner

In an attempt to influence the hearts and minds of German POWs in preparation for their return home, the Office of the Provost Marshal General secretly set up a reorientation program under the guidance of a vaguely named Prisoner of War Special Projects Division. The reason for the secrecy was Article 17 of the Geneva Convention, which sheltered prisoners from propaganda from their captors.[1] The American government did not want its servicemen in Germany subjected to such harassment. However, the convention did encourage "intellectual diversion . . . organized by the prisoners." That gave the Office of the Provost Marshal General an opportunity to step in and try to influence existing "intellectual diversion programs" already run by the prisoners. For this purpose, "assistant executive officers" (AEOs) were assigned to all POW base camps. Also a national bimonthly newspaper, *Der Ruf* [The Call], was created and written for POWs by cooperative prisoners with "liberal and democratic leanings" who were housed at Fort Kearney, Rhode Island. While *Der Ruf* was intended to change the attitudes of its national POW reading audience, the job of the AEOs was to subtly influence the prisoners through their apparent work as interpreters and assistants to camp chaplains. Under those guises, the AEOs were to reorganize POW recreational programs, select appropriate movies, and set up courses that would stress subjects appropriate to the reorientation program. The grandiose goals of the program were that German POWs "might understand and believe historical and ethical truth as generally conceived by Western civilization, might come to respect the American people and their ideological values, and upon repatriation to Germany might form the nucleus of a new German ideology which will reject militarism and totalitarian controls and will advocate a democratic system of government."[2]

To check on how the new program was going in the spring of 1945, Joseph H. Waxer and Richard Meyer of the Special Projects Division visited the POW camp at Camp Butner on 7–10 April. They were pleased to report that the camp commander, Colonel Alexander; the executive officer, Captain Morris; and the POW camp intelligence officer, 1st Lieutenant Spear, were "cooperating whole-heartedly with Captain Damio and Second Lieutenant Patman, the new AEO officers, in the promotion of the Intellectual Diversion Program." It seemed to them that the AEOs had made "considerable progress in the accomplishment of their mission." They had made good use of the media of radio, film, music, and literature. From the perspective of the reporting officers, "the influence of these media on the prisoners of war is apparent in their musical offerings, their purchase of books on America, their keen delight in American films and the avid interest they display in a variety of radio programs. The Assistant Executive officer has used tact, initiative and ingenuity in organizing and promoting the reorientation program."[3]

The Special Projects visitors were especially enthusiastic about the Camp Butner AEOs' efforts to segregate individuals who might disrupt the program:

> A separate compound has been set up for the segregation of pro-Nazi prisoners of war. The commanding officer and his intelligence officer have conscientiously pursued a policy of immediately removing subversives and incorrigible Nazi prisoners of war from the other compounds as soon as they are uncovered. These prisoners are transferred to the pro-Nazi compound aptly referred to as "Little Siberia."[4]

When the German camp spokesman requested removal of POWs who openly denounced Hitler and Nazism, the intelligence officer instead transferred "subversive elements threatening violence rather than the removal of prisoners of war who had expressed anti-Nazi views. In short, segregation of subversives has contributed considerable impetus to the reorientation program."[5]

The AEOs felt that the Americans had to gain intellectual control by confronting the opposition on its own terms and overcoming it. At Camp Butner, shortly after the AEOs arrived, they faced a show of force by former members of the Wehrmacht who found the postwar defeatism of some of their number disgusting and even traitorous. Smarting at the rise of anti-Nazi sentiment in the wake of peace in Europe, loyalists and Nazis threatened violence. Their target was an especially vocal anti-Nazi named Krudl. One morning they plastered the camp with posters stating "Comrades, beware of this man, a traitor to his Fatherland—Krudl." The AEO responded in kind. As he later reported, "The next morning there was quite a hubbub. New posters had been distributed in the night: 'Comrade, know you a man who lives only for freedom and his Fatherland—Krudl.' . . . Only three persons at Camp Butner know the origin of those presumptuous follow-up posters—the AEO who wrote them, the S-2 and the EM who tacked them up at 0300 hours."[6] In the discussions within the camp that followed, the anti-Nazis discovered the real influence they had in the camp. That new confidence, along with the transfer of the most belligerent Nazis to another camp, gave a major impetus to the new reorientation program. Even the inhabitants of "Little Siberia," the "Nazi Camp," began participating in some of the "intellectual diversion" classes.[7]

Because the AEO at Camp Butner first devoted himself to the improvement of radio, film, and musical facilities, "the prisoners of war . . . accepted Captain Damio and his assistant without suspicion." At least this is what the Special Projects Division visitors thought. They knew, however, that winning the hearts and minds of the German POWs would not be easy. In order that the POWs would not feel propagandized, they had to feel that the films that were shown to them were the result of their own choices. Some trickery was necessary. The AEO at Butner noted that "in December [1944] the PWs were being shown whatever German films were available because that was what they wanted. We knew, of course, that at best these films would be neutral or slightly antagonistic as far as the program was concerned. . . . We contracted for half a dozen of the oldest films in the German language we could get and followed them with Deanna Durbin in *It Started with Eve*. The next day the Spokesman asked us for more American films, about fifty-fifty."[8] The AEO knew that given the choice of the oldest German-language films the AEO could find and a sexy new American film, the Germans would chose the American films. With their good friend, the AEO, looking after their interests, the German POWs would be soon seeing many American films. More and more of them would be about America's National Parks, it democratic form of government, or American heroes like Abraham Lincoln.

With the Germans made receptive to American-selected "educational" films, the AEOs began to concentrate on the development of a new set of educational programs. This included arrangements with the University of North Carolina to be the sponsoring university of the camp and to provide films and travelogues for the POWs. Faculty members at UNC-Chapel Hill campus came as lecturers to Butner and some of its side camps.

One of these lecturers was the Jewish German émigré Professor Helmut Kuhn, a professor of philosophy at Chapel Hill and a native of Berlin. Kuhn presented lectures at the base camp in the summer and fall of 1945 and in the winter of 1946 as well as at least one at the side camp in Monroe. The summer 1945 series was entitled "Cosmopolitanism and National State: The Foreign Policy Orientation." It included lectures like "Twilight of the Gods: Concerning the Greatness and Decline of the National State in Europe"; "The New Masters: Germany, Europe, and the Great Powers"; and "The Charter of the United Nations." A series of ten fall lectures had a variety of American and European themes: "America, You Have It Better"; "The American Dream"; and "The American Reality." Several others included "Anti-Semitism"; "Albion, Is She Perfidious?" "Hereditary Enemy, Hereditary Neighbor"; and "Russia, Once and Now." Professor Kuhn also presented four lectures during the winter of 1945–1946. They were "Recompense and Absolution" on 25 November, "Once Again Potsdam" on 11 January, "The Atomic Bomb and World Politics" on 25 January, and "The Nuremberg Trial" on 1 February.[9] His efforts aroused interest among the POWs, left memories that remain today among some, and attracted favorable comments in the Butner POW camp newspapers, which were influenced by the watchful AEOs.[10]

The event that was most favorably commented upon in the AEO-influenced Camp Butner newspaper, one that has attracted some controversy among historians, was a political election at the camp. It was designed to demonstrate and reinforce changing POW attitudes toward democracy, a form of government they were encouraged to discuss after the collapse of Nazi Germany. The election "proved" that the POWs at Camp Butner were overwhelmingly in favor of democracy. What was heralded positively by democratic enthusiasts among the POWs and by some later historians was roundly castigated even by some of the POWs at Fort Kerney who published *Der Ruf*. Historian Ron Robin, whose book is critical of what he considered to be the utopian and naive efforts of the reorientation program, quotes from an angry article that one of the *Der Ruf* POW staff members wrote and scheduled for publication in the 15 November 1945 edition of that national POW newspaper. The proposed article was deleted by American authorities. The message of the deleted article was summed up in one sentence: "So Camp Butner, North Carolina, voted ninety-five percent in favor of democracy, thereby obediently falling into the ranks of a new ideology. Nine-five percent—it sounds like an old well-know fairy tale. As you know, Goebbels never allowed lower figures."[11] The POW writer was saying that claims of a 95 percent electoral victory were worthy of Hitler's propaganda minister, Joseph Goebbels, and unworthy of a truly democratic society. The writer was even more concerned that if his fellow prisoners were so easily switching from support of Nazism to democracy, they were expressing less the spirit of true conversion and more a too-rapid willingness to attach allegiance to any new ideology that seemed to be gaining the upper hand. True democrats should be more skeptical and reserved in their enthusiasms.

## Camp Mackall and Fort Bragg Special Projects: Hints in Changing POW Newspapers

### Camp Mackall

Some hint of the impact of the American reorientation program undertaken by the Special Projects Division of the PMG can be seen in the changes in the POW camp newspapers that appeared at Camp Mackall and Fort Bragg in the spring and early summer of 1945. Both camps had POW newspapers in the spring of 1945, *Die deutsche Insel* [The German Island] at Camp Mackall and *Der Drahtberichter* [The Wire Reporter] at Fort Bragg. But shortly after the end of the war in Europe in May 1945, these two newspapers ceased publication and were replaced by *Das Freie Wort* [The Free Word] and *Der Aufbruch* [The Beginning/Start]. The names of the newspapers suggest the editorial departures that occurred at each of the POW camps under the guidance and encouragement of American AEOs.

A description of the iconography, allusions, and types of articles that appeared in the camp newspapers of Camp Mackall and Fort Bragg both before and after the end of the war is illustrative. *Die deutsche Insel* of Camp Mackall is a good place to begin. The iconography of the first page of each issue indicates their political ideology. *Die deutsche Insel* stressed the heroic, "insular" quality of German POW life in America. The frontispiece shows four large four-man tents. A guard tower stands behind the barbed wire in the background. Behind the tents and overshadowing them in size is the outline of a great German eagle. In the stillness of the sleeping camp behind the barbed wire, the German eagle, the symbol of Germany, is a towering presence. In contrast stands the iconography of *Das Freie Wort*, which replaced *Die deutsche Insel* on 15 August 1945. It has as its frontispiece a globe with clouds, a star, and a shooting star. Gone is the German insularity and the heroic nationalism of the otherwise sleeping POW camp. In its place is the image of a larger world within a happy solar system.

The articles that characterized the old and new Camp Mackall POW camp newspaper reflect these iconographic changes as well. While not all of the articles of the earlier *Die deutsche Insel* are easy to categorize as soldierly or Nazi, there was a focus and tone in *Insel* that stressed soldierly and uniquely German qualities. In the seventh issue, on 15 May 1945, Unterofficier [corporal] Robert Kern, the editor of the newspaper, wrote of the camp's celebration of yet another Pentecost far from home in circumstances [the end of the war in Europe] that few wished. He called on his comrades to show what he called the "particularly German characteristic" of "not hanging one's head, even in the face of the greatest adversity." He urged them to face their fate stoically.[12] For him and for his beloved comrades, the war was over, but their good German character and soldierly virtues would help them to soldier on. Good German virtues rather than cosmopolitan ones should sustain them.

In the 15 June issue of the newspaper, Gefreiter [private first class] Schweiger wrote "A Reflection on Pentecost," which reviewed a POW assembly and concert by the camp choir, the purpose of which was the celebration of "der Heimat" [home/Vaterland], good old comrades, and the old flag. "Again the camp choir in its usual manner created a bridge for us with our *Heimat* and allowed us to forget for several moments our hard fate. . . . The beautiful march, 'Old Comrades' reminded us of the time when young, spirited blood rose in us as we were forged into men. . . . The concert ended with 'Under the Old Flag.' Its renewed performance served as a greeting of welcome to our newly arrived comrades. We thank the choir for their hard work. Their melodies from home awakened in us our duty to remain brave and upright even in the mightiest storms."[13]

Yet even as these brave soldierly words were printed to encourage the "old-timers" as well as the new arrivals at Camp Mackall, the editorial staff noted that the paper was changing. It was henceforth to be a monthly publication. In truth, however, it faced imminent demise and replacement by a newspaper of a different name and under different editorial leadership.[14]

Even under the old editorial leadership, new voices representing the soon-to-be-dominant ones in a renamed and "new" paper were making themselves heard. The July issue of *Insel* retained the frontispiece portraying the lonely tents behind the barbed wire with the overshadowing German eagle, but there were several remarkable changes. One was that below the standard iconography stood in bold print the saying "NO ONE IS MORE A SLAVE THAN ONE WHO THINKS HE IS FREE." Additionally there were at least two articles that ran directly against the earlier grain of Wehrmacht coherence and soldierly loyalty to the Vaterland. One instance was an article, "Das Leben in Österreich nach dem 13. März 1938" [Life in Austria after 13 March 1938] by two obviously Austrian POWs, Kurt Granichstaedten-Czerva and Gerald Kummer.[15] In none-too-subtle terms the writers suggested that most Austrians knew before their nation was incorporated into Germany, or learned shortly afterward as they were forced into party organizations, the problems of such developments. They also mentioned not only early privations under German rule but also the evils of the "so-called Jewish solution," which had caused a wave of Jewish suicides in Austria. The article did not mention the real horrors of the death camps or the problems that were brought to Austrians through their service in Hitler's Wehrmacht. But this tip of the iceberg was enough to suggest a postwar sea change within the POW enclosure at Camp Mackall. Austrians were encouraged to recall their oppression by Hitler's Germany and Germans were encouraged to see that oppression for what it was. A new wind was beginning to blow in the camp. Patriotism toward the Third Reich was being undermined. New questions and new values were being advanced.

An article about Nazi newspapers in the July issue of *Insel* criticized the rabid propaganda of the press of the Nazi era. The writer suggested that his article was the first of its kind to appear in the newspaper and that he anticipated that it would arouse quite a storm. But he expressed the hope that it would lead others to write similar articles in the near future. He encouraged future writers to make contributions with no expectations that their writing had to be masterworks. The old Greater Germany was gone and it was up to the writer and his comrades to prepare for a new Germany that could take its place among the peoples of the world.[16] The call was going out for the anti-Nazis to raise their voices and for the unquestioning loyalties of the past to be questioned and openly criticized.

The announcement in the July issue of the new intellectual opportunities that were to begin in August 1945 was indicative of coming changes and the growing power of the AEO in the last issues of *Insel*. That issue announced a new simplified set of English-language courses. Their stated goal was to help POWs make the most of their time in America to learn more about its people, its history, and its system of democracy. One of the courses was to be for advanced learners, one for moderates, and one for those who wanted to "tehk it isi" [Take it easy]. For those taking the course—and for them alone—there would be a series of lectures and movies on America for entertainment and insights. There was also an announcement that copies of books that might be of interest were available at the PX. Tellingly, these included:

Adams, *Der Aufstieg Amerikas* (Epic of America)

*Meyers-Blitz-Lexikon* (Dictionary for Quick Information)

Windelband, *Geschichte der Philosophie* (History of Philosophy)

Schnabel, *Weltgeschichte* (World History)

Fischer, *Amerikakunde* (America—Its History, Geography, and Civilization).[17]

The takeover of the "intellectual diversion program" by the AEOs was complete. The hook was baited and in the water. The hook was the English-language course that would be the vehicle for propagandizing the Germans about the virtues of the American people, their history, and their system of democracy. The bait was the opportunity for students of the English-language courses to hear stimulating guest lecturers and view entertaining movies. Even the books about America were sold rather than given away. It was thought that the Germans would be more likely to overlook the propaganda features of the new literature if they had to pay for it. Literature distributed for free was too politically and intellectually suspect.

It was obvious that the American reorientation program was about to move into high gear, and part of that change was to be the demise of *Insel* and the emergence of *Das Freie Wort* on 15 August 1945. The last issue of *Die deutsche Insel* revealed the future writers as well as the themes of the upcoming camp paper. It featured an article, "Wir Neuen" [We New Guys], by Willy Bartik, who would soon be the editor of *Das Freie Wort*. Bartik expressed his amazement after arriving fresh from the battlefields of Europe and a Germany disillusioned by the feckless propaganda of Hitler and company to find the POWs who had spent more time in America than him still adhering to the beliefs and perceptions of the early war years. He encouraged these longer-term POWs to give up their misguided and outmoded views of a homeland that was now destroyed. Instead, he urged them to prepare to rebuild a new Germany of the future.[18]

On 15 August 1945, the first issue of *Das Freie Wort* appeared. The changes that had been hinted at in the waning issues of *Insel* became the dominant themes in the new newspaper at Camp Mackall. This did not occur without at least a last gasp from the diehards. A printed letter to the editor revealed the intellectual struggles going on within the camp, as they were within all of the German POW camps in America. In a letter/article entitled "Ich liebe den Verrat und hasse den Verraeter" [I love treason and hate the traitor], Kurt Niezel vented his anger and confusion at the "treason" and "traitors" that were appearing in his POW world. He wondered aloud if someone could sleep at night if he had been so willing to believe and even fight for one ideal but had then changed ideals in order to gain personal advantage.[19] He was clearly accusing the emerging anti-Nazis of the camp of changing their allegiances in a cynical attempt to gain the favor of their American captors. In an editorial response to Niezel, the staff of the new newspaper expressed the view that it was hard to believe after the horrors of the last years one could still follow the ideals of leaders who had disobeyed their own orders and either fled, committed suicide, or surrendered. Comrades with the same feelings as the letter-writer were urged to think clearly and be prepared to help Germany rebuild in a world that no longer wished to see Prussian military boots.

What had happened to make these changes possible in the camp newspaper at Camp Mackall? There is evidence that goes beyond the obvious changes in the editorial leadership, style, focus, and content of the camp's newspaper. The Special Projects Branch people had visited Camp Mackall in April 1945 and made suggestions and applied pressure to ensure that necessary changes would be made within the camp. When Special Projects Division Field Service officers 1st Lt. Joseph H. Waxer and 1st Lt. Richard N. Meyer visited Camp Mackall on 5–6 April 1945, they were convinced that "progress in organizing the intellectual diversion program is slow and generally unsatisfactory." One of the reasons was the AEO officer at the camp. 2nd Lt. Richard P. Mellman was trying to serve as the camp intelligence officer as well as the AEO. He could hardly be expected to do both jobs well. It was deemed necessary for Lieutenant Waxer to contact Col. L. R. Hathaway, post commander; Major H. Konigmark Jr., executive officer; and 1st Lt. William McCraw, POW camp commander, and explain the objective of reorientation and the role of the AEO in that program. During their visit, the field service officers learned that Lieutenant Mellman's efforts to rid the camp of subversives had begun but were constantly undermined by the arrival of transfers from other camps. Mellman had uncovered "several ardent Nazis" and transferred these undesirable prisoners. However, "within a short time many more ardent Nazis were transferred to this camp. This action has served to nullify the efforts of the Intelligence Officer to segregate troublemakers." Discouraged by these developments, Lieutenant Mellman had made no attempt to develop the education program until undesirable prisoners of war could be segregated. The Field Service visitors decided to help. In their report they noted that editors of *Die deutsche Insel* and the camp spokesmen "will be sent." And where were such individuals "sent"? In their report under the category of "Segregation," Waxer and Meyer noted that twenty-two of Mackall's POWs had been transferred for subversive activities: five noncommissioned officers to Aliceville, Alabama, and seventeen enlisted men to Camp Butner.[20] It is likely that some of those sent to Butner wound up in the famous Company 11 along with Fritz Teichmann and others mentioned elsewhere in this volume.[21]

## Fort Bragg

Developments in the Special Project Branch's reorientation program surfaced at Fort Bragg at the same time as they appeared at Camp Mackall. As at Mackall, the POWs at Fort Bragg had their own POW newspaper by the spring of 1945. The first weekly issue of *Der Drahtberichter* [The Wire Reporter] appeared on 1 April 1945. Its iconography featured a lonely prisoner standing behind the barbed wire as two radio towers beamed signals in the distance behind him. The observant reader of the paper did not need an editorial explanation of the double meaning of that frontispiece, which appeared in each issue. But Gustav Bieck, the POW editor, stated that the purpose of the paper was "the informing, the strengthening, the education, and the development of our camp inhabitants, and along with that their diversion and entertainment." The first edition suggested that as many comrades as possible would cooperate and contribute to the paper: "Old 'Afrikaner' will tell us their first encounter with a lion without moats and bars, Russian fighters will report on Cossack choirs and of Circassians in the Caucasus, comrades from southern France will tell us something of bull fights or about a day on the Riviera as it does not occur in novels."[22]

The articles that appeared in *Der Drahtberichter* were what one would expect in a German POW camp paper in a camp where a war was still going on and where within the barbed-wire enclosures, the Germans, led by their noncoms, still ran the camp as though it was located in the heart of Germany. When he reviewed the kinds of educational opportunities within the camp in April 1945, one writer gave no hint that the entire intellectual diversion program was on the brink of a major overhaul. As late as April, there were no courses on America, its peoples, its politics, and its national parks. Instead, he reviewed past and current educational endeavors:

> The instruction in our camp began on 24 July 1944 with a German course and in September 1944 several other courses were added. In October 1944, because of the possible transfer of all prisoners of war to another camp, instruction was suspended. But because this camp was not dissolved, there began on 11 December a planned course of studies in German, English, Spanish, and French, as well as book keeping, stenography, a commercial course, mathematics, algebra for high school graduates and officer candidates, mathematics for university students, physics, economics, and mathematics and German for non-commissioned officers. And, since February 1945, space studies. The number of students participating a week is about 230 men.[23]

The intellectual diversion program at Fort Bragg was still being run by the Germans for the Germans. The courses taught and studied were the kind that would have been given in a German military camp in Germany. The education program, like the camp newspaper, was still in the hands of loyal members of the Wehrmacht. With the appearance of an AEO at Fort Bragg, the publication of a new camp newspaper, and a very different educational program, things would change.

The last days of German control of the educational programs and free-time activities within the camp featured few clues of the monumental changes that would soon occur. The 1 April 1945 edition of *Drahtberichter* still featured the story of a "Concert for Heroes" on German Memorial Day [Heldengedenktag]. It was reported that the camp orchestra under Emil Rothfuss had put together an hour-long program of classical music by Wagner, Beethoven, Mozart, and Handel. Along with the music were "moving recitations" by Gerhard Shoenfelder and Alfred Mostert, "which brought the seriousness of this time to our attention and allowed us to feel the music more deeply."[24] German classics for the edification of patriotic Germans were still on the agenda.

German army bravery medals were still conferred and proudly reported in the POW camp newspaper. The 15 April 1945 edition of the paper announced that Maj. Paul Becker, who served the camp as a pastor, was awarded a Knights Cross with Oak Leaves, which was sent to the prisoner of war camp.[25] The editors of the camp paper, as well as their readers, were still loyal German soldiers and celebrated German heroism and martial duties. The tone of the camp was still set by loyal members of the Wehrmacht, if not outright Nazis.

But things were changing. Allusions to disharmony within the camp appeared in the 22 April 1945 edition in a dark essay by the editor, Gustav Bieck. He described a new and oppressive atmosphere that hung over the camp. "Unpleasant events," which he did not specifically mention, caused distress in the Notgemeinschaft [community of the distressed]. "Some thoughtless people disturbed the community and tore it apart." Unity was destroyed at a time when it was more necessary than ever, in Bieck's view. What did he mean? He seems to have been alluding to the emergence of divisions within the camp between those like himself who insisted on soldierly solidarity and those who with the end of the war voiced their criticisms of the Nazi regime. Bieck's editorial suggested that "everyone in this camp is old enough to decide his own course. He who at the time of greatest calamity wishes to separate himself from his cultural community [Volk], should in God's name go. The step is a difficult one, and he who would make it should consider all the possibilities before taking it. But there can be no conversions with a mallet."[26] Bieck was saying that those who wished to declare their alienation from their former German government and from their comrades should do so, but they should be aware of the implications of those steps. They should also not try to force their new convictions on their former comrades. However, they would and they did with the help of the army's Special Projects Division and the camp's AEO. The changes would be immediately obvious in the last issues of the POW camp newspaper and new issues of the camp paper that would replace it.

The last issues of *Der Drahtberichter* appeared in a changed atmosphere. The war was lost, Nazism could be and was freely denounced within the POW camps, and revelations regarding Germany's concentration camps were being made known to the world. The German POWs in America were forced to view films made during the liberation of these places of horror. In the 10 June 1945 issue of *Der Drahtberichter*, one of the German POWs soon to be associated with the new anti-Nazi atmosphere within the camp wrote "Thoughts Concerning the Film-Showing 'The Horrors in the German Concentration Camps.'" Leo Josef Bylicki of the 3rd Company wrote, "Whether we want or not, we must consider that the unbelievable has occurred in the land that is our home and where in the past being human, human worth, and humanity were not only represented, but also passionately defended when attacked." He noted that "our trust was misused in a frightful way. . . . The justice and the humanity that we thought to be defending was reversed behind our backs and barbarisms committed that threaten to take away our belief in the good of humanity. . . . We will struggle with ourselves and our future until we have overcome the catastrophe of the last years and until we can honestly and freely look the people of the world in the face."[27]

Bylecki's article appeared in the last issue of *Drahtberichter*. On 24 June, Bylecki, as editor of a new POW paper for Fort Bragg, introduced *Der Aufbruch* [New Beginning]. Gone was the picture of the lonely POW behind the barbed wire. Replacing it was the icon of three marching men bearing the banner proclaiming "Aufbruch." According to Bylecki, the purpose of the paper was to bring the POWs together to rethink their past and "begin the building of a Germany that will enjoy again in the world and among the family of nations the respect that it once possessed and win again that love which it misses so badly because of its own guild and the mistrust of others."[28]

At the Fort Bragg POW camp, as at Camp Mackall, these changes in the camp newspaper were not solely the result of the POWs themselves. The Special Projects Division people had their hands on the educational machinery of the camps. In the third issue of *Der Aufbruch*, on 22 July, the paper announced new evening courses for the POWs. They would focus on English and on American geography, history, and politics. It announced that while the courses were voluntary, there was an expectation on the part of the American camp administration that all prisoners would take part in these new courses. It was suggested further that the Americans felt that now that the war was over it was time for Americans and Germans to work together. Joining in the courses would be evidence of such cooperation; reluctance to participate would be seen as opposition to the Americans. The *Aufbruch* editor forthrightly issued a strongly implied American threat: prisoners who resisted cooperation would be deemed unworthy and not reliable enough to be sent back to Germany soon.[29] Clearly, the American administration at Fort Bragg, at least as it was portrayed by the new editor of *Aufbruch*, was close to "using the mallet for purposes of persuasion." What the editor of *Drahtberichter*, Gustav Bieck, had warned against was already coming true. A new day had dawned for the German POWs at Fort Bragg.

# 9

## WINDING DOWN

### Late-War and Postwar Reactions

The last days of the war in Europe did not mean the end of war for the American people. As the war on one front drew to a close, the war in the Pacific continued. Wartime austerity also continued, including rationing of gasoline, favorite foods, beverages, and cigarettes. Choice cuts of meat and certain vegetables did not appear on American tables unless they were grown at home. But they did seem to appear on the tables of German prisoners of war. That would not go long unnoticed by the American press, the public, and Congress.

The problem of German POWs receiving what the American public could not have was aggravated by the fact that information about such disparities came to the attention of the public just as American troops were liberating malnourished American POWs in Germany and discovering the Nazi concentration camp system. The horrors uncovered at places like Ohrdruf, Dachau, Bergen-Belsen, and Mauthausen shocked Americans. The immediate result was popular revulsion toward Germans and things German. German POWs, who appeared to some to have been coddled, suddenly were looked upon with new eyes and attitudes. Uncle Sam's smiling laborers became detestable "Nazis." In response to this public reaction, a period of austerity was introduced in the American POW camps that manifested itself in reduced daily caloric allotments and renewed enforcement of labor rules. The reduction of treats in POW canteens combined with reduced calorie levels gained the attention of International Committee of the Red Cross and Swiss visitors as well as the German POWs, who suddenly began to lose weight rapidly on the reduced diets. Some of the POWs perceived their new diets as America's childish revenge against defeated enemy forces.[1] In retrospect it is easy to see why they might have seen things that way.

A former POW from Camp Davis remembered that with the end of the war the Americans became unfriendly because they suddenly saw in every German a "Nazi." One day a documentary photo book showing the horrors of the concentration camps was circulated among the prisoners and each had to confirm by his signature that he had viewed the book. "It often happened that Americans spit on us from their vehicles to show their animosity."[2]

There was a nationwide reduction in food supplies to POWs during a period from spring through early fall 1945. The decision to change POW menus had been made in February, though further reductions in calories were introduced in April and May in light of civilian rationing and in reaction to a rising national protest against the sense that German POWs were being coddled. The changes called for substitutions of foods that were not available to civilians on menus for POWs. Additionally, the calorie level for working POWs was set at 3,000 a day. Margarine replaced butter, rations were cut to a maximum of four ounces of meat per man per day, and scarce items like fats, canned fruits and vegetables, and sugar were reduced.[3] From a report of a visit to the Monroe branch camp, Camp Sutton, came word that "rations, until recently, were drawn from Morris Field [in Charlotte], but the Quartermaster Sales Officer there was so highly arbitrary in red-lining items for technical reasons and refusing to make normal substitutions, that the prisoners lost weight at an alarming rate and arrangements were made to draw rations from Fort Jackson [Columbia, South Carolina]."[4]

Eventually the calorie levels in the camps nationally sank to between about 2,000 and 2,600. An International Committee of the Red Cross delegate reported from Wilmington a level of about 2,630 calories, which he noted was higher than that of the base camp at Camp Butner. The Red Cross man reported that the POWs received 2,250 calories on workdays and 2,140 on Sundays in mid-June 1945.[5]

How and why these changes came about was reflected in the pages of the *Charlotte Observer* during the month of April 1945. First there were reports of "special menus" for POWs at Easter. Then there were pictures and editorials revealing the ill treatment of American prisoners by the Germans and the contrasting "coddling" of German prisoners within the United States. The angry public reaction to this contrast forced the American military to take drastic measures. First, it took measures to negate the charges of "coddling," then it began public relations campaigns to inform the American public about the "true" nature of the POW program. Finally, a congressional hearing focused public attention on the "coddling" charges and helped explain them away.

The story that caught the eye of *Charlotte Observer* readers on 5 April 1945 was "Nazi Prisoners Feast on Ham at Easter Meal." The report originated in Boston and came through the Associated Press wire service. The title speaks volumes: In the eyes of the press and of most Americans, Germans were "Nazis," so German prisoners of war in America could be described as "Nazi prisoners." Neither the popular press nor the man in the street then nor now worries much about such generalizations. Fine differentiations have traditionally been left to moralists and historians. The fact that many Germans served in the Wehrmacht because of their sense of patriotic duty, despite their differences with the Hitler regime, did not trouble the American press. Nor did it trouble newspaper readers during World War II. The real issue was revealed in the title of the newspaper article: "Ham at Easter Meal." The only thing missing in the title is the implied exclamation point. The story revealed and shared the writer's sense of outrage: "The public relations office confirmed a Boston *Traveler* article to the effect that ham, virtually unavailable to citizens in the Boston metropolitan area on the Sabbath, had been served in practically all the prisoner of war camps. . . . The Germans ate ham for Easter Sunday—a luxury denied all but a few Americans."[6]

In a letter to the editor in the *Charlotte Observer* on 5 April, Mrs. James O. Hall of Elizabethtown wrote,

> Why do our American people show so much concern for the German prisoners over here in giving them every comfort they can, while our own dear boys are being treated like a bunch of dogs in the various prison camps in Germany? . . . The German prisoners over here are being handled with kid gloves while our own boys

over there are being treated like animals in that heartless, brutal ungodly land. I have no tender spot in my heart for the German race for they have caused more broken homes and heartaches than any civilized nation that ever existed. May God grant that a day of reckoning may soon come when Hitler and all of his clan will be wiped off the face of the earth forever.[7]

Charges that German POWs were being coddled went back to June 1943 with an article in the *New York Times* titled "Axis Captives Find Ease in Tennessee." The article, with phrases like "piles of juicy hams, plenty of butter, steaks and sausages," was sure to arouse the public.[8] In fact, the U.S. government was upholding Articles 10 and 11 of the Geneva Convention that "the conditions shall be the same as for the troops at base camps of the detaining power. The food rations of prisoners of war shall be equal in quantity and quality to that of troops at base camps." The American public did not know that. The army's attempt to keep the POW program out of the public eye and at the same time assure that the German government would give reciprocal treatment to American prisoners in its hands left the American government at a distinct disadvantage in defending itself against charges of coddling. It would take a series of national press attacks and two investigations by the House Military Affairs Committee, one in the summer of 1944 and the other in the spring of 1945, before the public could be convinced that "we do not coddle prisoners of war, but we treat them fairly and firmly."[9]

But Carolinians, like Americans in general, first went through a paroxysm of anger and vituperation against Germans in reaction to the very real evils that were uncovered in liberated Europe. On 8 April 1945, the *Charlotte Observer* carried a biting column by famous and nationally syndicated Walter Winchell, a writer who prided himself on the praise he received for his "one man campaign against coddling." Within the next few days newspaper readers saw the publication of stories and pictures of the scarecrow-like bodies of American servicemen liberated from a prison camp in Ohrdruf, Germany. Four days later, the *Observer* carried on its front page two Associated Press stories that it juxtaposed for shock effect, as did a number of newspapers across the country. One story was entitled "Allied Prisoners Suffered Brutality to Shock World on Forced March in Snow." The other was "Striking Nazi Prisoners Get

Their 'Smokes.'" The latter told of 250 German POWs in Belle Glade, Florida, who staged a strike at a bean plant over the lack of cigarettes in their PX.[10]

On 13 April 1945, the *Observer* printed an Associated Press story that mirrored popular wrath while noting the U.S. government's efforts to dampen the fires of resentment. "Well, Well, At Long Last: U.S. Warns Reich of Prisoner Crimes," by J. W. Davis, repeated the story of POWs' strike for cigarettes and reiterated the "shockingly inhuman treatment" of prisoners in Germany. Davis noted, however, that Secretary of War Stimson made a formal statement at a news conference suggesting that "the deplorable conditions under which many of these 70,000 men are living today are due to a large extent to Germany's fanatical determination to continue a hopeless war with resultant disintegration under disastrous military defeat." With apparent glee, the writer proclaimed that "the statement did not say so, but it was learned at the War Department that a general tightening up is underway at various prisoner of war camps in this country. It was emphasized, however, that even if the Germans are cruelly mishandling helpless men, the United States intends to stick to the conventions of humane treatment of prisoners."[11]

On 16 April, the editors of the *Observer* printed an editorial entitled "Study in Startling Contrasts" that featured pictures of an emaciated GI liberated from a camp in Germany and photos of well-fed and neatly clothed German prisoners of war marching in a formal funeral procession for one of their number at Camp Como in Mississippi. Lest the reader miss the point, "The *Observer* is herewith printing again two pictures which have already appeared in its news columns. Our purpose is one of emphasis and not one which we believe to be overemphasis. It comes down to this: American prisoners of war in Germany have been living in hell. But German prisoners of war in America have been living in paradise and our people are sick of it."[12]

Three articles that appeared in the *Greensboro Daily News* on 29 and 30 April and 1 May 1945 must be seen in the light of such negative articles regarding the American handling of German POWs. It is obvious that the American military as well as at least one staff writer for the Greensboro paper felt that another side to the story had to be told. James F. Reynolds, a *Daily News* staff writer, set another tone with his three articles. The first was entitled "War Prisoners at Bragg Treated Strictly, Firmly, Fairly, Justly: Regulations of Geneva Convention Followed Closely in Handling Them." This article and the two that followed are examples of efforts by the American military to gain some sympathy for their treatment of POWs. As Reynolds said, "There arose rumors of how American prisoner of war camps were coddling the Germans. Statements based on these rumors were carried in certain sections of the press, in magazines, in radio comments, and were even heard in the halls of Congress. A public opinion poll of national reputation conducted a survey, the results being announced early this month, in which the majority expressed the opinion that too much 'pampering and freedom' was allowed in our prisoner camps." Reynolds noted that misunderstandings among the public had grown because one widely read national magazine carried a story during the fall of 1944 about how "the Nazis were dominating the prisoner camps." But the writer of the article, as far as Reynolds or the Office of the Provost Marshal General could tell, had never been inside a POW camp. Nor had he talked with anyone at the Office of the Provost Marshal General or the Office of the Bureau of Public Relations. Worse, according to Reynolds, was that the article by the poorly informed writer "got further wide publicity through its re-publication in a magazine digest with several million readers."[13]

Reynolds noted that "the house military affairs committee conducted an investigation which failed to substantiate any of the numerous coddling rumors." Instead, he reminded his readers, the congressional hearing determined that the provisions of the Geneva Convention of 1929 were carried out "to the letter," because "the slightest deviation therefrom on our part would instantly result in more than retaliation measures on the part of our enemies against American prisoners of war in their hands." Reynolds stated the highlights of the Geneva Convention: "Prisoners of war must at all times be humanely treated. . . . The food ration of prisoner of war shall be equal in quantity and quality to that of troops at base camps . . . etc."

According to Reynolds, the prisoners at Fort Bragg were good workers. "Work of prisoners on jobs at the army post releases many soldiers for other duties. . . . POWs meanwhile worked at KP duty, cooking, baking, working in warehouses and the automotive repair shop, carpentry shop. . . . Officers and civilian supervisors who direct these activities say the Germans perform excellent work."

The wording and content of Reynolds's article bears repeating because it reveals what the government wanted the American public to know about the POW program in the spring of 1945 and the degree to which that public could have been aware of the program if they were newspaper readers:

> One detail of 35 men is engaged cutting and loading pulpwood on a tract in Harnett County several miles from the army base. This is an outside contract, supervised by W. D. Christian of Moncure, who said he was highly pleased both with the attitude displayed by the prisoners and the thoroughness of their work. . . . In company with Captain Nast, assistant executive officer of the prisoner of war camp; Capt. A. T. McLean and T/Sgt, C. O. Jeffress, of the public relations office; a signal corps photographer, Pvt. Kenneth S. Rollins; and a spokesman for the prisoner of war compound, we visited the woods detail in mid-afternoon and observed the systematic method these men follow in their work. . . . Contractors on such jobs as this pay the treasury of the United States the prevailing local wage for the type of labor as certified by the war manpower commission. The prisoners receive only the 80 cents per day proposed by this country to Germany at the beginning of the war and are paid in canteen coupons only. . . . Punishment is meted out to any prisoner of war qualified to work who refuses to work, slows down or deliberately loafs on the job. Such a prisoner at the Ft. Bragg camp is put on bread and water and locked up. . . . In the early stages of the war, emphasis was placed on the security of prisoners, causing a heavy drain on the army's manpower for guard duty. Later on, as the number of prisoners rapidly increased, the war department began to look upon them as an untouched pool of available manpower and as a result made security secondary to work. . . . Only one guard is provided for each working detail. The men simply do not want to get away, and during the approximately one year since the camp was established here there have been no escapes and only one attempted escape. Asked what would motivate a man to escape, Captain Nast said the main

reason would be to get away from the sight of a wire fence, even for a brief time.

Reynolds concluded:

The GIs on duty at the prisoner of war camp have what is probably the toughest assignment in the army. They have a thankless job in which there is little or no glory. The routine is monotony of the worst sort—the same grinding task day after day, handling enemy prisoners from every walk of life. The Germans look like any American group of similar size would look. Imagine, if you can, handling a crowd of Americans of the same make-up, mentally and physically, and you will have a pretty fair picture of what the GI's at Fort Bragg's prisoner of war camp have to contend with.[14]

The second article that appeared in the *Greensboro Daily News*, on 30 April 1945, continued the positive evaluation of the POW program at Fort Bragg in its title: "Prisoner of War Spokesman Keeps Contact with Camp Authorities: Food Is Ample But Not Abundant; Prisoners Not Allowed to Have Cash." The article presented details that helped personalize prisoner images for the article readers:

This spokesman, an intelligent fellow who has a good command of our language, told us he was a student of civil engineering and had gone "half way" through the university before he was called into the army eight years ago. He recently "celebrated" his 29th birthday. He was a member of the Afrika Korps and was brought to Ft. Bragg last September. . . .

The prisoners, whose ages range from 18 to 55 years, come from practically every walk of German life. Some were well-trained veterans, while others had not been in the army very long when captured. Some are bitterly pro-Nazi, some are outspokenly anti-Nazi, others take the middle-of-the-road course.

The article emphasized the nature of POW meals:

The prisoners are furnished an ample ration, in compliance with the articles of the Geneva convention, consisting principally of non-critical foodstuffs. . . . Although the Germans say their favorite meat is pork chops, they have not received any for five or six weeks, and beef is equally as scarce. Except for bologna, which comprises 60 to 65 percent of their meat ration, they are issued meat of any kind only once or twice a week. . . .

Of the vegetables, the prisoners prefer cabbage, potatoes and green peas, and apparently make good use of onions. They get no butter, but are occasionally issued oleomargarine; rarely receive sugar, and other sweets, such as syrups, are scarce articles with them. They receive a plentiful supply of bread and milk and are issued breakfast cereals, which they say they do not care for.

The inherent nature of the German race for economy, however, makes it possible for the prisoner mess hall attendants to prepare a delectable menu from the rations issued them.

In the kitchen we picked up a menu, freshly mimeographed in German, which we were told was the one for that particular day. It contained the following:

Breakfast—Coffee. Milk. Corn Flakes. Bread.
Lunch—Milk and rice soup. Bologna. Mayonnaise. Bread.
   Orange.
Supper—Mutton stew. Potato soup. Bean salad. Red beets.
   Coffee. Bread.[15]

The third and final article in the *Greensboro Daily News* appeared on 1 May. Its title summed up the thesis and tone of the series: "No Coddling Given Nazis at Ft. Bragg."

Maj. Morgan F. Simmons, who heads the prisoner of war camp for Germans at Ft. Bragg and members of his staff are obeying orders from the war department by putting work first and security second in their system of handling the prisoner.

The war department inaugurated the prisoner of war work program the latter part of 1942 and it has paid dividends in two ways: It helped to solve an acute manpower shortage and boosted the morale of the prisoners by keeping them from idleness and its consequent depressive effects.

A reclamation department is maintained near the camp compound and from 108 to 210 depending on the need, are worked there reclaiming tools, tents, rain coats, overcoats, typewriters, adding machines, mess kits, and a variety of other articles used by American soldiers. The supervisor of the reclamation department told us that within eight months 70,000 water canteens, 100,000 canteen cups and more than 100,000 mess kits had been reclaimed. In three months, he said more than 5,000 flashlights had been repaired by three men alone, while 25 others working in the carpentry shop had built 5,000 coal boxes. Many thousands of general purpose boxes, fly screens and ladders have been made in this shop during a year's time, the amount of lumber used totaling more than one million feet.

A number of prisoners work at the post sawmill, where timber produced on the Ft. Bragg reservation is converted into lumber, which, in turn, is used for repairs and other purposes for which lumber otherwise would have to be bought. . . .

On our tour of the many phases of activity of the prisoner we visited the quartermaster warehouses where shoes and other articles worn or used by the soldier are classified and packed, the automotive classification warehouse where parts are put in proper condition, the automotive repair shop, the post carpentry shop, and a number of other places where the Germans are employed. Those in charge all spoke highly of the prisoners as steady workmen and agreed that they were well worth their pay. . . .

In this series of stories we have tried to present the facts as found during two days spent, not only with the officers of the prisoner of war camp, but among the prisoners themselves, in the privacy of their barracks, in their mess halls, in their canteen, in their recreation hall, in their library, in their study hall, even in the hospital wards where something like 20 of their number are ailing and at many of the places where prisoner labor is employed. We slept just outside the strong wire fences which keep these German captives secure at night, we walked the streets of their compound, we observed them at work and play.

No opinion has been advanced except that based on facts as we found them.

There has been a lot of talk—apparently loose talk base on hearsay that came from somewhere across the creek—about coddling of Germans in American prisoner of war camps.

The Ft. Bragg prisoner of war camp does not.[16]

It was obvious that James F. Reynolds and the *Greensboro Daily News* saw and described the POW program at Fort Bragg as the army wanted them to. In fact, that is exactly the way International Committee of the Red Cross and YMCA visitors described the American POW program in North Carolina and the United States as a whole. What the media commentators and an angry public perceived as "coddling" was the deliberate attempt by the American government to uphold the Geneva Convention in order to protect American prisoners in German hands. When public pressure at the end of the war forced the army to reduce POW rations, International Committee of the Red Cross delegates noticed and complained. By then, of course, there was no Nazi government to retaliate. Nor was there any legal German government that might complain. Good sense, the needs of American farmers for healthy workers, and the realization that demoralized German POWs would be poor subjects for an American reorientation program ended the brief period of "hunger rations" for the POWs by the late summer of 1945.

By that point, the POW program was winding down at Fort Bragg and Camp Butner and their branch camps. But that was not obvious to contemporaries. German POWs would be in North Carolina until at least April 1946. In the meantime, problems would continue for American POW administrators and their German captives. The number of incoming prisoners would increase and peak during the last days of the war in Europe. During the summer of 1945, the Germans continued to suffer from hunger rations imposed by a vindictive America. And as the war in Europe ended, followed several months later by the end of the war with Japan, postwar lethargy affected both the Germans and their American guards.

A visit by Dr. Bubb of the International Red Cross on 10 July 1945 revealed that the number of POWs in Fort Bragg had multiplied, a minor crisis had passed, and the POW facility at Fort Bragg was, in the eyes of the Swiss visitor, "an excellent camp."[17] The "minor crisis" he referred to was the reduction of rations to POWs in the United States.

"After having been very limited in the last several weeks, the nourishment had improved markedly over about the last week. Now it is considered sufficient in quantity. . . . The spokesman affirmed that the rations formerly had been 2400 calories per day per man, whereas now they had reached a little more than 3000 calories. . . . In general, the state of health [of the prisoners] is perfectly satisfactory. Most prisoners lost notable amounts of weight in the last weeks, but few noticed the changes precisely."

It was also noted that although the location and arrangements of the camp had not changed much since the last Red Cross visit, the number of POWs had quadrupled. There were now two compounds with four companies each. Each company had more than 250 men for a total of 2,324 German POWs. Of these there was one officer, 694 noncommissioned officers (of whom only 269 were officially recognized by the Americans), and 1,623 regular soldiers. Nearly 1,200 worked within the bases in its kitchens and canteens. Three hundred worked in the forest felling trees, and another 500 were involved in the peach harvest. The German spokesman privately told the Red Cross visitor that he had asked that about 300 prisoners who were more than forty years old should not be employed except on light duty and that the camp authorities had taken that into consideration. "In any case, the spokesman and the medical doctors hope that these prisoners will be repatriated rapidly, for an appropriate employment for them has presented a difficult problem."

Planning for a return home was on the minds of both the German POWs in the Camp Butner system and the International Committee of the Red Cross visitors. The last Red Cross visitor to inspect the POW camp at Camp Butner was Guy S. Métraux. At the time of his visit on 3 April 1946, the number of prisoners at the main camp was 1,460 and those in six remaining side camps totaled 2,283. Even on the eve of its dissolution, the Camp Butner facility still administered 3,743 men. The remaining branch camps were at Ahoskie, Moore General Hospital in Swannanoa, New Bern, Roanoke Rapids, Williamston, and Wilmington. These side camps supplied POW services that were still urgently needed even as large numbers of the former Wehrmacht were being processed for return to Europe, if not immediately to their homeland.[18]

Things were changing. Col. Thomas Alexander was no longer the

POW camp commander at Camp Butner. In this postwar period, his replacement was Capt. D. J. Morris. The postwar Camp Butner POW camp henceforth occupied what had formerly been only the "A" compound. "Allied prisoners of war" were in a segregated portion of this enclosure. These were the remaining French, Dutch, Poles, Czechs, and Luxembourgers who had been segregated from their Wehrmacht comrades because of their desire to rejoin national forces fighting against the Nazis. Now they, like the rest of the men of the camp, were awaiting their journey home. At the time of the Red Cross visit, it was expected that this "nationalities group" would leave about 10 April for a port of embarkation. The other prisoners would soon follow. The side camps at Williamston and New Bern were to be closed sometime between 9 and 15 April and their prisoners redistributed to other side camps. These camps were to be reassigned to another base camp because Camp Butner was to be closed about 15 April and would therefore cease to be their base camp for administration and supply. The library at Camp Butner had already been packed for shipment to the International YMCA and study courses had stopped. "The prisoners of war buried at Camp Butner are to be moved to the cemetery at Fort Bragg, North Carolina, in the near future."[19]

There were still "eight prisoners of war in the prison stockade. Two [had] been confined for three months protective custody, two for attempted escapes, two for writing notes to American girl employees, one for writing an unauthorized letter, one for insubordination."[20] The POW program was winding down, but its problems remained until the end.

# 10

# IT'S NOT OVER UNTIL IT'S OVER

## Memories of France and England

What happened to the 10,000 German POWs who spent time in the Tar Heel State? Did any stay? When were they returned home? Uncertainty lay ahead for the German POWs in North Carolina in 1945. Even though the war in Europe ended in May 1945, the American war against Japan continued. Beyond that, American domestic economic needs and the problems of early postwar Europe combined to prolong their stay in America and continue their uncertainty about when they would return home.

Further complicating the issue was the fact that some 180,000 of the 378,000 German POWs on the shores of America were either "owned" by the British and temporarily held by the Americans in the United States or promised to the French and Belgians.[1] They were held in America because originally there was no place to keep them in wartime Europe, even though most had been captured in North Africa by the British. These German POWs were in the temporary custody of the Americans. At the end of the war, America's British, French, and Belgian allies assumed that large numbers of these prisoners would be turned over to them to help rebuild ravished countries and economies. What German POWs denounced as "slave trading" was an exaction of reparations in the form of labor from former European enemies. About 123,000 German POWs who had spent time in America would spend a year or more working in postwar Britain, and about 55,000 would do the same in France. A small number were also sent to Belgium.[2]

The 178,000 German POWs shipped to France, Belgium, and Britain at the end of the war were just a small fraction of the German POWs

the United States turned over to Allied nations from its POW enclosures in the United States and in Europe. Because American troops
captured many German prisoners at war's end, the vast majority of
them were never taken to the United States. There were between 2–5
million German soldiers in American hands in Europe in June 1945.[3]
Of the 975,000 POWs that the Americans turned over to its Allies after
the war 797,000 of them were already in Europe; 178,000 came from
captivity in the United States. From American-held POWs, both in the
United States and Europe, France received 700,000 German prisoners—of which 200,000 worked on farms, 55,000 in mines, 40,000 in
construction, and 30,000 in forestry. The British received 175,000 prisoners, which added to their own German captives for a total of 385,000
men. Of these, 85,000 were used to clear rubble, 35,000 to mine coal,
20,000 were employed by the Air Ministry for unnamed tasks, and the
rest worked in agriculture. Belgium received approximately 50,000
prisoners. An additional 50,000 German POWs who had be held by the
Americans in the United States or Europe were divided between the
Netherlands, Norway, Czechoslovakia, Yugoslavia, and Greece.[4]

The "slave-trading" by America and the Allies at the end of the war
remains one of the most controversial aspects of the POW program
and deserves some discussion. In retrospect it seems a serious trans-
gression of Article 75 of the Geneva Convention that stated that "repatriation of prisoners shall be effected with the least possible delay
after the conclusion of peace."[5] It must be remembered that no peace
treaty was concluded with Germany at the end of war. The peace treaty
occurred only in 1990 with the agreement between the Allies and the
two German states to reunify Germany. There was no legally recognized
German government in 1945. Of course, all that sounds like post facto
justification.

Edward Pluth's work on the administration and operation of the German Prisoner of War camps offers a valuable analysis of the development of U.S. and Allied use of German POW labor.[6] He points out that
the Allies made plans to use German labor in postwar Europe at least as
early as the Quebec Conference in September 1944. Henry Morgenthau
Jr., the U.S. secretary of the treasury, proposed a plan for reparations
that used "forced German labor, outside Germany." The plan was accepted in principle and at Yalta, the Protocol on German Reparations

provided for reparations in kind, which included use of German labor. Allied governments could use POWs outside Germany for "agricultural and rehabilitation work in liberated nations." The Allied Reparations Commission agreed to turn over 1,750,000 German prisoners of war to the French by July 1946. Belgium, Luxembourg, and Russia were also to receive POW labor. But the largest number of German POWs held by American troops went to France and Britain. In June 1945, it was believed that the United States held about 2,100,000 German POWs in Europe and the Americans agreed to release or turn over to the French or British all of these men except for about 600,000 who were to be kept as labor for the United States Army in Europe. In April 1945 the *Washington Post* editorialized that such POW labor was a violation of the spirit of the Geneva Convention. But the reaction of the American public to Allied plans was positive: a Gallup Poll published in May 1945 showed that 82 percent of Americans polled favored requiring German men to spend two or three years helping rebuild cities in Russia. This was an increase from an earlier poll in March, which indicated that 71 percent favored the idea compared to 20 percent opposed. No doubt the change occurred because of intervening press reports of "coddling" of the Germans in the camps in America, German maltreatment of American prisoners in Germany, and the discovery of the concentration camps. In the spring of 1946, a year after the Allies' decision to use POW labor was made public and German POWs from the United States were already being turned over in large numbers to British and French authorities, the *Christian Century* condemned the American government's collaboration with its European allies on the POW labor program. The periodical informed its readers that the prisoners in the United States had been told that they would be sent home but in fact were becoming unpaid laborers in Britain and France. By then, however, the German POWs had left American shores and Americans were forgetting the fate of their recent German visitors.

Another moral dilemma concerned the repatriation of Soviet citizens. But unlike the "slave-trading" issue, repatriation was largely overlooked by the American public at the time. As with citizens of other Eastern European nations, some former citizens of the Soviet Union had been captured in the uniforms of the Wehrmacht. The Soviets wanted these "traitors" back home and the American government felt compelled to return them to whatever fate awaited them. This was less callousness on the part of the American authorities than the realization that the Russians had just liberated several thousand American POWs from Nazi hands in central Europe. If the United States wanted its sons back home, it needed to recognize the valid claims of its Soviet ally for the return of its own citizens.[7] The Soviet citizens held in Camp Butner, like those from all American-run POW camps, faced forced shipment and almost certain death in Soviet Europe. While their resistance to that fate is not evident in the records of the North Carolina camps, the resistance was obvious at such transit camps as Fort Dix, New Jersey, where on 29 June 1945 armed American guards had to use teargas and storm a barracks housing former Wehrmacht soldiers who were to be repatriated as Soviet citizens. Seven prisoners were wounded, and three committed suicide. The incident led to discussions at the highest level of the American government, but it was decided that because of agreements made at Yalta, the repatriation of Allied nationals was mandatory. The most that could be done was to refuse to return by force former citizens of the Baltic countries (Estonians, Latvians, and Lithuanians) and western Ukrainians (Poles), who had not been Soviet citizens before the seizure of their homeland by Soviet forces in 1939 and 1940. After seven of the Fort Dix "Russians" were determined to be Balts or Poles, they were removed from the list of those to be forcefully repatriated. Eventually, 146 men were put on a ship at New York on 31 August 1945 to be handed over to Soviet authorities in Europe.[8]

Not all of the German POWs in North Carolina were Soviet citizens or candidates for a prolonged work experience in France, Great Britain, or Belgium. POWs in certain categories were given early repatriation to their homelands. Some were considered too young or too old to be useful to their captor nations. Others were considered "useless" by the Americans because they were officers and noncommissioned officers (who could not be required to work), the sick or insane, and, finally, "Nazis," who were considered to be untrustworthy.[9] Not surprisingly, when the decision was made public, the "Nazi" category aroused the ire of the *New York Times*, the American public, and German POWs alike.[10] Additionally, some workers were deemed by the Allies to be immediately necessary to rebuild the Germany economy: miners, construction workers, policemen, and civilian administrators. Men in these categories were among the first to be repatriated beginning in the fall of 1945. There were others, too, who because of accident of birth were citizens of the restored Austrian republic. These men were returned home by the spring of 1946 to help rebuild their freshly re-created state. That was the experience of Max Reiter, the Camp Butner prisoner from near Linz, and Erich Moretti, the Camp Butner prisoner from Graz. Reiter, as a member of the Hitler Jugend and later of the Waffen-SS, never thought of himself as an Austrian until he was returned to Germany in the spring of 1946. There, as an "Austrian," he was designated for quick separation and transport across the border to his homeland. His unexpected and rapid repatriation came in time for him to begin his delayed education in the fall of 1946. Moretti, who was from a Pan-German and illegal Nazi family even before the Anschluss, never thought of himself as "Austrian" during his early life and military career with the Luftwaffe. He, too, was returned to Austria and to Graz in time to begin work toward a doctorate in economics in the fall of 1946.[11]

Much the same happened to the Bavarian medic who had spent time in Camp Sutton and Camp Butner. Because he was born in the Sudetenland, formerly a part of Czechoslovakia, he found a surprise in store for him. When he was sent to France in the spring of 1946, he learned that, like Austrians, those who had been born in Czechoslovakia were not to be held in France but were to be sent to Germany for repatriation to the places of their birth. Because of his accident of birth, he was not exposed to the chicanery of his former enemies. However, he did encounter the chicanery of his former comrades. Jealous fellow Wehrmacht members sought to relieve him of the "burden" of the sixty-five pounds of goodies that he was entitled to take back to Europe from America. In Babenhausen, near Darmstadt, he and his fellows were exposed to the thievery of a German-run but American-administered camp.[12]

He was still among the lucky ones. Almost half of the German POWs in the United States returned to Germany only after prolonged detours in France or England. Those who spent time in Britain were the more fortunate of these remaining groups. Though the British had suffered the Blitz, they had not endured the German occupation that the French had. The British government and its citizens were quicker to see their postwar German POWs as useful reconstruction workers and guests rather than as objects of scorn, anger, and abuse.

What was in store for the 55,000 "Americans," as the German POWs from the United States were called, when they arrived in France in the late winter and spring of 1946? First, for them there was surprise and dejection. When they embarked from America via Camp Shanks, New York, they were not told that they were not headed for Germany. It was an awful shock when they landed at Le Havre and were sent to the massive holding camp nearby at Bolbec. Even those like the Bavarian medic who spent only a brief time there before shipment to Germany and early release remembered that the food was in short supply and that the treatment of the POWs there was much worse than in America. As he and many others like him remembered, it was not necessarily because of the French themselves but because of the Eastern European guards and German camp leaders that the newcomers often suffered. Individual former prisoners, while they are consistent in their denunciations of the machinations, thievery, and maliciousness of their German comrades who had lived in France and had found their way into the administration of the postwar French camps, differ in their descriptions of the nationalities of their guards at Camp Bolbec. One Bavarian described them as Poles, while an Austrian thought that they were Yugoslavs.[13]

Bolbec was only the first of the unhappy surprises for men like the former Aliceville, Camp Davis, New Bern, and Butner prisoner who landed at Le Havre and "began a path of misery."[14] The lucky ones, the Austrians and men over forty years of age, were separated and released. But he and a contingent of those to be retained in France were sent south by train to near Lyons. Others were sent to a multiplicity of French camps. In the camp at Rouanne, the Camp Davis man and his fellows were given medical examinations to see if they were fit for work in the mines. In that work he discovered "hunger in its worst forms: in the morning there was a piece of bread that was to weigh 200 grams, mid-day a bowl of watered soup, and evening the same for five weeks long." Along with that came abuse: "standing for hours in the night, and if someone moved, immediately there was a guard with the butt of his rifle." Later he was sent to St. Etienne on the Loire and base camp St. Etienne 148. "We marched with our luggage. If we had known that those in the camp would take everything from us, then we would have left everything lying."

On 20 April 1946, he and his comrades arrived at their intended work camp. "The relationship to the civilians in France was never good. Beatings in the mines occurred frequently. Once a young Frenchman threw a stone at my head even though no conflict had occurred beforehand. The fact that one was a *Boche* [French slang for a German, a thickhead] sufficed."[15]

He was finally released on 16 October 1948. During his time in French captivity, especially when his physical and spiritual powers seemed at their lowest point, he was inspired by a fellow German POW who was a camp pastor: "I always compared him with Saint Paul."[16] His splendid example more than what he said gave the soldier the inner strength that he so badly needed at the time.

Matthias Buschheuer, a fellow Afrika Korps man and onetime cook at Camp Sutton, was more fortunate than the former prisoner from Camp Davis. He would get home sooner. But first he would transit through four French camps—Bolbec, Rouanne, Annecy, and Chedde. Finally, he was employed in an aluminum works as an oven worker. Buschheuer was returned home to Brühl near Cologne on 31 August 1947, beating the Bavarian corpsman by more than a year.

Buschheuer, who was transferred from Camp Sutton to Butner on 28 December 1945 and then left on 6 March 1946 for Camp Shanks, New York, and embarkation on 9 March 1946, had also believed that he was on his way home. He had no idea that it would be more than a year before he would arrive back in his hometown as a free man. He had anticipated that his arrival in Germany would be triumphal and had carefully preserved his Afrika Korps uniform. On his voyage back to Europe, he carried the maximum allowable luggage, complete with plenty of cigarettes and nylons acquired through purchase with his POW earnings. He arrived in Le Havre on 18 March 1946. Within the first four days in France, he was relieved of everything he had brought back from his stay in America except for his Afrika Korps uniform. In August 1947, he would wear it proudly, somewhat defiantly, at his homecoming. Decades later he told an interviewer, "Only the best were in the Afrika Korps."[17]

The experiences of the POWs from North Carolina who were sent to Britain were very different from those of their comrades who spent time in France. Fritz Teichmann of Camp Butner, Company 11, began his journey home in early 1946 with a train ride to New York and a Liberty Class C transport over the Atlantic. He and his comrades expected to land at a German port. To their shock they were deposited in the United Kingdom as prisoners of the British. Teichmann recalled that the British camp officers were "very correct." Food was sufficient, given the still-rationed civilian standard of living.[18]

By 1946, German POWs in Britain were sent out on work assignments without guards. For the entrepreneurial Teichmann, that meant that while walking through the city of Ripon in Yorkshire, he could engage in undocumented work for private individuals in the late afternoon or evening before returning to camp. He also enjoyed the fact that a number of kind people for whom he worked sent food parcels to Germany, something the prisoners themselves were not allowed to do.

Fraternization between the German POW workers and their English hosts developed as the representatives of the two nations shared the tasks of rebuilding the war-ravaged British economy. In Teichmann's area of Yorkshire, Dr. G. A. Chase, the bishop of Ripon, broke the ice for members of his Anglican congregations by entertaining German prisoners in his home at Christmas. Fritz Teichmann still treasures a clipping from the front page of the *Yorkshire Post and Leeds Mercury* of 30 December 1946. Along with a story under the headline "Bishop Entertains German Prisoners," there is a picture of the bishop and his guests posing while enjoying tea and cake. On the left side of the photo is a young Fritz Teichmann.

According to the report of "Our Special Correspondent,"

> Eight Germans felt somewhat shy as they climbed a hill outside Ripon in the misty December twilight of yesterday. They were not quite at ease in meeting English civilians; and to be entertained by the Bishop was a prospect likely to make anyone just a trifle nervous.
>
> When Dr. Chase welcomed them with a smile into the lounge of Bishop's Court all their apprehensions vanished. Though still wearing the distinguishing brown jackets of their comrades at Ure Camp, these men forgot for several hours that they were prison-

ers of war. Their host, a holder of the Military Cross from the First World War, was equally at home with his guests.

All in this small private party could speak English, but the international language of music was the real medium of good fellowship. After distributing a few small gifts from the Christmas tree, the Bishop drew the party round his grand piano. One of the Germans, a skilled musician played a little Bach. Then Dr. Chase produced some of the choicest gramophone records from his collection.

There were no speeches, no ceremonies, no formalities during this tea party, but out of hearing of his guests, the Bishop told me: "Believing that Christianity knows no boundaries of nationality, a number of Churchmen in Ripon, in co-operation with the Commandant of the camp, have offered Christmas hospitality to groups of German prisoners now stationed in Ripon."[19]

Letters to America from former German inmates of the Wilmington camp give additional insights about the disposition of the Tar Heel prisoners after the war. All but one of the letters to be discussed here were from the United Kingdom and sent to Mr. Arthur Ezold of Holyoke, Massachusetts. These letters, written to a trusted and beloved former American army friend and instructor in the Wilmington camp's reorientation program, reveal highlights of the odyssey that faced these men on the long trek back to Germany.

At least one of the letters Arthur Ezold received from former Wilmington POWs came not from Britain but from Germany. It was from Helmuth Schimmelpfennig and was written on 16 October 1946 from his home in Stuttgart:

This is going to be the first letter I have the chance to write from here at my home in Stuttgart. Many times I remembered you as the man I would write as the first thing after I'd arrived here. But I think it's not too late yet though I have been discharged about 10 days ago. It was rather long way back and not quite easy either, for I had to stay in France for another period of 3 months before they sent me home. Now I'm just lucky and my folks too.[20]

Klaus Bockhacker, formerly of the Wilmington camp, wrote to Ezold in care of the YMCA in Holyoke, Massachusetts on 21 May 1946 from No. 116 POW Camp, Great Britain (in Essex).[21]

Dear Mr. Ezold, You probably will be surprised to get a letter from England and not from my home address. But here, in short, is the time from our departure at Wilmington up to now. From Wilmington over Base Camp [Butner] to New York where we were embarked at Staten Island on the 18 March. Over the Atlantic in 9 days, disembarked in Belgium, from where after a few weeks we were brought to England. You may imagine, how disappointed we were, but the time goes over everything, and so also don't mind another year or perhaps more. Personally I am well. I am working as Clerk in a British headquarters, a work that suits me more than anything else. Shortly before I left America I had a letter from my mother who is living in the Rhineland; she has not any news from my father and my sister since May 45 and she seemed not to [sic] good. I hope, I will have more mail from her in the next time. I wonder what you are doing now. Are you discharged from the Army? The weather in England is not as good as in the sunny South, it rains a lot, but it is very nice in the countryside here, green and full of blossoms. As everywhere in Europe you can see that there has been a war for 6 years, there is a shortage of everything you may think of. So far I have come along all right, I got used to the new circumstances very quickly. I will close for today. With the best wishes and hoping to receive an answer form you I remain Yours Klaus Bockhacker.[22]

Rudolf Haynk, the noncommissioned officer who served as the spokesman for the Wilmington camp, wrote in German to Arthur Ezold from P.O.W. Camp 19, Happendon, Douglas, Lanarkshire, Great Britain [actually Lanarkshire, Scotland], on 14 December 1946:[23]

Dear Uncle Arthur, Just a short note to inform you that I hope to leave for home on 18 December. Perhaps after seven years I can again celebrate Christmas with my dear wife. It was a very great disappointment in April of this year when we were sold [verkauft] from America to here. But I have taken to heart these words, "He can help." These words I will never forget. They have helped me here too. Daily I thank God for his grace and for all that he gave me in America. Again I say to you and the pastor my special thanks for all that I received in America in soul and body. I wish you and the pastor a best happy Christmas and a happy and healthy new year. If it would be possible for you and the pastor, I would like to stay in correspondence with you. My address for mail [near Dresden, Saxony, Russian zone] . . . .

Another letter, written in English on 22 December 1946 and sent to Ezold from Rudolf Wellein from No. 101 German PW Working Camp, Newton, Montgomeryshire, Wales, is worthy of an extensive excerpt:

As you know I arrived in this country on May 14th. After five weeks being in camp I went to a farm in Wales in Billet. Was quite a bit disappointed the first day on the farm when I learnt [sic] that people speak Welsh a language of which I could not understand any word. Although everybody has learnt [sic] to speak English at school they never talk English to each other. Therefore I have not had a very good chance to get ahead with my little English knowledge. My brother Jakob got home on March 8th. I'm receiving quite a bit of mail from home. Things are allright [sic] there. When I came back to this camp a few days ago I found only a few men from W[ilmington]. Walter Werner, Hermann Werthmüller, and Oskar Uberrhein (Rakete) ["Rocket"]. That's all what is left from W[ilmington]. Helmut Pausinger wrote to me from Austria he arrived home on June 2nd. I think that men from Austria were all sent home straight from America. All the other men I have been with in W[ilmington]. have been scattered all over this country and I think not many of them have returned home yet. Only a few more days and we will have Christmas again. I hope it will be the last in prisonership. Now I wish you a Merry Christmas and a happy New Years. Herzlichen Gruss, Rudolf Wellein.[24]

An equally revealing letter was written by Gerhard Bachmann, 276 G.P. W.W. Camp, Nissen Creek, Pinhoe, Nr. Exeter, Devon, Great Britain, to Mr. Ezold on 20 January 1947. It too bears extensive quotation:

There are a few things you ought to know. First I am still in England and I don't even know when my time comes to go home. Do you remember what you told me about our meetings in camp, when you told us about American History and Democracy and what more? You told us, that in attending those lessons we would have a sure fact, that it would help us everywhere to get along and that it was very important for us for our future as Prisoners. Well, all I think, that we were sent over here to England without anything definite about our political gradings. We were never screened in America, though I think that you kept a certain record of every P.O.W. [This reference suggests that Ezold was the AEO at Wilmington]. So as we came to England we were considered as kind of black sheep that had to be screened. I got away with B– (B-minus) that means that with my membership to the Hitler Youth I was not free from any black spots. There is still a chance that we are up-graded again and I might go up to a better group.— Another item on my list tonight is the fact that Konrad Bertram is home at last. He went home in December as sick, and I think that was the best for him, because he got worried very much about his wife and kids and there wasn't any sense in keeping him any longer. You will be glad to hear that I suppose.

I had a nice Christmas with an English family, and I learned a lot about the ways the English have to make strangers comfortable and at home in their houses. It was the happiest Christmas I ever spent as a P.O.W. and I can still go and see them any time I like to [sic].[25]

Finally, there was the homecoming for former North Carolina prisoners. For some, after years in captivity there was the peculiar feeling of being time travelers returning to a future that was unfamiliar. Former Winston-Salem POW Captain Fritz Lempp recalled arriving at the Munich train station. People stared at the returnees because some were still wearing their uniforms and decorations. "They were looking at us with hostility. Someone finally approached me, and touching my uniform whispered 'It's no longer the time to wear that!'"[26]

# 11

## GRAVES AND MEMORIES

### Graves

An article in the *Charlotte Observer* on 23 June 1995, entitled "They Were Our People" focuses on eight German POW graves at the post cemetery at Fort Bragg. They were still being remembered by loyal countrymen in a memorial service each October. The graves were first tended by a German-born war bride living in Fayetteville, Ottilie Kriby, who died in 1993. She organized a group to visit the graves and honor the dead with a memorial service. In 1995, there were some ninety members of the memorial club, "German-born wives or widows of American soldiers, and most have a child's perspective on the war."[1] The *Observer* writer was suggesting that the grave tenders cherished romantic images of heroic deaths. He implied that the stories of the deceased Germans were rather prosaic. Prisoners, like most humans, usually die from diseases and accidents, even suicides, instead of being struck down while in the pursuit of heroic deeds.

The *Observer* article noted the grave sites, names, ranks, and death dates of the eight former POWs buried at Fort Bragg. It indicated that little was known about each of the deceased other than what could be found in four death certificates at the local Cumberland County courthouse. One was a cancer victim and others were killed in job-related accidents—falling trees and vehicular accidents.

There were originally nineteen graves of German POWs in North Carolina—the eight that are still at Fort Bragg and eleven others at the post cemetery at Camp Butner. After the war, the eleven bodies at Butner were disinterred and reburied at the large National Cemetery in

Chattanooga, Tennessee, on 13 March 1947; the army made it a policy to bury POWs in cemeteries of permanent federal installations. When Camp Butner ceased to be a federal installation, the bodies of the POWs were moved to the National Cemetery in Chattanooga. The transfer of the bodies was documented by the German authorities entrusted with maintaining information about deceased members of the former German Wehrmacht for their next of kin, the Deutsche Dienststelle für die Benachrichtigung der nächsten Angehörigen von Gefallenen der ehemaligen deutschen Wehrmacht (German Office for the Notification of the Next of Kin of the Deceased of the Former German Armed Forces, formerly the WASt, Wehrmachtauskunftsstelle).[2]

Using figures through December 1945, the Prisoner of War Operations Division stated that nationally there had been a total of 735 German deaths: 72 suicides, 4 murders, 3 homicides, 40 shootings, and 126 accidental deaths. Additionally there were 490 deaths "from natural causes, including wounds received in action outside the continental United States."[3] In light of the fact that two of the deaths among German POWs in North Carolina occurred after December 1945, those of Johann Zokan and Josef Wimmer in January and February of 1946, and that large numbers of Germans remained in the United States through the spring of 1946, these national statistics are probably not complete. But they do put developments in North Carolina into a national perspective.

Only Werner Friedrich Meier of Camp Sutton, who was shot while trying to escape a work detail, can be included among the forty German prisoners who were shot. No murders or homicides are listed among the North Carolina POWs, though initially the army was suspicious about one of the "suicides" at Camp Butner. Three deaths are listed as "suicides" by WASt: Kilian Kernberger at Camp Butner in January 1945, Paul Schmidt at New Bern in April 1945, and Erwin Frantz at Camp Butner in June 1945.

Two of these deaths were suicides by hanging. It was decided that Kernberger took his life because of depression: "He had been quiet and moody for some time. His despondency was said to be the result of worry over old wounds and family troubles. The deceased had written several letters immediately prior to his death indicating that he planned suicide."[4] In the case of Erwin Frantz, the verdict was that he was psychotic: "The prisoner was found hanging in an empty latrine in a compound to which he had been assigned on a work detail. His death was apparently a suicide. The prisoner was classified as a psychotic, although not an extreme case. He had been kept under close observation but evaded surveillance on this occasion."[5] Paul Schmidt's death was assumed to have been the result of the prisoner's demented state and self-destructive flight into the swampland around New Bern. Schmidt escaped on 18 July 1944; his remains were found on 27 November 1946. One additional death that the WASt lists as an accident was reported initially by American authorities as a suicide because the troubled soldier seemed to have intentionally fallen in front of a moving vehicle.[6]

The "suicide" of Kilian Kernberger originally was suspected to have been a murder. His body was found on 16 January 1945 in a Camp Butner barracks. Initially camp authorities were concerned because when the body was found hanging from a shoestring, there appeared to be signs of two rings around the victim's neck and Kernsberger's neck was broken. Foul play was suspected:

> There is a definite indication that he was murdered because a shoe-string won't break a man's neck. We immediately dispatched two investigators from our Durham, North Carolina, office which is about thirty miles from Camp Butner, to the scene. We have also dispatched two special agents who are experts in the subject of murders, both of whom worked on the murder case at Aiken, South Carolina, at Camp Gordon, and broke that case. We now have four special agents on the scene working on the whole matter.[7]

However, ultimately the army decided that there was no need to be so suspicious regarding Kernberger's death. He had written several letters indicating that he was contemplating suicide. The report that they sent to the Special War Problems Division of the Department of State for communication to the International Committee of the Red Cross and through them to the German government read as follows:

> Reference is made to letter SPMGO (17) 383.6 dated 16 January 1945 from the Office of the Provost Marshal General to the Legation of Switzerland, a copy of which was forwarded to your

department, concerning the death of German Prisoner of War Kilian Kernberger, 81G-271502H, at Prisoner of War Camp, Camp Butner, North Carolina.

A report of investigation discloses that a fellow prisoner found the deceased dead at 1140 on 16 January 1945 in the empty room of a non-commissioned officer on the second floor of unoccupied Barracks T-140, where the deceased together with seventeen other prisoners of war, had been working on a paint detail. The body was found slumping from a bed post from which a strong string had been fastened around the deceased's neck and all evidence led the investigating officers to conclude that the death was a suicide. A knife was found near the prisoner's right hand, but the medical officer's report reveals that the death was attributed to strangulation, as cuts on the deceased's neck were only superficial, apparently made before the hanging, in a futile effort of the deceased to cut himself down afterwards.

No evidence of coercion, threats, or foul play was found and investigation disclosed that Prisoner of War Kernberger had had no controversies or arguments with fellow prisoners, although he had been quiet and moody for some time. His despondency was said to be the result of worry over old wounds and family troubles. The deceased had written several letters immediately prior to his death indicating that he planned suicide.[8]

The remaining deaths among POWs in North Carolina are listed as due to illness (10) and accidents (5). Specifics about illness and accidents are difficult to obtain from official statistics and must be gleaned from searching incomplete army reports to the State Department, which handled communications with the International Committee of the Red Cross. Some additional details can be obtained from POW camp newspapers.

The accidents most common in North Carolina, as well as nationally, were the result of motor vehicles or falling trees. Wilhelm Burghardt died on 26 October 1944 at the Regional Hospital at Fort Bragg because of injuries sustained in a vehicular accident:

The accident occurred near Prisoner of War Camp, Fort Bragg, North Carolina, when Burghardt and nine other prisoners were being taken to work at the Post Ordnance Shop. As the truck approached an intersection and attempted to pass another vehicle stalled on the highway in front of it, the stalled vehicle started up and turned to the left directly in front of the prisoner of war truck. The two vehicles collided and Prisoner of War Burghardt was thrown from the back of the open truck to the highway, fracturing his skull and causing concussion of the brain. He was dead upon admission to Station Hospital #2, at Fort Bragg, North Carolina.[9]

Vinzent Bednarski died on 8 September 1945 at Camp Butner, also in a vehicular accident:

At approximately 3:30 P.M., Saturday, 8 September 1945, German Prisoner of War Bednarski, Vincenz [sic], 8WG 55075 MI, accidentally met his death by falling off a moving truck while enroute from his work detail at the Convalescent Hospital Ration Breakdown, Camp Butner, NC to the Prisoner of War Camp. Upon questioning other prisoners who were riding in the truck at the time of the accident, it was revealed that since all the seats on the 2½ ton truck had been taken, it was necessary for three (3) men, one of whom was Bednarski, to stand. These three (3) prisoners, instead of standing inside the truck, however, elected to stand on the tail gate, holding onto the canvas and frame. As the truck neared the entrance to the Prisoner of War Camp, the driver, Euralee Harrison, civilian, made a short turn and Prisoner of War BEDNARSKI fell to the ground suffering a fractured skull. An ambulance was immediately summoned and he was taken to the Camp Butner General Hospital where he died at 7:10 P.M. the same date. Prisoner of War Bednarski was buried at the Prisoner of War cemetery, this camp, 11 September 1945.[10]

*The European*, the POW camp newspaper for "Allied" prisoners at Camp Butner, noted that:

Our comrade, Winc. [sic] Bednarski fell victim to a tragic auto accident. In the bloom of his life he died far from his beloved *Heimat* [Homeland]. His death is so much the sadder for he was fortunate enough to have survived the risks of the war and now was about to have the long desired return home. . . . So many comrades attended the funeral mass that the chapel could not contain them. . . . At the open grave our camp pastor held a short homily and amid prayers and the song "Ich hatt'einen Kameraden" [I Had a Comrade], the casket was lowered into the ground. A salute, fired in honor of the deceased by American soldiers, ended the simple service.[11]

Wilhelm Schäffer died on 20 June 1945 at Fort Bragg due to a timbering accident. "While on a work detail engaged in clearing timber at Fort Bragg, North Carolina, Prisoner of War Schaeffer was struck on the back of the head by a limb of a falling tree. The medical report states the cause of death to have been 'Hemorrhage, intra-cranial resulting from accidental fracture of base of skull.'"[12] The POW camp newspaper at Fort Bragg on 8 July 1945 reported the accident and the attendant funeral:

On 22.6.1945 at 14:00 the funeral mass for our unfortunate comrade Willi Schaffer [sic] was held. All of the comrades who were in camp at this time and were available took part in the ceremony. It transpired in the most impressive manner. The funeral music was very affective and the word of farewell to the deceased presented by our pastor, Major Paul Becker, touched our hearts. Amid the resounding strains of Chopin's funeral march our comrade was carried out and buried in the soldiers' cemetery at Fort Bragg. We will not forget you when we return to der Heimat [the Homeland], comrade![13]

The danger of accidents and even a death in the woods like that of Willi Schäffer aroused the War Department to create a special film warning POWs of the dangers of accidents on the job. The POW newspaper at Fort Bragg, Der Aufbruch, mentioned this film and the need for work safety in its first issue on 24 June 1945:

Recently the number of accidents at the work places of prisoners of war has risen. In response to this fact the War Department has created a film, also shown in our camp, that especially relates to woods workers. . . . What the film says is that every Kamerad, whatever his work place, must be careful with his materials and tools so that he is not injured. Carelessness is often the cause of disastrous accidents.[14]

There were ten deaths from illnesses at the North Carolina POW camps. Four led to graves at the Fort Bragg post cemetery and six to graves at Camp Butner (and later at the National Cemetery in Chattanooga). Finding information on the specific causes of death is a bit difficult. Some details are to be found in Swiss Legation reports and some in information given to the International Committee of the Red Cross. Not all the records seem to have survived. There are often hints rather than specific details. For instance, a report of a visit to Fort Bragg on 9 December 1944 by a representative of the Swiss Legation and a member of the State Department indicated that there had already been two deaths at Fort Bragg and its branch camps: "Prisoner Wilhelm Burghardt died as the result of an automobile accident. Prisoner Wilhelm Blum died from a brain abscess. Both of these deaths were reported."[15]

The case of Heinrich Hoffer [spelled Hofer in official German files], who died of leukemia on 13 August 1945 in the army hospital at Camp Butner, is instructive because of the vagaries of fate it reveals. Hofer, a Panzergrenadier with an armored artillery unit who was captured in Tunisia on 24 April 1943, was born in Strassburg in 1922. He was an "Alsacien," ethnically German but a citizen of France before the Nazi takeover of the region in 1940.

Hoffer was at Camp Butner because he was placed in the unique "Allied" compound of POWs who volunteered to join the forces of their native countries against the forces of Germany. To their fellow Wehrmacht comrades they were "Überlaufer," "turncoats and traitors." To themselves and their fellow nationals they were victims of the German mobilization who sought freedom from those German associations and a return to their own nationalist folds. Hoffer's death prevented him from joining the French army for which he had volunteered. Unlike his fellow Alsacien, Pierre Mertz (mentioned in Chapter 4), he would not join in the liberation of his homeland and in its final victory over the German forces in which he had once served.

Heinrich Hoffer's father sought information about his son's death and final resting place. His letter to American POW authorities indicated the Hoffer family's last communications from their son and the limited information that they had on his fate.

He sent his last letter from Camp Butner and he posted it on 2-4-1945 [2 April 1945]. One of his fellows came back from America and advised Hoffer's Family that Henry Hoffer was dead in General Hospital of Camp Butner on 13-8-1945 [13 August 1945]. I should be grateful for your seeking if Hoffer's death is true. In this case, you can advise officially his family which first of all wishes to recover its property of Henry Hoffer's personal things, to know what are the death circumstances, where is the grave and looks for the possibilities of bring back the body to France.[16]

The reply from America was:

Former German Prisoner of War Hoffer died 13 August 1945 at the United States General Hospital, Camp Butner, North Carolina, of Leukemia Lymphatic acute, secondary Anemia. The decedent's remains are interred at Grave 34, Section 2, Prisoner of War Cemetery, Camp Butner, North Carolina. A report of death was forwarded to the International Committee of the Red Cross on 25 August 1945, List No. 407. The death certificate was also forwarded to the International Committee of the Red Cross. It is suggested that you contact the French Embassy regarding the return of the decedent's remains to France.[17]

Apparently the family decided against returning their son's body to France. His body was relocated when Camp Butner no longer was a federal facility. Heinrich Hoffer has been interred since 13 March 1947 at the National Cemetery in Chattanooga. He and his fellow deceased POWs are far from the North Carolina POW camps where they died and farther still from their European homes. They are "Americans" forever.

## Memories

For many of the former Wehrmacht "guests" in North Carolina, memories and American friendships were lasting. Correspondence and visits to former campsites have not been unusual, and they continue today.

It is well to remember, however, that the evidence of positive memories that have influenced this historian may cause him to underestimate the degree to which for some POWs the experiences in North Carolina (as elsewhere in the United States) were not positive ones. As one of my German colleagues, Matthias Reiss, has said, "Perhaps it should be mentioned that there were also disgruntled POWs (they formed a short-lived club in Germany in the 1950s) but that it is difficult to track them down. I talked to a few of them, but the vast majority refused to be interviewed in detail, partly (I think) because they feared being branded as anti-American, partly because they did not wish to speak about what they considered a 'lost' period of their life."[18] This author has encountered or learned of similarly alienated former POWs who spent time in POW camps in other states. The evidence about the POW experience in the North Carolina camps, however, has been overwhelmingly positive.

German POWs from the Williamston camp continued to correspond with their American friends after their departure for Europe. Arturo Morasut wrote from the Russian sector of Berlin that "life was better in Williamston than here. I will never forget the beautiful time I stay with you and your friends. The day I left Williamston I was rather unhappy because I left all my good friends behind. You all treated me better than brothers. I can't ever forget you." Another, Dr. Gunther Hermann, wrote, "The time I was in America was the best for me. . . . I will ever remember the nicest time of my imprisonment when I was sitting on the Roanoke River and will remember you and your brother who have been so kind to me."[19]

In January 1947, Johann Mattfeldt, a former POW at Camp Sutton and resident of Bokel, Germany, in the British zone, wrote to the mayor of Monroe asking for the addresses of two of his former American civilian supervisors:

Dear Mayor! During the years 1944 to 1946 I was a POW in Camp Sutton in the neighborhood of your town. I have stayed there during my whole captivity and have been treated always correctly and decently. My Camp Commander was Lieut. Schmidt [Smith]. Every POW in the camp estimate [sic] this gentleman because he acted honestly. I have worked the whole time in the motor-pool with Mr. Twitti [Twitty] and Mr. Murray. When in 1946 the first 20,000 POW were discharged I was amongst them. After my return to Germany I found my family healthy and alive. Only life is not so as it should be. Perhaps you over there have also learned of our distress. Now I should like to ask you a favor, Sir. Could you perhaps send me the addresses of Lieut. Schmidt [sic], Mr. Twitti [sic] of Monroe and Mr. Murray. These gentlemen have asked me to write them. Unfortunately I was not allowed at my return to take the addresses along.[20]

It is difficult to determine how many former German POWs kept in touch with friendly Americans they encountered while in the North Carolina camps. Newspaper articles over the years reveal such instances and jog pleasant memories. One such article, which appeared in the *St. Petersburg Times* in June 1984, was entitled "D-Day Spotlights the Power to Forgive." The article focused on how some forty years after D-Day, the differences between Americans and Germans seemed to be fully healed. The author, Robert Pittman, mentioned seeing TV coverage of former German soldiers returning to the small town in Louisiana where they had been held as prisoners of war. Pittman remembered that there had been two German POW camps near his home in North Carolina.

He remembered the POWs working in the peanut fields of his father's place and being warned to stay away from them but also being fascinated by "these young men with deep tans who spoke a strange language." What Pittman remembered most was how "even in wartime, human kindness sometimes prevailed over fear." His wife's parents hired POWs to remove a barn from their property in Ahoskie. They treated the Germans kindly and gave them refreshments as they worked. After the war one of the POWs wrote a thank-you letter along with a plea for care packages during the early years of postwar German reconstruction. The result was that Pittman's wife's family "adopted" the former German POW's family and sent them what was needed. Later, the son of the American family visited the German family in the early 1950s and the former POW brought his family back to Ahoskie for a visit in 1983.

Pittman concluded: "In war, the differences that separate nations seem to be great, irreconcilable causes. Yet in human terms, in the relationship between one family and another family, they are small and short-lived. If nations could apply those human characteristics to their diplomacy, there would never need to be another D-Day."[21]

One former Camp Sutton prisoner, Matthias Buschheuer, long kept in touch with a farm couple who had treated him well while he worked on their dairy farm northeast of Charlotte. For several months in 1944 and 1945, 33-year-old Hugh Harris would drive to Camp Sutton in Monroe and pick up five POWs to help him on his farm. They would all cram into his two-door 1942 Ford. "They came every morning with their shoes shined and creases in their britches," Harris recalled. Matthias Buschheuer, the former Afrika Korps member who had been captured by the British in North Africa and served as a cook at the POW camp at Camp Sutton, worked with the Harrises for only two weeks, but he was struck by their kindness. Despite army orders not to feed the Germans, Hugh Harris and his wife Mary Elizabeth shared their food with their Wehrmacht workers. Buschheuer never forgot their kindness, and just after Christmas 1947 he wrote to the Harrises from Germany. Buschheuer's plea for assistance during a time of deprivation in the late 1940s led the Harrises to send care packages. Buschheuer claimed that "the food kept his family from starving to death." As a result of the growing friendship, over the years the Harrises and Buschheuer exchanged letters, packages, and visits. One of Harris's sons visited Buschheuer in Brühl in 1961. In 1969, Buschheuer visited the Harrises in Charlotte. Visits continued to be exchanged in both countries over the years until Matthias Buschheuer died in 1991 at age 69. Even after Buschheuer's death, his granddaughter came to visit the Harrises.[22]

Other former North Carolina POWs have made trips back to the sites where they were incarcerated in the Tar Heel State. That was the case of Werner Luck of Berlin, who visited Fort Bragg in 1989 for the first time since 1946. Luck, a former Luftwaffe corporal, was captured in North Africa in May 1943 when he was not yet twenty-one. He was shipped to New York in July, and his American POW odyssey took him first to Camp Livingston in Louisiana, then Fort Jackson, South Carolina, before he ended up at Fort Bragg. There, in 1945 and 1946, he spent the final days of the war and the early postwar period before being returned to Berlin. Luck, who had trained as a caterer before the war, became a police officer and worked with American military police patrolling the border of the Soviet sector. Later he managed a British officers' club in Berlin. He was sixty-six when he returned to Fayetteville, accompanied by his son, Wolfgang. Because he had written to ask permission to tour the post at Fort Bragg, he and his son were met by Lt. Col. Marcel J. Lettre and provided with a tour and dinner party. Luck also watched a parachute drop, lunched with U.S. soldiers, and swapped memories with American veterans. He also watched a parade at the post and participated in a memorial service. He told reporters that what he particularly remembered about being at Fort Bragg was that "at Christmastime, we had cake, apples, oranges, and many, many books. With Hitler, these books were forbidden." Though the wartime buildings where Werner Luck was incarcerated no longer existed, he felt that his return visit was very meaningful. "I wanted to say 'thank you' for what you have done for me. . . . Maybe someone will remember they have done something for the prisoners. It is nice that there are people who are willing to help others."[23]

Happy memories of the German POW presence in North Carolina are by no means the exclusive property of the German visitors. Americans hold dear some of their wartime contacts with Tar Heel POWs as well. A Raleigh lawyer, Armistead J. Maupin, remembered a family story about three anonymous POWs: "My uncle, the late William B. 'Buck' Jones, was a practicing lawyer in Raleigh and for fun owned a farm on what is now known as Buck Jones Road. It was operated by a marvelous man named Zebadee Jeffers who had a grandson named Peter. Peter fell into a farm pond and was drowning when three German Afrika Korps troopers who were working on the farm jumped in and saved him."[24]

In May 1992 there was a commemoration by former enemies of the sinking of the first German U-boat off America's shores forty years earlier, the *U-352*. The U-boat, which sank in 110-foot waters about twenty-six miles south of Beaufort, had a crew of forty-five, ten of whom went down with the vessel. The others were taken prisoner and briefly held at Fort Bragg. Thirteen Germans—eight from the U-boat, four wives, and Heinrich Ruhe, the brother of Hermann, one of the Germans who died in the engagement—met with five members of the crew of the Coast Guard cutter that sank the *U-352*, only one of whom, John Ostensen, was on the ship when it encountered the submarine. The Germans and the Americans tossed a wreath in memory of those who died. On the dive boat *Olympus*, divers Robert Purifoy and his father, George, who discovered the wreck of the *U-352* back in 1975, took other members of the former German submarine crew to lay a wreath directly on the wreck. "The Germans said that they came to North Carolina for the 50th anniversary of the sinking of the *U-352* in a spirit of friendship and remembrance. 'We thought about our comrades, while they are still lying down there,' said Ernst Kammerer, 67. 'We think that since we came as friends . . . mutual understanding between our two nations is the only way to avoid nonsense wars.'"[25] All of the former submariners who were quoted by name or whose pictures were shown at the dive site were listed in Fort Bragg POW detention lists in July 1942. They included Kurt Kruger, former sonar operator and medic, and Walter Grandke, Edgar Herrschaft, Ernst Kammerer, Willi Link, and Hans Neitsch.[26]

Local communities and their newspapers continue to highlight the happy return visits of former German POWs to the Tar Heel State. *Caravan*, published for employees and retirees of R. J. Reynolds Tobacco Co. and their families by the Public Relations Department, noted in its March 1995 issue: "German POW visits R. J. Reynolds." Accompanying a picture of Gunter Schikora, a former POW who worked for R. J. Reynolds for six months in 1945, was a brief article that mentioned the POW's first return trip to the city and the plant since World War II. "With a smile, Schikora remembered the six months he spent in Winston-Salem during 1945. 'I wanted to stay here,' he says, 'because I felt freer in this city as a prisoner of war than I did in my own homeland.'"[27]

The *Winston-Salem Journal* covered another such return visit on 28 March 1997. The visitor was Erwin Sommerfeld, who had "said goodbye to the armed guards and barbed wire that held him in Winston-Salem" some fifty-one years before.[28] He returned with a son, Albert, and grandson, Martin, to look for the places that he lived and worked as a POW in that city. Little was left. The National Guard Armory on Patterson Avenue and Ninth Street, where Sommerfeld and his comrades were kept, had been bulldozed in 1973. Warehouses had replaced the armory and neighboring houses and the former POW found nothing recognizable. Much had changed since Sommerfeld's capture in northern Italy, shipment to New York, and train ride to Winston-Salem in October 1944.

Pleasant and funny memories remained for the 72-year-old German, who had come to Winston-Salem as a nineteen-year-old and who had served only three days of active duty in a communications division of the Wehrmacht before his capture in 1944. Sommerfeld told of one of the American guards at Winston-Salem who liked to sleep on the job but who would ask the prisoners to wake him if they saw an officer coming. On one occasion, the Germans decided to play a trick on this guard: they disassembled his rifle while he slept and left the pieces lying in front of him. Waking up suddenly, he was unable to put the rifle back together himself. "'You good fellows, you help me,'" Sommerfeld said the guard pleaded with them.[29]

Sommerfeld mentioned a theme that seems to have been a recurring one among Germans as they remembered their wartime experiences in the American South: the special relationship that the German POWs seemed to develop with American black workers. The *Winston-Salem Journal* noted that "Sommerfeld said that black workers at Reynolds seemed especially nice to the men. He believes that that is because the blacks sympathized with them for being an underclass in America, he said."[30]

Despite increasing age, the former POWs of the Tar Heel State keep returning with relatives to visit their old stomping grounds. Former 2nd Lt. Werner Lobback was one of these. He came in May 2004 to revisit the R. J. Reynolds Company in Winston-Salem. He then stopped by the North Carolina Archives in Raleigh for a video interview with Sion H. Harrington III, the military collection archivist. Accompanied by his granddaughter during the interview, Lobback recounted his American odyssey between 1944 and 1946. That odyssey we encountered in the opening chapter of this book when the "German visitors" were first introduced. Here is the rest of the Lobback story. Following the advice of British officers at Munsterlager, one of the British POW camps in Germany that he transited through on his way to release, the former North Carolina POW decided not to return to his hometown in Russian-occupied Saxony. Instead, he accepted an invitation from his former battery commander to come home with him to Walldorf, near Frankfurt and in the western Allied zone. Lobback has thought of this area as his home ever since. He pursued a variety of jobs around West Germany after the war until he found his niche as an airport manager at Düsseldorf.

He finished his career in Frankfurt and retired at age fifty-nine. He has enjoyed travel thereafter. His visit to the Tar Heel State, to his former employer R. J. Reynolds Tobacco in Winston-Salem, and with an archivist in Raleigh became part of his pleasant memories of a time long ago when he was a POW. He was only one of the many former POWs from North Carolina who continued to cherish the good treatment and fine memories that they took back with them to Europe after their stay in the Tar Heel State.

Lobback, like many of the German POWs who came to North Carolina, learned that their American enemies were human. North Carolinians learned a similar lesson. The result was that often "Nazi" enemies of the wartime years became lifelong German friends.

Table 11.1. Deaths of POWs in North Carolina Camps, May 1942 to February 1946

| Name | Date of Death | Date of Birth | Details of Capture | Cause of Death | Place of Death | Initial Burial Location | Final Burial Location |
|---|---|---|---|---|---|---|---|
| Gerd Ruessel | 10 May 1942 | 17 September 1921 | U-352 sunk off Cape Hatteras, 9 May 1942 | Wounds | Died at sea on way to interment at Charleston, South Carolina | National Cemetery, Beaufort, South Carolina | National Cemetery, Beaufort, South Carolina |
| Werner Meier | 11 July 1944 | 28 January 1919 | Luftwaffe, Mateur, Tunisia, 6 May 1943 | Shot while trying to escape from Camp Sutton | Camp Sutton | Post Cemetery Camp Butner | National Cemetery, Chattanooga, Tennessee |
| Wilhem Blum | 23 September 1944 | 11 September 1904 | Wehrmacht, Normandy, France, 27 June 1944 | Station Hospital, Seymour Johnson Field | Illness | Post Cemetery Fort Bragg | Post Cemetery Fort Bragg |
| Karl Helmut Haeberlein | 3 October 1944 | 1 February 1913 | Wehrmacht, Tunisia, 11 May 1943 | Drowned after escape from Camp Davis, 3 July 1944 | New Jersey | National Cemetery Long Island, Pinelawn, New York | National Cemetery Long Island, Pinelawn, New York |
| Wilhelm Burghardt | 26 October 1944 | 1 January 1912 | Navy, Cherbourg, France, 27 June 1944 | Accident | Regional Hospital Fort Bragg | Post Cemetery Fort Bragg | Post Cemetery Fort Bragg |
| Kilian Kernberger | 16 January 1945 | 2 December 1904 | Wehrmacht, Gap, France, 20 August 1944 | Suicide | Camp Butner | Post Cemetery Camp Butner | National Cemetery, Chattanooga, Tennessee |
| Rudolf Sieben | 29 January 1945 | 22 May 1900 | Wehrmacht, Dinge, France, 22 August 1944 | Illness | Regional Hospital Fort Bragg | Post Cemetery Fort Bragg | Post Cemetery Fort Bragg |

| Name | Date of Death | Date of Birth | Details of Capture | Cause of Death | Place of Death | Initial Burial Location | Final Burial Location |
|---|---|---|---|---|---|---|---|
| Paul Schmidt | 12 April 1945 | 26 April 1916 | Wehrmacht, Caen, France, 18 July 1944 | Suicide; remains found on 27 November 1946 seventeen months after escape from New Bern | New Bern | Post Cemetery Fort Bragg | Post Cemetery Fort Bragg |
| Ernst Bautz | 27 April 1945 | 15 April 1919 | Wehrmacht, Cherbourg, France, 27 June 1944 | Illness | Bluethenthal Field, Wilmington | Post Cemetery Camp Butner | National Cemetery, Chattanooga, Tennessee |
| Erwin Frantz | 14 June 1945 | 21 July 1912 | Wehrmacht, Paris, France, 26 August 1944 | Suicide | Camp Butner | Post Cemetery Camp Butner | National Cemetery, Chattanooga, Tennessee |
| Wilhelm Schäffer | 20 June 1945 | 10 January 1916 | Wehrmacht, Dorsten, Germany, 31 March 1945 | Accident | Fort Bragg | Post Cemetery Fort Bragg | Post Cemetery Fort Bragg |
| Heinrich Hofer | 13 August 1945 | 9 August 1922 | Wehrmacht, Tunisia, 24, April 1943 | Illness | U.S. Army General Hospital Camp Butner | Post Cemetery Camp Butner | National Cemetery, Chattanooga, Tennessee |
| Vinzent Bedrarski | 8 September 1945 | 23 March 1914 | Wehrmacht, Zaghuan, Tunisia, 13 May 1943 | Accident | Camp Butner | Post Cemetery Camp Butner | National Cemetery, Chattanooga, Tennessee |
| Hermann Bürger | 14 September 1945 | 13 January 1897 | Volkssturm [Home Guard], Essen, Germany, 9 April 1945 | Accident | Camp Butner | Post Cemetery Camp Butner | National Cemetery, Chattanooga, Tennessee |
| Roland Fuhrmann | 20 October 1945 | 18 October 1923 | Paratrooper, Baustert/ Rheinland, 25 February 1945 | Illness | U.S. Naval Hospital Edenton | Post Cemetery Camp Butner | National Cemetery, Chattanooga, Tennessee |

Table 11.1—*Continued*

| Name | Date of Death | Date of Birth | Details of Capture | Cause of Death | Place of Death | Initial Burial Location | Final Burial Location |
|---|---|---|---|---|---|---|---|
| Gustav Alfing | 15 November 1945 | 21 October 1923 | Wehrmacht, Metz, France, 18 December 1944 | Illness | AAF Regional Hospital Greensboro | Post Cemetery Camp Butner | National Cemetery, Chattanooga, Tennessee |
| August Rüter | 20 December 1945 | 10 January 1910 | Luftwaffe, Brest, France, 8 September 1944 | Accident | Pope Field, Fort Bragg | Post Cemetery Fort Bragg | Post Cemetery Fort Bragg |
| Johann Zokan | 8 January 1946 | 21 November 1923 | Wehrmacht, Tunis, Tunisia, 9 May 1943 | Illness | Army General Hospital Camp Butner | Post Cemetery Fort Bragg | Post Cemetery Fort Bragg |
| Josef Wimmer | 20 February 1946 | 15 May 1899 | Landesschutz [Home Guard], capture place and date not known | Illness | Fort Bragg | Post Cemetery Fort Bragg | Post Cemetery Fort Bragg |

Source: Records of the Deutsche Dienstelle für die Benachrichtigung der nächsten Angehörigen von Gefallenen der ehemaligen deutschen Wehrmacht(WASt) and in the National Archives and Records Administration, College Park, Maryland, as cited in notes accompanying the text concerning individual deaths mentioned in Chapter 11. Information on the individual grave locations, dates of death, and dates of interment can be found under the individual POW's name through the Nationwide Gravesite Locator created by the U.S. Department of Veterans Affairs at http://gravelocator.cem.va.gov/j2ee/servlet/NGL_v1.

# APPENDIX
# THE JAKOB FISCHER CASE

In a letter of 2 October 1945 to E. Tomlin Bailey, the acting chief of the Special War Problems Division of the Department of State, Alfred L. Cardinaux, a delegate of the International Committee of the Red Cross in Geneva, Switzerland, brought up the matter of prisoner of war Jakob Fischer, 31G-51796, Camp Butner, North Carolina. Cardinaux recommended that Fischer's case be given serious consideration in light of an autobiographical essay he had obtained from Fischer. To get the State Department's attention, Cardinaux quoted from Fischer's letter:

> From the enclosed biography of mine, it appears that I'm most probable [sic] the only one full-blooded Jew, who by the irony of providence, after indescribable sufferings in Germany, also has not been saved the fate of being a publicaly [sic] known fact, that German prisoner of war are already being repatriated, one could call it almost nonsense, that I, as a home and futureless Jew, also have to bear the aggravated restrictions, applying to German war prisoners. After waiting now for the period of more than a year, that I may be granted the human right to be transferred into an internment camp, I repeat once more my earnest request, to intervene at the proper authorities in my affair.
>
> Hoping that I have not caused you too much trouble and in advance very grateful for your efforts.[1]

Fischer's autobiographical essay, which Cardinaux sent to Bailey, reads as follows:

> Fischer, Jakob
> Present Address: Camp Butner, North Carolina
> Autobiography
> The undersigned, Jakob Fischer, mistakenly known until my twentieth year as Jakob Jaenchen, was born on 26 April 1920,

the illegitimate son of Jasof Abraham Jaenchen and Klara (really Chafe Basche) Fischer (the widow Kuzinski).[2] My mother, who emigrated from Kaunas, Russia (Tr. Note: now Lithuania) to Czechoslokia [sic] in 1919, died in Northern Bohemia on 27 May 1927. When I was nineteen I discovered for the first time that because of my mother's emigration, and my own illegitimacy, I had never had citizenship rights in any country whatsoever. I think I should mention here that my parents, as well as myself, were members of the Jewish religious community.

After my mother's death my sister, who was three years younger than myself, and I were put into the Jewish Orphans' Asylum in Prague XII, Belgicka 16. We remained there, in complete unawareness of our confused family relationships, until 1937.

A few months later the Nazis marched into Northern Bohemia. Only dimly did we suspect the fate that was in store for us. For the time being, however, I was able to deceive the authorities. When the Germans began to deport foreign labor to Germany, I was sent to work at forced labor in a chemical manufacturing plant in central Germany (The Westphalian Munitions Works, the Elsnig Torgau plant). In July 1939 the Gestapo in Halle a/d Salle established the fact of my Jewish origin—easily enough, in view of my personal documents. And after that I, too, experienced the sufferings visited upon the Jews of Germany.
Further investigations by the Gestapo brought out these facts:

1. My illegitimacy, of which I had been hitherto unaware.
2. My mother had never been legally married to my father.
3. According to the Nuremberg racial laws I was a full-blooded Jew.
4. My statelessness.

Points 1, 2, and 4 were established from the Czechoslovakian records, and received legal confirmation in a decision handed down by the Lower Court of Leipzig in 1939.

The Gestapo deported me to Dresden and put me under the protection of the Jewish Cultural Community. Here I was loged [sic] in a house occupied only by Jews, the front of which defaced by an abominable caricature with the Star of Judah. Little by little those of us who lived here were deprived of the last remnants of our personal freedom, until finally we were reduced almost to the state of outlaws.

My only hope now lay in being able to emigrate. But since I was without means, the only thing I could do was to try to enter Palestine illegally through (Hascharia), the Palestine office in Berlin. I was summoned to a Jewish training camp near Berlin (Dobbrikow, companion camp to Trebbin in Luckenwalde). A few months later a loaded transport left Bratislava (Slovakia). But it never reached its destination. The survivors landed in an Italian concentration camp. As we discovered later, this was the last transport taking refugees to Palestine. Through the efforts of the "Jewish Community of the Reich" in Germany I was placed in an emigrant's camp (Pilgram, in Frankfurt-on-the-Oder), a branch of the main camp "Neuendorf" at Fuerstenwalde-on-the-Spree. In these camps we were guarded like prisoners, we had no freedom of movement whatsoever, and we were forced to do heavy labor.

There were two possible places to which the internees in these camps might emigrate: the Mindanao, in the Philippines, and as farm laborers to the Dominican Republic. After a few weeks, however, we were told that the Germans had suspended all movements of transports from Germany. And so all hope of my being able to leave Germany vanished. At the same time we were informed that the entire camp was to be sent to Germany. (This was the beginning of the deportation of German Jews to the eastern occupied provinces).

With great difficulty I obtained permission for a two-weeks' leave from the camp, to go to Dresden, in an effort to clarify my stateless situation. A conversation with the head of the Jewish Cultural Community made clear to me the fearful fate that would be mine in Poland. And so, summoning every weapon at my disposal, I succeeded in outwitting the Nazis. By means of false testimony and personal papers, and with the aid of an employe [sic] of the Jewish Cultural Community, I obtained papers which identified me, at least until some one investigated further, as a "half-Jew." This saved me from being deported to Poland, and thus from certain death. But in spite of all this, I really owe my life to a beneficent Fate; for in spite of my interim passport, a high administrative official—the president of the administrative district of Dresden—after an examination such as only German authorities know how to give, declared me a full-Jew. And it was only because of the lack of agreement between the administrative and party officials that I escaped being arrested. This was in 1941.

The President of the Dresden Police issued me a foreigner's passport (stateless), which kept me under police supervision, as a foreigner and half-Jew, until April 1944. I spent three terrible years as a laborer in the coal mines, under the constant fear that at any moment the authorities might discover their mistake. The strain of those years on my nerves was so great that I almost became a physical and nervous wreck.

In the spring of 1944 came the decree that all persons not eligible for service in the Wehrmacht (this included persons with a political or criminal record, as well as gypsies and the few half-Jews still left in the Reich) were to be taken into custody and sent to do forced labor in the occupied territories in the East, or at the front. I was caught by this decree. On the surface these people were designated as "Civilian Auxiliary Service Forces under the Supervision of the Todt Organization." Actually, however, the uniformed and armed troops of the Todt organization were the guards of these forces. And so I realized my desire to escape from the Paradise of the Third Reich, although in a manner far different from what I had ever visualized. We were taken from Berlin to Paris under strict guard. Now I was really a political prisoner. Part of the group, myself included, were sent to Valognes, near Cherbourg, in Normandy. There we were tossed into a prisoners' camp and given prisoners' garb. Our activities consisted of replacing defenses and clearing up debris following the Allied air attacks. As these attacks increased in intensity we were detailed only to clear up the debris caused by them. Conditions in this camp, insofar as the care and treatment we received were concerned, were barely human.

Our expectation and hope was that the "invasion" which was so often spoken of, would soon become a fact. For then, we thought, that would mean our release. During the night from 5 to 6 June 1944, which marked the beginning of the Allies' heaviest military action, I knew that for me the hour of freedom had struck. And yet we still had a good many difficulties to overcome. We found ourselves in a state of almost indescribable joyful excitement. With pleasure we noted that the high officers and the entire construction force of the Todt Organization had left their posts and fled. With the aid of French civilians we helped free those who had been buried beneath the ruins caused by the air attacks (6 June). On 7 June 1944 our camp commandant promised that eventually the political prisoners would be turned over to the Allies. A few hours later, however, he received an order to send us to Paris and turn us over to the SS (Schutzstaffel: Elite Guard).

Because of the transportation difficulties we were forced to start this march on foot, while Russian forced laborers by the thousands were taken back in trucks. In spite of my ignorance of the French language, I was determined to escape. But I found no opportunity to put my determination into effect. We spent the night in an NSKK [Nationalsozialistisches Kraftfahrkorps: Tr. Note: Nazi Motor Corps] camp in Rouville, about 17 kilometers from Valognes. On the morning of 8 June our camp commandant appeared, accompanied by an officer of the military police of the 709th division and told us the invasion could be regarded as practically stopped. Against our will, and under forces of arms, we were loaded into trucks and taken to Colomby, six kilometers east of Valognes. Without any formality, and in complete disregard of human feelings and rights, we were there compelled to put on German uniforms. Laughing cynically, the German soldiers, but that, because of unfortunate military necessity, we were to do military duty. However, after the invasion had been stopped we would again be regarded as political prisoners.

For my part, I should like to make it clear that I have always regarded myself as a civilian, even today, when for some inexplicable reason I am confined here in the United States as a prisoner of war. For I cannot be regarded as a German soldier, from either from ammoral [sic] or a legal standpoint

From 9 to 12 June 1944 we were put to work in the troop dressing station at Valognes, burying fallen German as well as Allied soldiers. From 12 to 14 June we were forced to dig the so-called "one-man dug-outs" at Vanderville, near Mountebourg, under constant shelling from the enemy artillery. Finally, on this last day, we refused to work any longer; but under the last of constant reviling, and the threat of armed force, we were compelled to resume our labors.

On the morning of 15 June, however, we managed to accomplish our long-cherished plan of escaping. After many detours we reached Cherbourg on the morning of the next day (16 June). We represented ourselves to the German authorities there as laborers assigned to the Todt organization, and because of the chaos that reigned there, were able to remain undetected until the Allies took Cherbourg on 26 June 1944.

On 27 June 1944 I was subjected to my first examination at the hands of an American officer in Sainte Mere l'Eglise. After I had been issued a special passport, on which was indicated my ignorance of any military information, my faith, and also that I was to be delivered to an internment camp, I was taken to Devices [sic, Devizes], an American transit camp for prisoner of war in southern England. Here I was again interrogated by 1st Lt. Forest, an intelligence officer. All of my papers, including my passport as a stateless individual and my special passport, were taken away from me and kept, with the comment that after they had been more carefully examined in Washington they would be returned to me. I was also assured again that I would be placed in a civilian internment camp in the United States.

On 17 July 1944 I arrived in Boston, whence I was sent to one of the notorious Nazi prisoners' camps at Fort Custer, Michigan. However, by good luck I was, a few hours later, put with a small group of so-called anti-Nazis. Four weeks later I was sent to a so-called camp for anti-Nazis at Camp Ellis, Illinois. My repeated attempts to be put into an internees' camp were unsuccessful, even here. Since I no longer had my personal papers, they having been taken away from me, as I indicated above, to be examined in Washington, or so I was assured by Headquarters, at Camp Ellis I was asked to proof to show that I was really a citizen of the Reich. They could not believe it possible that I, a Jew, had been brought to the United States as a prisoner of war.

Finally I was able to furnish evidence that [I] had never been a German citizen. I was then placed in the nationalities' camp at Camp Butner, North Carolina.

Since all my efforts to date to obtain justice in my peculiar situation have been fruitless, I humbly beg of you to intervene for me in support of my cause with the authorities.

I swear upon my oath that all of my statements are truthful.

I hope that my request for your aid will not cause you too much inconvenience. Thanking you for any assistance you may be able to give me, I am,

Yours,

Jakob Fischer, POW

31 G 51 769

The ultimate fate of Jakob Fischer remains unknown. His immediate fate in the fall of 1945 was clear from a letter of 22 October 1945 from Brigadier General B. M. Bryan, the acting provost marshal general, to E. Tomlin Bailey in the Special War Problems Division of the State Department:

Gentlemen:

This will acknowledge receipt of your letter SWP 711.62114/10-245 dated 11 October 1945 inclosing a copy of a letter from Mr. Alfred L. Cardinaux, Delegate, International Committee of the Red Cross, Washington, D.C., dated 2 October 1945, concerning German prisoner of war, Jacob [sic] Fischer.

Records in this office reveal that this prisoner is presently interned in the "Special Compound" at Prisoner of War Camp, Camp Butner, North Carolina. For your information, the prisoners interned in the "Special Compound" at that installation are prisoners of war claiming Allied citizenship.

Recently, the Screening Commission composed of the Military Attaché and his assistants from the Czechoslovakian Embassy,

Washington, D.C., interviewed this prisoner of war and rejected him as not being qualified for return to Czechoslovakia.

Therefore, under these circumstances, this prisoner of war will be detained in the "Special Compound" at Prisoner of War Camp, Camp Butner, North Carolina, and will be returned to Europe for disposition at a subsequent date.

# NOTES

## Preface

1. Billinger, "Mysterious Nazi Prisoners," 10–12. See also "German POW Camp Historical Marker Dedication Ceremony Set for February at 10:00 a.m.," *Bulletin of the World War II Home Front Heritage Coalition* 4 (January 30, 2002); and interview of Margaret Rogers, 2 December 1998.

2. Jung, *Die deutschen kriegsgefangenen in amerikanischer Hand, USA*, 7, cites the figure of 378,000 and says that there were 155 base and 511 side camps in August 1945. However, he also notes that the number of branch camps continually changed and that there were at least 760 in existence at one time or another. He located German POW camps in all but three states: Vermont, North Dakota, and Nevada. (However, in the appendix, two maps, Karte 7 and 9, show a side camp just outside Bismarck, North Dakota.) One camp was outside the forty-eight states in Alaska at Excursion Inlet (p. 24). For Army Signal Corps photos of the camp at Excursion Inlet, search on "Prisoners of War Camp" at the Alaska Digital Archives Web site, http://vilda.alaska.edu/index.php.

3. See Pluth, "The Administration and Operation of German Prisoner of War Camps in the United States during World War II"; Krammer, *Nazi Prisoners of War in America*; and Ganzberg, *Stalag: U.S.A.*

4. See Robin, *The Barbed-Wire College*; Carlson, *We Were Each Other's Prisoners*; Koop, *Stark Decency*; Billinger, *Hitler's Soldiers in the Sunshine State*; and Fiedler, *The Enemy Among Us*.

5. Georg Gaertner, the last POW to surrender, did so in 1985. See Gaertner and Krammer, *Hitler's Last Soldier in America*.

6. Krammer, *Nazi Prisoners of War in America*, vii.

7. Fritz Landauer, "Sind wir alle Nazis?" *Der Ruf*, 15 February 1946, 8.

## Chapter 1. The German Visitors: An Introduction

1. Erich Moretti, telephone interview with the author, 1 May 2004; and Erich Moretti, interview with the author, Graz, Austria, 4 June 2004.

2. Billinger, "Behind the Wire," 483.

3. Jung, *Die deutschen kriegsgefangenen in amerikanischer Hand, USA*, 7–8.

4. Matthias Reiss argues that American historians (including this one), like American military men of the 1940s, have entertained exaggerated stereotypes of the veterans of the Afrika Korps. He suggests that "only some of the German soldiers captured

in North Africa belonged to the Deutsches Afrika-Korps, and only a tiny fraction of the units captured there had known any special discipline." He also rejects the notion that the prisoners captured in France after D-Day were dispirited, undisciplined, and less indoctrinated with Nazi ideology. Reiss argues that that is "a simplification, as large numbers of soldiers from Waffen-SS or other elite units were also captured in France and brought to the United States." See Reiss, "Bronzed Bodies behind Barbed Wire," especially 476 and 488. Despite Reiss's insight, the American military, surviving "Afrikaners," and former German POWs who were captured in Italy and France mention the discipline, soldierly character, and peer-pressuring attitudes and demeanor of the "Afrikaners" within the American camps.

5. Matthias Buschheuer, interview with the author, Brühl, Germany, 22 August 1980.

6. Fritz Teichmann, Unterleinleiter, Germany, to the author, 2 March 2003.

7. Ibid.

8. Fritz Teichmann, Unterleinleiter, Germany, to the author, 10 March 2003.

9. Costelle, *Les Prisonniers*, 118.

10. Max Reiter, interview with the author, Schwertberg, Austria, 24 January 2004. Matthias Reiss comments on the frequency with which Americans used stereotypes of Nazis with horns in "Bronzed Bodies behind Barbed Wire," 478–79.

11. Teichmann to the author, 2 March 2003.

12. Fritz Teichmann, Unterleinleiter, Germany, to the author, 9 April 2003.

13. English translation of report of Dr. Werner Bubb, International Committee of the Red Cross, of his visit to Camp Butner, North Carolina, on 7, 17, and 18 June 1945, RG 59, Entry 1353, Lot 58D7, Box 23.

14. Reiss, *Die Schwarzen waren unsere Freunde*; Teichmann to the author, 9 April 2003.

15. Teichmann to the author, 10 March 2003.

16. Ibid.

17. For more on Kurt Rossmeisl, see Krammer, *Nazi Prisoners of War in America*, 138–39.

18. Teichmann to the author, 10 March 2003.

19. Teichmann to the author, 2 March and 10 March 2003.

20. Alexander's warm feelings toward Teichmann are evident in a letter Alexander wrote to him on 7 January 1965, a copy of which was enclosed in Fritz Teichmann, Unterleinleiter, Germany, to the author, 11 February 2003. In the 1965 letter, Alexander noted that "I remember quite well and enjoyed hearing you play the organ. I imagine you have made considerable progress with your music and I would enjoy hearing you again."

21. Teichmann to the author, 2 March and 10 March 2003.

22. Teichmann to the author, 10 March 2003. Since members of military units of different nationalities were not kept together, Teichmann's reference to "the Italian" must mean a comrade captured in Italy.

23. Ibid.

24. Ibid.

25. Teichmann to the author, 2 March 2003.

26. Max Reiter, Schwertberg, Austria, to the author, 19 February 2003.

27. Reference to Reiter's arrival at Pier 33 in Max Reiter, e-mail to the author, 4 February 2003.

28. Ibid.

29. Reiter to the author, 19 February 2003.

30. Reiter e-mail to the author, 4 February 2003.

31. Information on Werner Lobback from his video interview with Sion H. Harrington III, North Carolina Office of Archives and History, Raleigh, North Carolina, 21 May 2004, and copies of menus and other materials Lobback left with Harrington at that time and shared with the author when he visited the North Carolina archives on 16 June 2004.

32. Friedrich Wilhelm Hahn, "Die Hölle von Dachau," *Das Freie Wort*, Mackall, N.C., 1 October 1945, 5–6.

33. For the first of the two articles on Hahn's experiences in Dachau see Hahn, "Die Hölle von Dachau," *Das Freie Wort*, 1 September 1945, 1–2.

34. Nikolaus Ziegelbauer, "Meine Erlebnisse im Konzentrationslager," *Der Lagerfackel*, 5 August 1945, 4–6.

35. This point is a major theme in my study of German POWs in Florida, *Hitler's Soldiers in the Sunshine State*.

## Chapter 2. POW Camps in the Tar Heel State: An Introduction

1. For Fourth Service Command boundaries, see Karte 8 in appendix of Jung, *Die deutschen kriegsgefangenen in amerikanischer Hand, USA*.

2. Col. Willis M. Everett Jr., Acting Director, Security and Intelligence, Headquarters Fourth Service Command, to Commanding General, Army Service Forces, Washington, D.C., 5 July 1945, RG 389, Entry 459A, Box 1608.

3. For National Archives pictures of Rathke and his men as they landed at Charleston and later were fingerprinted and processed for interrogation, see *http://www.uboatarchive.net/U-352POW.htm* (accessed 22 September 2003). This is an excellent site for pictures and information on U-boats. It is maintained by Capt. Jerry Mason, USN.

4. Col. B. M. Bryan, Chief, Aliens Division, to Special Division, Department of State, 28 August 1942, RG 389, Entry 434, Box 422, File 680.2. See also T. L. Lewis, Commanding Officer, Atlantic Fleet Anti-Submarine Warfare Unit, to Commander in Chief, United States Atlantic Fleet, 18 May 1942, and accompanying memorandum by J. T. Hardin, Lieutenant Commander, U.S. Navy, to Commanding Officer ASW Unit, U.S. Atlantic Fleet, 16 May 1942, available at http://www.uboatarchive.net/U-352IcarusReport.htm.

5. See report of visit by Mr. Weingärtner, First Secretary, Swiss Legation, Department of German Interests, and Bernard Gufler, Assistant Chief, Special Division, Department of State, to the prisoner of war camp at Fort Bragg, North Carolina, 17 September 1942, RG 59, Entry 1353, Lot 58D7, Box 23.

6. Memorandum by J. T. Hardin, Lieutenant Commander, U.S. Navy, to Commanding Officer ASW Unit, U.S. Atlantic Fleet, 16 May 1942 noted in footnote 4.

7. Report of Weingärtner and Gufler visit to Fort Bragg, 17 September 1942.

8. Geo. V. Strong, Major General, AC of S, G-2, to Provost Marshal General, 31 July 1942, RG 389, Entry 461, Box 2476.

9. Moore, *Faustball Tunnel*, 35.

10. Full name and rank of Bollmann from Annex B: List of Crew of U-352 in Navy Department, Office of the Chief of Naval Operations, Washington, Final Report of Interrogation of Survivors From *U-352* Sunk by *U.S.C.G. Icarus* on May 9, 1942 in Approximate Position Latitude 34.12.05 N. Longitude 76.35 W. available at http://www.uboatarchive.net/U-352INT.htm.

11. See pictures of the German POWs alone and photographed with Swiss and American diplomats in B. N. Bryan, Colonel, F. A. Chief, Aliens Division, to Special Division, Department of State, Washington, D.C., 30 September 1942, RG 59, Entry 1353, Lot 58D7, Box 23.

12. Six prisoners at Fort Bragg ordered transferred to Fort Devens, Copy of General Gullion to Commanding General, Fourth Service Command, 18 September 1942, RG 389, Entry 434, Box 422, File 383.6, Fort Bragg; and File 141.7, Fort Devens, 10 November 1942 note referring to request for information on custody of items belonging to crew members of *U-352*, who were recently transferred from Fort Devens to Camp Forrest, also in RG 389, Entry 434, Box 422.

13. Copy of secret air mail from Services of Supply, Office of the Provost Marshal General, Washington, to Commanding General, Fourth Service Command, Atlanta, 14 November 1942, Subject: Transfer of Prisoners of War, RG 389, Entry 461, Box 2476.

14. The story of Wattenberg and his fellow escapees is the heart of Moore's *Faustball Tunnel*.

15. Copy of secret airmail from Office of the Provost Marshal General, Washington, to Commanding General Fourth Service Command, Atlanta, 1 December 1942, Subject: Transfer of Prisoners of War, RG 389, Entry 461, Box 2476.

16. Moore, *Faustball Tunnel*, 45.

17. Ibid., 9–13, 45.

18. Hans C. Larsen, Lt. Col., Infantry, Dir. Int. Sec. Div., Headquarters, Fort Bragg, North Carolina, to Adjutant General's Office, War Department, Washington, D.C., 22 June 1943, RG 389, Entry 434, Box 422, File 314.2, Fort Bragg.

19. Krammer, *Nazi Prisoners of War in America*, 26–27.

20. Ibid., 82–83, 86–88.

21. See "Davis Troops Rebuked for Taunting Germans," *Durham Morning Herald*, 28 February 1944, 2.

22. Report of visit by Captains R. V. Estes and D. L. Schweiger, Field Liaison Officers, to Prisoner of War Base Camp, Camp Mackall, North Carolina, 31 August and 1 September 1944, RG 389, Entry 461, Box 2660.

23. Report of visit by Dr. R. W. Roth, Swiss Legation, and Eldon F. Nelson, Department of State, to the prisoner of war camp at Camp Davis, North Carolina, 22 June 1944, RG 389, Entry 461, Box 2660; also in RG 59, Entry 1353, Lot 58D7, Box 25.

24. Report of visit by Maurice Perret, International Committee of the Red Cross, to the prisoner of war camp at Camp Sutton, North Carolina, 12 July 1944, RG 389, Entry 461, Box 2673.

25. Report of visit by Maurice Perret, International Committee of the Red Cross to the prisoner of war camp at Fort Bragg, North Carolina, 19 June 1944, RG 389, Entry 461, Box 2656.

26. Report on visit by Dr. R. W. Roth, Swiss Legation, and Eldon F. Nelson, Department of State, to the prisoner of war camp at Camp Butner, North Carolina, 28–29 June 1944, RG 389, Entry 461, Box 2657.

27. "State Faces Grave Shortage in Farm Labor This Season: Draft, Migration Takes Heavy Toll, Hamilton Reveals," *Durham Morning Herald*, 10 March 1944, 1:3.

28. Labor reports from Hendersonville camp, RG 389, Entry 461, Box 2494.

29. Labor reports, RG 389, Entry 461, from New Bern, Box 2520; Scotland Neck, Box 2495; and Seymour Johnson Field, Box 2495.

30. Labor reports, RG 389, Entry 461, from Moore General Hospital, Box 2520; Whiteville, Box 2495; Greensboro, Box 2520; Roanoke Rapids, Box 2520; and Edenton, Box 2493.

31. Report of visit by Captains R. V. Estes and D. L. Schwieger, Field Liaison Officers, to Prisoner of War Base Camp, Camp Mackall, North Carolina, 31 August and 1 September 1944, 19 September 1944, RG 389, Entry 461, Box 2666.

32. Report of visit by G. Métraux, International Committee of the Red Cross, to Camp Mackall, North Carolina, 26 September 1944, RG 389, Entry 461, Box 2666.

33. Ibid.

34. PW Daily Work Schedule, Tuesday, 26 September 1944, Headquarters, Prisoner of War Camp Mackall, North Carolina, RG 389, Entry 461, Box 2666.

35. Report of visit by G. Métraux, International Committee of the Red Cross, to Camp Mackall, North Carolina, 26 September 1944, RG 389, Entry 461, Box 2666.

36. Report of visit by Verner Tobler, Swiss Legation, and Carl Marcy, Department of State, to the prisoner of war camp at Camp Mackall, North Carolina, 7 December 1944, RG 389, Entry 461, Box 2666.

37. Ibid.

38. Report of visit by Dr. R. W. Roth, Swiss Legation, and Eldon F. Nelson, Department of State, to the prisoner of war camp at Camp Davis, North Carolina, 22 June 1944, RG 59, Entry 1353, Lot 58D7, Box 25; and English translation of report on visit by G. Métraux of the International Committee of the Red Cross to the prisoner of war camp at Camp Davis and the work detachment at Wilmington, North Carolina, 23 and 24 September 1944, RG 59, Entry 1353, Lot 58D7, Box 25.

39. "Davis Troops Rebuked for Taunting Germans," *Durham Morning Herald*, 28 February 1944, 2.

40. Report of visit Dr. R. W. Roth, Swiss Legation, and Eldon F. Nelson, Department of State, to the prisoner of war camp at Camp Davis, North Carolina, 22 June 1944, RG 59, Entry 1353, Lot 58D7, Box 25.

41. English translation of report of visit by G. Métraux of the International Committee of the Red Cross to the prisoner of war camp at Camp Davis and the work

detachment at Wilmington, North Carolina, 23 and 24 September 1944, RG 59, Entry 1353, Lot 58D7, Box 25.

42. Report of visit by Verner Tobler, Swiss Legation, and Carl Marcy, Department of State, to Camp Davis, North Carolina, 8 December 1944, RG 389, Entry 1353, Lot 58D7, Box 25.

43. Report of visit by Dr. Werner Bubb, International Committee of the Red Cross, and Mr. Toohey, State Department, to the prisoner of war camp at Camp Davis, 12 June 1945 RG 59, Entry 1353, Lot 58D7, Box 25.

44. Report of visit by Captains R. V. Estes and D. L. Schwieger, Field Liaison Officers, to Prisoner of War Base Camp, Camp Sutton, North Carolina, 29, 30, and 31 August 1944, RG 389, Entry 459A, Box 1622, File 255.

45. Report of visit by Maurice Perret, International Committee of the Red Cross, to the prisoner of war camp at Camp Sutton, North Carolina 12 July 1944, RG 389, Entry 461, Box 2673.

46. Report of visit by Dr. R. W. Roth, Swiss Legation, and Eldon F. Nelson, Department of State, to the prisoner of war camp at Fort Bragg, North Carolina, 21 June 1944, RG 389, Entry 461, Box 2656.

47. Report of visit by Verner Tobler, Swiss Legation and Carl Marcy, Department of State, to the prisoner of war camp at Fort Bragg, North Carolina, 9 December 1944, RG 389, Entry 461, Box 2656.

48. Report of visit by Captain R. V. Estes and Captain D. L. Schwieger, Field Liaison Officers, to Prisoner of War Base Camp, Fort Bragg, North Carolina, on 1, 2, 3 and 4 September 1944, RG 389, Entry 461, Box 2656.

49. English translation of report of visit by Maurice Perret, International Committee of the Red Cross, to the prisoner of war camp at Fort Bragg, North Carolina, 19 June 1944, RG 389, Entry 461, Box 2656.

50. Report of visit by Dr. R. W. Roth, Swiss Legation, and Eldon F. Nelson, State Department, to the prisoner of war camp at Camp Butner, 28–29 June 1944, RG 59, Entry 1353, Lot 58D7, Box 23.

51. Ibid.

52. Report of visit by Verner Tobler, Swiss Legation, and Carl Marcy, Department of State, to the prisoner of war camp at Camp Butner, North Carolina, on 11 December 1944, RG 59, Entry 1353, Lot 58D7, Box 23.

53. Report of visit by Emil Greuter of the Legation of Switzerland and Louis S. N. Phillipp of the U.S. State Department to the prisoner of war camp at Camp Butner, North Carolina, 26–27 April 1945, RG 59, Entry 1353, Lot 58D7, Box 23.

54. Report of visit by Dr. R. W. Roth, Swiss Legation, and Eldon F. Nelson, State Department, to the prisoner of war camp at Camp Butner, 28–29 June 1944, RG 59, Entry 1353, Lot 58D7, Box 23.

## Chapter 3. The Afrika Korps Comes to Monroe

1. On 1 May 1944, North Carolina had four German POW camps: Camp Davis in Onslow County had 500 prisoners; Camp Mackall in Richmond and Scotland counties had 300; Wilmington in New Hanover County had 278; and Camp Sutton in Union

County had 750. Report of 1 May 1944, in Weekly Reports on Prisoners of War, July 1944–June 1946, RG 211, War Manpower Commission, Series 176, Civil Archives Division. For more on Camp Sutton, see Billinger, "Behind the Wire."

2. Description of location, set-up, and original conditions and staffing of the Camp Sutton by Captains R. V. Estes and D. L. Schwieger, Field Liaison Officers, Report of Visit to Prisoner of War Base Camp, Camp Sutton, North Carolina, on 29-30-31, August 1944, RG 389, Entry 461, Box 2673 (Estes and Schwieger visit, 29-31 August 1944).

3. Capt. William J. Bridges, Labor & Liaison Officer, Report of Inspection of Prisoner of War Labor at Prisoner of War Camp, Camp Butner, North Carolina, and five Branch Camps, 17 October 1945 thru 23 October 1945, for the Provost Marshal General, RG 389, Entry 461, Box 2657.

4. Lerch, "The Army Reports on Prisoners of War," 546. On 30 June 1944, the rate of escape from federal prisons was 0.44 percent; for POW camps, the comparable figure was 0.36 percent. During the entire period in which German POWs were detained in the United States, 2,222 of 378,000 POWs escaped, or roughly 0.59 percent (a rate of .0059). See Krammer, *Nazi Prisoners of War in America*, 117 and 146.

5. Estes and Schwieger visit, 29–31 August 1944.

6. On the history of the camp and the closing of the engineering center at Camp Sutton, see Coll, Keith, and Rosenthal, *The Corps of Engineers*, 310–13. The camp was closed in part because of racial incidents between segregated black troops and townspeople in Monroe; military authorities were concerned that a race war might erupt within the segregated military camp.

For specific details about the history of Camp Sutton, see Colonel Raymond C. Ball, Chief, Historical Services Division, U.S. Army, Washington, to Richard W. Iobst, 7 November 1963, Historical Highway Marker Files, Research Branch, Archeology and Historic Preservation Section, North Carolina Office of Archives and History, Raleigh.

7. Report of visit by Maurice Perret, International Committee of the Red Cross, to the prisoner of war camp at Camp Sutton, North Carolina 12 July 1944, RG 389, Entry 461, Box 2673 (Maurice Perret visit, 12 July 1944).

8. Regarding the "theater of operations" type buildings see Estes and Schwieger visit, 29-31 August 1944.

9. Maurice Perret visit, 12 July 1944.

10. Estes and Schwieger visit, 29-31 August 1944.

11. Maurice Perret visit, 12 July 1944.

12. Estes and Schwieger visit, 29-31 August 1944.

13. Maurice Perret visit, 12 July 1944.

14. Ibid.

15. "German Shot in Flight to be Buried at Butner," *Durham Morning Herald*, 13 July 1944, 1.

16. For more on Meier and his connection with the Aliceville Camp, see Cook, *Guests behind the Barbed Wire*, 90, 189, 347.

17. Jung, *Die deutschen Kriegsgefangenen in amerikanischer Hund, USA*, 7–8.

18. "WKG-012" is the code for a former POW who, through the Caritas organization, shared his story with the Maschke Commission, an officially sanctioned German research commission in the 1950s. WKG-012's seventeen typed pages of report were coded and his identity was protected. (Hereafter "WKG-012 Report.")

19. Matthias Buschheuer, interview with the author, Brühl, Germany, 22 August 1980.

20. Jung, *Die deutschen kriegsgefangenen in amerikanischer Hand, USA*, 24, 379; Krammer, *Nazi Prisoners of War in America*, 271.

21. The Geneva Convention was signed in Switzerland on 27 July 1929. Forty-two nations, including the United States and Germany, signed and ratified its ninety-seven articles, which were designed to protect prisoners of war from undue harshness or cruelty by their captors. Article 27 provided key guidelines regarding work: officers were not to be employed unless they specifically requested employment, noncommissioned officers were required to perform only supervisory labor, and only physically fit prisoners were to be put to work. See Article 27, Geneva Convention in Bevans, Treaties, II, 944. For further sources, see Billinger, "Behind the Wire," 486n13.

22. The prisoner's estimate of the number of POWs confined in the hold or holds of the ship seems low; perhaps there were several holds in each ship. The official history of the Transportation Corps noted that "the POW vessels were poorly equipped to move personnel" and had improvised sanitary facilities that included overside latrines. Each ship carried 300–500 POWs from Africa to the United States. Later transports from Europe carried as many as 1,000 POWs. See Reiss, *"Die Schwarzen waren unsere Freunde,"* 77, citing Bykofsky and Larson, *The Transportation Corps*, 180–81, 361–62.

23. "WKG-012 Report."

24. "Enemy Prisoners of War Under Sentences of Courts-Martial" (through 31 August 1945), Provost Marshal General's Office. Prisoner of War Division. "Prisoner of War Operations." Reel 2, Tab [Appendix] 115.

25. For the major peer-group killings see Krammer, *Nazi Prisoners of War in America*, especially 170–73.

26. Estes and Schwieger visit, 29–31 August 1944.

27. "WKG-012 Report."

28. We will have more to say about Camp Butner's Company 11 when we discuss Camp Butner and its interesting tripartite division into a regular camp, a "Nazi camp," and an "Allied" camp.

29. "WKG-012 Report."

30. Elbert Griffin, telephone interview, 21 June 1980.

31. Matthias Buschheuer, interview with the author, Brühl, Germany, 22 August 1980.

32. "WKG-012 Report."

33. James B. Potter, Captain, CMP, to Commanding General, Fourth Service Command, Atlanta, 1 December 1944, RG 389, Entry 461, Box 2485, Camp Sutton File.

34. Fourth Service Command forward to Commanding General, Army Service Forces, Washington, 2 December 1944; and Maj. Howard W. Smith Jr., CMP Chief,

Camp Operations Branch, Prisoner of War Operations Division for the PMG, to Commanding General Fourth Service Command, 14 December 1944, both in RG 389, Entry 461, Box 2485, Camp Sutton File.

35. *Mitteilungsblatt für die österreichischen Kriegsgefangenen* was published at Camp Butner for only six issues between late November 1945 and January 1946. See Billinger, "'Austrian' POWs in America," 127.

36. See Billinger, "Behind the Wire," 498.

37. Billinger, "Behind the Wire," 498.

38. Ibid., 500 and 483, Table 1.

39. Ibid., 501. State Department representative Louis S. N. Phillipp noted that "the camp commander stated that there had been some objections from organized labor to prisoners of war working in certain areas. Their objections were based on the statement that civilian labor could be obtained in these areas if adequate wages were offered. One of the projects was in connection with the grading work on the grounds of the Charlotte Memorial Hospital." Report of visit by Emil Greuter, Swiss Legation, and Louis S. N. Phillipp, State Department, to the prisoner of war camp at Camp Butner, North Carolina, 26–27 April 1945, RG 59, Entry 1353, Lot 58D7, Box 23. See the clipping from *Charlotte News*, 5 April 1945, attached to the first copy of this report.

40. Report of visit by Dr. Werner Bubb, International Committee of the Red Cross, and Mr. Toohey, State Department, to Monroe Side Camp, Camp Sutton, North Carolina, 15 June 1945, RG 389, Entry 461, Box 2657.

41. Elbert Griffin, telephone interview, 21 June 1980; N. B. Nicholson, telephone interview, 17 June 1980.

42. Douglas Hill, interview with the author, 1 April 1980; and Harold C. Funderburk, interview with the author, 12 February 1980.

## Chapter 4. North Carolina's Two Base Camps: Fort Bragg and Camp Butner

1. Location of the camp mentioned in report of visit by Dr. R. W. Roth, Swiss Legation, and Eldon F. Nelson, State Department, to the prisoner of war camp at Fort Bragg, North Carolina, 21 June 1944, RG 389, Entry 461, Box 2656.

2. Ibid.

3. Report of visit by Maurice Perret, International Committee of the Red Cross, to the prisoner of war camp at Fort Bragg, North Carolina, 19 June 1944, RG 389, Entry 461, Box 2656.

4. Report of visit by Dr. R. W. Roth, Swiss Legation, and Eldon F. Nelson, State Department, to the prisoner of war camp at Fort Bragg, North Carolina, 21 June 1944, RG 389, Entry 461, Box 2656.

5. Ibid.

6. Report of visit by Captains R. V. Estes and D. L Schwieger, Field Liaison Officers, to the Prisoner of War Base Camp, Fort Bragg, North Carolina, 1, 2, 3 and 4 September 1944, RG 389, Entry 461, Box 2656.

7. Addenda to report of visit by Captains R. V. Estes and D. L Schwieger, Field Liaison Officers, to the Prisoner of War Base Camp, Fort Bragg, North Carolina, 1, 2, 3 and 4 September 1944, RG 389, Entry 461, Box 2656.

8. Report of visit by Verner Tobler, Swiss Legation, and Carl Marcy, State Department, to the prisoner of war camp at Fort Bragg, North Carolina, 9 December 1944, Original in RG 59, Entry 1353 (Lot 58D7), Box 23, and copy in RG 389, Entry 461, Box 2656.

9. Ibid.

10. Report of visit by Edouard Patte of the YMCA to the prisoner of war camp at Fort Bragg, North Carolina, February 1945, RG 389, Entry 459A, Box 1609, Fort Bragg File.

11. Mutter, "Amerikafahrt Deutscher landser," 119–22.

12. Report of visit by Emil Greuter, Swiss Legation, and Louis S. N. Phillipp, State Department, to the prisoner of war camp at Camp Butner, North Carolina, 26–27 April 1945, RG 59, Entry 1353, Lot 58D7, Box 23.

13. Information on the Italian POWs in this and the next paragraph from Report of visit by George Bonetti and Dr. R. W. Roth, Swiss Legation, and Charles C. Eberhardt and Parker W. Buhrman, State Department, to the prisoner of war camp at Camp Butner, North Carolina, 11–13 October 1943, RG 389, Entry 461, Box 2657.

14. Ibid. *The Enemy Among Us* is the title of David Fiedler's very good study of the Italian and German POW presence in Missouri.

15. Ibid.

16. Ibid.

17. Bevans, *Treaties and International Agreements of the United States of America*, II, 938.

18. Report on visit by Dr. R. W. Roth, Swiss Legation, and Eldon F. Nelson, State Department, to the prisoner of war camp at Camp Butner, North Carolina, 28–29 June 1944, RG 389, Entry 461, Box 2657. This report gives the numbers and nationalities of men detained in the separate compound. Nelson or his typist set the number of POWs at 1,224, but then variously indicated the number at Williamston to be 235 and 335. Only if 335 prisoners were at Williamston would the camp total be 1,224. I use the term *Überlaufer* because that is one still used by Fritz Teichmann, a former Luftwaffe member and detainee at Camp Butner.

19. Report on visit by Edouard Patte of the YMCA to the prisoner of war camp at Camp Butner, North Carolina, 17–18 November 1944, RG 389, Entry 461, Box 2657.

20. Report on visit by Dr. R. W. Roth, Swiss Legation, and Eldon F. Nelson, State Department, to the prisoner of war camp at Camp Butner, North Carolina, 28–29 June 1944, RG 389, Entry 461, Box 2657.

21. Ibid.

22. For the designation of Compound C or Company 11 as the "Nazi Camp," see English translation of report of visit by Dr. Werner Bubb, International Committee of the Red Cross, to the prisoner of war camp at Camp Butner, North Carolina, on 7, 17, and 18 June 1945, RG 59, Entry 1353, Lot 58D7, Box 23.

23. Report of visit by Verner Tobler, Swiss Legation, and Carl Marcy, Department of State, to the prisoner of war camp at Camp Butner, North Carolina, 11 December 1944, RG 59, Entry 1353, Lot 58D7, Box 23.

24. Camp Davis was activated as a branch camp of the large camp at Aliceville,

Alabama, in March 1944 but was independent until it was transferred to the administration of Camp Butner. See RG 389, Entry 461, Box 2493 and the separate Camp Davis file in RG 59, Entry 1353, Lot 58D7, Box 25. Like Camp Davis, Camp Sutton in Monroe was also activated in March 1944 as a side camp of Aliceville but was also an independent camp before coming under the jurisdiction of Camp Butner. See RG 389, Entry 461, Box 2520.

25. English translation of report of visit by Dr. Werner Bubb, International Committee of the Red Cross, to the prisoner of war camp at Camp Butner, North Carolina, 7, 17, and 18 June 1945, RG 59, Entry 1353, Lot 58D7, Box 23.

26. Rations for German POWs were cut in camps across the nation. This was widely commented on by prisoners, the International Committee of the Red Cross, and the press. See, for example, Krammer, *Nazi Prisoners of War in America*, 240–42.

27. Bubb's report of June 1945 noted that "the rations are known and may be controlled to a certain degree. According to our approximate calculations the rations distributed on June 15, 16, and 17 represented 2250 calories per working day and 2140 per day of rest (Sunday)." English translation of report of visit by Dr. Werner Bubb, International Committee of the Red Cross, to the prisoner of war camp at Camp Butner, North Carolina, 7, 17, and 18 June 1945, RG 59, Entry 1353, Lot 58D7, Box 23.

28. Ibid.

29. Report on visit by Edouard Patte of the YMCA to the prisoner of war camp at Camp Butner, North Carolina, 17–18 November 1944, RG 389, Entry 461, Box 2657. The fate of POWs who were Soviet citizens is described in part in Bethell, *The Last Secret*, 166–70.

30. English translation of report of visit by Dr. Werner Bubb, International Committee of the Red Cross, to the prisoner of war camp at Camp Butner, North Carolina, 7, 17, and 18 June 1945, RG 59, Entry 1353, Lot 58D7, Box 23.

31. The story of Pierre Mertz is in Costelle, *Les Prisonniers*, 96–101.

32. Ibid., 98.

33. Ibid., 99.

34. Ibid., 99.

35. Ibid., 99.

36. Ibid., 99–101.

37. German POWs who were captured in the European theater were assigned serial numbers beginning with "31G." Some of them were processed later in one of the military regions of the United States, as was the case with Franz Antl of the nationalities camp, whose POW number was 4WG53-20487. This meant that Antl was not given his POW number until he arrived at the 4th Military District, whose administrative command was located in Atlanta.

38. English translation of report of visit by Dr. Werner Bubb, International Committee of the Red Cross, to the prisoner of war camp at Camp Butner, North Carolina, 7, 17, and 18 June 1945, RG 59, Entry 1353, Lot 58D7, Box 23.

39. Fritz Teichmann, Unterleinleiter, Germany, to the author, 10 March 2003.

40. English translation of report of visit by Dr. Werner Bubb, International Com-

mittee of the Red Cross, to the prisoner of war camp at Camp Butner, North Carolina, 7, 17, and 18 June 1945, RG 59, Entry 1353, Lot 58D7, Box 23.

41. Xerox of program for the *Zigeunerbaron*, enclosure in Fritz Teichmann, Unterleinleiter, Germany, to the author, 27 July 2003.

42. For a list of POW camp newspapers and the dates they appeared, see Böhme, *Geist und Kultur der deutschen Kriegsgefangenen im Westen*, 270–73. Many issues of these newspapers are available in a microfilmed collection at the Library of Congress: German P.O.W. Camp Papers (Washington, DC: Library of Congress Photoduplication Service, 1965), 15 microfilm reels. A microfilm guide and index by Karl John Richard Arndt, *German Prisoner of War Camp Papers Published in the United States from 1943 to 1946*, is on the first reel. The *European*, Der *Lagerfackel*, and *Mitteilungsblatt* are on Reel 2.

### Chapter 5. Branch Camps

1. Report of visit by Verner Tobler, Swiss Legation, and Carl Marcy, Department of State, to the prisoner of war camp at Camp Butner, North Carolina, 11 December 1944, RG 59, Entry 1353, Lot 58D7, Box 23.

2. See Labor Reports from Camp Wilmington in RG 389, Entry 461, Box 2520.

3. "The City and the Coalition Will Dedicate a Historical Marker at the Site of the First German POW Camp (February 1944)—Shipyard Boulevard and Carolina Beach Road—on February 6 [2002]," *Bulletin of the World War II Wilmington Home Front Heritage Coalition*, 4 (20 January 2002).

4. English translation of report of visit by G. Métraux, International Committee of the Red Cross, to Camp Davis and Work Detachment at Wilmington, North Carolina, 23 and 24 September 1944, RG 59, Entry 1353, Lot 58D7, Box 25.

5. See labor reports from Camp Wilmington in RG 389, Entry 461, Box 2520. For information on Bluethenthal Field, see "Aerofiles: Army and Air Force Flying Fields in the USA," available at http://www.aerofiles.com/usaf-bases.html (accessed 14 March 2007); and "The Home Front: Places—NC War sites," available at http://www.cmstory.org/homefront/places/warSites.htm (accessed 14 March 2007).

6. Report of visit by Verner Tobler, Swiss Legation, and Carl Marcy, Department of State, to the prisoner of war camp at Camp Butner, North Carolina, 11 December 1944, RG 59, Entry 1353, Lot 58D7, Box 23.

7. English translation of report of visit by G. Métraux, International Committee of the Red Cross, to Camp Davis and Work Detachment at Wilmington, North Carolina, 23 and 24 September 1944, RG 59, Entry 1353, Lot 58D7, Box 25. This report is also found in RG 389, Entry 461, Box 2657.

8. Ibid.

9. Report of visit by Verner Tobler, Swiss Legation, and Carl Marcy, Department of State, to the prisoner of war camp at Camp Butner, North Carolina, 11 December 1944, RG 59, Entry 1353, Lot 58D7, Box 23.

10. Report of visit by Dr. Werner Bubb, International Committee of the Red Cross, and Mr. J. L. Toohey, State Department, to the prisoner of war camp at Camp Wilmington, North Carolina, 13 June 1945 RG 389, Entry 461, Box 2657.

11. POWs at Wilmington worked, among other places, for the New Hanover Mutual Exchange and Southern Box and Lumber. See Robert E. Isaacson, 2nd Lt. CMP, Administrative Officer, labor report for 31 May 1945. A 15 September 1945 labor report listed 25 man-days for the Department of Health in Wilmington working on mosquito control and 12 man-days for the National Cemetery in Wilmington preparing graves. See Labor Reports for the Wilmington Camp in RG 389, Entry 461, Box 2520.

12. Report of visit by Dr. Bubb, International Committee of the Red Cross, and Mr. Toohey, State Department, to prisoner of war camp at Camp Wilmington, North Carolina, 13 June 1945 RG 389, Entry 461, Box 2657.

13. Ibid.

14. Roberson, "Our Friends the Enemy," 9.

15. Report of visit by George Bonetti and Dr. R. W. Roth, Swiss Legation, and Charles C. Eberhardt and Parker W. Buhrman, State Department, to prisoner of war camp at Camp Butner, North Carolina, 11–13 October 1943, RG 389, Entry 461, Box 2657.

16. Roberson, "Our Friends the Enemy," 9–10.

17. Labor reports from Williamston, North Carolina, RG 389, Entry 461, Box 2520; and Roberson, "Our Friends the Enemy," 10.

18. Report of visit by Emil Greuter, Swiss Legation, and Louis S. N. Phillipp, State Department, to the prisoner of war camp at Camp Butner, North Carolina, 26–27 April 1945, RG 59, Entry 1353, Lot 58D7, Box 23.

19. When the camp was deactivated, the building was purchased by the Standard Fertilizer Company, whose property adjoined the camp. Later it was acquired and used into the 1980s by the Tom Crockett Irrigation Company. Roberson, "Our Friends the Enemy," 10–11.

20. Ibid., 11.

21. Ibid., 11–12.

22. Report of visit by Guy S. Métraux, International Committee of the Red Cross, and Louis S. N. Phillipp, State Department, to the prisoner of war camp at Camp Butner, North Carolina, and branch camps, 3 April 1946, RG 59, Entry 1353, Lot 58D7, Box 23.

23. Report of visit by Verner Tobler, Swiss Legation, and Carl Marcy, Department of State, to the prisoner of war camp at Camp Butner, North Carolina, 11 December 1944, RG 59, Entry 1353, Lot 58D7, Box 23.

24. Ibid.

25. Labor reports for New Bern, North Carolina, RG 389, Entry 461, Box 2520.

26. Report of visit by Emil Greuter, Swiss Legation, and Louis S. N. Phillipp, State Department, to the prisoner of war camp at Camp Butner, North Carolina, 26–27 April 1945, RG 59, Entry 1353, Lot 58D7, Box 23.

27. Labor report from New Bern, 31 August 45 RG 389, Entry 461, Box 2520.

28. Report of visit by Dr. Werner Bubb, International Committee of the Red Cross, and J. L. Toohey, State Department, to the prisoner of war camp at New Bern, North Carolina, 11 June 1945, RG 389, Entry 461, Box 2657.

29. Information on Paul Schmidt's flight and presumed suicide and the date when

the remains were found were part of the information the Deutsche Dienststelle für die Benachtrichtigung der nächsten Angehörigen von Gefallenen der ehemaligen deutschen Wehrmacht [German Office for the Notification of the Next of Kin of the Deceased of the Former German Armed Forces, formerly the Wehrmachtauskunftsstelle, or WASt] shared with the author in its communication of 3 August 2004.

30. Report of visit by Guy S. Métraux, International Committee of the Red Cross, and Louis S. N. Phillipp, State Department, to the prisoner of war camp at Camp Butner, North Carolina, and branch camps, 3 April 1946, RG 59, Entry 1353, Lot 58D7, Box 23.

31. See Labor Reports for Scotland Neck in RG 389, Entry 461, Box 2495.

32. See Labor Reports for Seymour Johnson Field, RG 389, Entry 461, Box 2493.

33. Report of visit by Verner Tobler, Swiss Legation, and Carl Marcy, Department of State, to the prisoner of war camp at Camp Butner, North Carolina, 11 December 1944, RG 59, Entry 1353, Lot 58D7, Box 23.

34. Ibid.

35. See files for the camp at Seymour Johnson Airfield in RG 389, Entry 461, Box 2494.

36. Report of visit by Dr. Bubb, International Committee of the Red Cross, and Mr. Toohey, State Department, to the prisoner of war camp at Seymour Johnson Airfield, 9 June 1945, RG 389, Entry 461, Box 2657.

37. Labor report for Seymour Johnson Airfield, 15 March 1946, RG 389, Entry 461, Box 2494.

38. Labor report for Ahoskie, 31 August 1944, RG 389, Entry 461, Box 2520.

39. Report of visit by Verner Tobler, Swiss Legation, and Carl Marcy, Department of State, to the prisoner of war camp at Camp Butner, North Carolina, 11 December 1944, RG 59, Entry 1353, Lot 58D7, Box 23.

40. Labor reports for prisoner of war camp at Ahoskie, January and February 1945, RG 389, Entry 461, Box 2520

41. Jack H. Hagerty, 1st Lt., Commanding, POW Camp Ahoskie, report to Army Service Forces Headquarters, 16 April 1945, RG 59, Entry 1353, Lot 58D7, Box 23.

42. Report of visit by Emil Greuter, Swiss Legation, and Louis S. N. Phillipp, State Department, to the prisoner of war camp at Camp Butner, North Carolina, 26–27 April 1945, RG 59, Entry 1353, Lot 58D7, Box 23.

43. Captain William J. Bridges, Labor & Liaison Officer, Report of Inspection of Prisoner of War Labor at Prisoner of War Camp, Camp Butner, North Carolina, and five Branch Camps, 17 October 1945 thru 23 October 1945, for the Provost Marshal General, RG 389, Entry 461, Box 2657.

44. Report of visit by Guy S. Métraux, International Committee of the Red Cross, and Louis S. N. Phillipp, State Department, to prisoner of war camp at Camp Butner, North Carolina, and branch camps, 3 April 1946, RG 59, Entry 1353, Lot 58D7, Box 23.

45. RG 389, Entry 461, Box 2520, Winston-Salem File.

46. Report of visit by Emil Greuter, Swiss Legation, and Louis S. N. Phillipp, State

Department, to the prisoner of war camp at Camp Butner, North Carolina, 26–27 April 1945, RG 59, Entry 1353, Lot 58D7, Box 23.

47. Notes accompanying photocopy of POW art, North Carolina Office of Archives and History, Raleigh, North Carolina. The notes and artwork were originally held in the archives at R. J. Reynolds. The archivist there gave them to Werner Lobback, who passed them on to the Office of Archives and History in Raleigh in 2004.

48. Report of visit by Verner Tobler, Swiss Legation, and Carl Marcy, Department of State, to prisoner of war camp at Camp Butner, North Carolina, on 11 December 1944, RG 59, Entry 1353, Lot 58D7, Box 23.

49. Labor report from Winston-Salem, 10 December 1944, RG 389, Entry 461, Box 2520.

50. Location on Patterson Avenue documented in Christopher Quinn, "A Few Recall POWs at RJR," *Winston-Salem Journal*, 31 May 1993, 1, 6.

51. Report of visit by Dr. Werner Bubb, International Committee of the Red Cross, and Mr. J. L. Toohey, State Department, to the prisoner of war camp at Winston-Salem, North Carolina, 16 June 1945, RG 389, Entry 461, Box 2657.

52. Captain William J. Bridges, Labor & Liaison Officer, Report of Inspection of Prisoner of War Labor at Prisoner of War Camp, Camp Butner, North Carolina, and five branch camps, 17 October 1945 thru 23 October 1945, for the Provost Marshal General, RG 389, PMG Entry 461, Box 2657.

53. Labor report from Winston-Salem, 15 August 1945 RG 389, Entry461, Box 2520.

54. Werner Lobback, video interview with Sion H. Harrington III, North Carolina Office of Archives and History, Raleigh, North Carolina, 21 May 2004.

55. Notes accompanying photocopy of POW art. For the location and description of Shed 112, see Quinn, "A Few Recall POWs at RJR," *Winston-Salem Journal*, 31 May 1993, 1; and Associated Press, "German POWs Labored at Reynolds," *News & Record* [Greensboro. North Carolina], 1 June 1993, B2.

56. Report of visit by Dr. Werner Bubb, International Committee of the Red Cross, and Mr. J. L. Toohey, State Department, to the prisoner of war camp at Winston-Salem, North Carolina, 16 June 1945, RG 389, Entry 461, Box 2657.

57. HQ, Fourth Service Command, ASF, Atlanta, to Commanding General, Army Service Forces, Washington, DC, 28 March 1946, Winston-Salem File, RG 389, Entry 461, Box 2520.

58. Labor report, Hendersonville, North Carolina, 15 July 1944, RG 389, Entry 461, Box 2494.

59. Labor report, Hendersonville, North Carolina, 21 September 1944, RG 389, Entry 461, Box 2494.

60. Labor reports, Hendersonville, North Carolina, 15 July–12 October 1945, RG 389, Entry 461, Box 2494.

61. For the opening date of the camp and its state on 7 April 1946, see report of visit by Guy S. Métraux, International Committee of the Red Cross, and Louis S. N. Phillipp, State Department, to the prisoner of war camp at Camp Butner, North Carolina, and branch camps, 3 April 1946, RG 59, Entry 1353, Lot 58D7, Box 23.

62. Labor reports, 15 November 1945–30 April 1946, Moore General Hospital, Swannanoa, 15 July–12 October 1945, RG 389, Entry 461, Box 2520.

63. Report of visit by Guy S. Métraux, International Committee of the Red Cross, and Louis S. N. Phillipp, State Department, to the prisoner of war camp at Camp Butner, North Carolina, and Branch Camps, 3 April 1946, RG 59, Entry 1353, Lot 58D7, Box 23.

64. Ibid.

65. Labor report from Whiteville, 30 November 1945, Whiteville, North Carolina File, RG 389, Entry 461, Box 2495.

66. Report of visit to Prisoner of War Camp Whiteville, North Carolina, by Dr. Bubb and Mr. Toohey, 14 June 1945, RG 389, Entry 461, Box 2657.

67. Labor Report, Whiteville, North Carolina, 31 May 1945, RG 389, Entry 461, Box 2495.

68. Labor Report, Whiteville, North Carolina, 31 August 1945, RG 389, Entry 461, Box 2495.

69. Report of visit to Prisoner of War Camp Whiteville, North Carolina, by Dr. Bubb and Mr. Toohey, 14 June 1945, RG 389, Entry 461, Box 2657.

70. Labor Report, Whiteville, North Carolina, 30 September 1945, RG 389, Entry 461, Box 2495.

71. Labor stopped at Whiteville on 30 November. Labor report, Whiteville, North Carolina, 30 November 1945, RG 389, Entry 461, Box 2495.

72. Labor report, Greensboro, North Carolina, 15 March 1946 RG 389, Entry 461, Box 2520.

73. Labor reports from Edenton, 15 August 1945–15 March 1946, Edenton, North Carolina, File, RG 389, Entry 461, Box 2493.

74. Labor reports from Roanoke Rapids, 15 August 1945–31 March 1946, Roanoke Rapids, North Carolina, File, RG 389, Entry 461, Box 2520.

75. Report of visit by Guy S. Métraux, International Committee of the Red Cross, and Louis S. N. Phillipp, State Department, to the prisoner of war camp at Camp Butner, North Carolina, and branch camps, 3 April 1946, RG 59, Entry 1353, Lot 58D7, Box 23.

76. Ibid.

77. Krammer, *Nazi Prisoners of War in America*, 238.

78. Ibid., 245, 255.

## Chapter 6. Uncle Sam's Willing and Unwilling Workers

1. For a discussion of the POW labor program, see Krammer, *Nazi Prisoners of War in America*, 79–113.

2. Report of visit by George Bonetti and Dr. R. W. Roth, Swiss Legation, and Charles C. Eberhardt and Parker W. Buhrman, State Department, to the prisoner of war camp at Camp Butner, North Carolina, 11–13 October 1943, RG 389, Entry 461, Box 2657.

3. Lewis and Mewha, *History of Prisoner of War Utilization by the United States Army*, 108.

4. Capt. Richard E. Smith, Asst. Chief, Labor Branch, Fourth Service Command, to all farm labor officers in the peanut-growing states, 3 August 1944, RG 389, Entry 467C, Box 1574.

5. Fickle and Ellis, "POWs in the Piney Woods," 699, from *Der Aufbruch*, 8 July 1945.

6. Report of visit by Verner Tobler, Swiss Legation, and Carl Marcy, Department of State, to the prisoner of war camp at Camp Butner, North Carolina, on 11 December 1944, RG 59, Entry 1353, Lot 58D7, Box 23.

7. Fritz Lempp quoted in Costelle, *Les Prisonniers*, 118.

8. Werner Wampler quoted in Costelle, *Les Prisonniers*, 114–15.

9. Report of visit by Dr. R. W. Roth, Swiss Legation, and Eldon F. Nelson, State Department, to the prisoner of war camp at Camp Butner, North Carolina, 28-29 June, RG 389, Entry 461, Box 2657.

10. Report of visit by Maurice Perret, International Committee of the Red Cross, to the prisoner of war camp at Camp Sutton, North Carolina, 12 July 1944, RG 389, Entry 461, Box 2673.

11. Translated in Fickle and Ellis, "POWs in the Piney Woods," 702, from *Der Aufbruch*, 8 July 1945.

12. Translation from the IRC Inspection Report of 13 June 1945 in Jung, *Die deutschen kriegsgefangenen in amerikanischer Hand, USA*, 194.

13. Translation in Fickle and Ellis, "POWs in the Piney Woods," 703.

14. English translation of report on visit by G. Métraux, International Committee of the Red Cross, to the prisoner of war camp at Camp Davis and the work detachment at Wilmington, N.C., 23 and 24 September 1944, RG 59, Entry 1353, Lot 58D7, Box 25.

15. "DCV 3023 Report." Like "WKG-012," "DCV 3023" was an anonymous interviewee and former POW who provided information to the Maschke Commission.

16. Labor report, Hendersonville, North Carolina, branch camp of Camp Forrest, Tennessee, 15 July 1944, RG 389, Entry 461, Box 2494.

17. Labor report, Scotland Neck, North Carolina, Fort Bragg branch camp, 30 September 1944, RG 389, Entry 461, Box 2495.

18. Labor report, Camp Butner, North Carolina, 31 October 1944, RG 389, Entry 461, Box 2520.

19. 1st Lt. Burton Spears, S-2 Officer, to Commanding General, Fourth Service Command, Atlanta 3, Georgia, 30 January 1945, RG 389, Entry 452, Box 1370.

20. "Negro Knocks Out Hitler 'Superman,'" *Wake County Journal and Apex Booster*, 25 January 1945, 4. Thanks to archivist Tom Belton of the North Carolina Office of Archives and History for bringing this article to my attention. See also "Nazi 'Superman' Dislikes Verdict in Slapping Case: Camp Butner Negro Pops So-Called Member of 'Master Race' for Cursing," *News and Observer* [Raleigh, North Carolina], 13 January 1945, 9.

21. The incident is reported in Reiss, *"Die Schwarzen waren unsere Freunde,"* 276.

22. Fritz Teichmann, Unterleinleiter, Germany, to the author, 10 March 2003.

23. "DCV 3023 report."

24. Mutter, "Amerikafahrt Deutscher Landser," 133–34.

25. Major Howard W. Smith Jr. to Director, Prisoner of War Operations Division, 2 February 1945, RG 389, Entry 461, Box 2570, Deaths & Escapes File.

26. Major Howard W. Smith Jr., Prisoner of War Operations Division, Memorandum for the Director, Prisoner of War Operations Division, 23 March 1945, RG 389, Entry 461, Box 2570, Deaths & Escapes File.

27. 1st Lt. Burton Spear, S-2 Officer, Prisoner of War Camp, Camp Butner, North Carolina, to Office of the Provost Marshal General, Prisoner of War Division, Washington, D.C., 27 April 1945, RG 59, Entry 1353, Lot 58D7, Box 23.

28. Ibid.

29. For information on the Articles of War, see http://loc.gov/rr/frd/Military_Law/pdf/A-W_book.pdf (accessed 14 March 2007).

30. See "Jendricke, Wilhelm, listing on Disciplinary Punishment, March 1945," list with Spear to Office of the Provost Marshal General, 27 April 1945.

31. 1st Lt. Jack H. Smith, Executive Office at POW Camp Sutton, April 1945 disciplinary report accompanying report by 1st Lt. Burton Spear, S-2 Officer, Prisoner of War Camp, Camp Butner, North Carolina, to Office of the Provost Marshal General, Prisoner of War Division, Washington, D.C., 27 April 1945, RG 59, Entry 1353, Lot 58D7, Box 23.

32. Report of visit by Emil Greuter, Swiss Legation, and Louis S. N. Phillipp, State Department, to the prisoner of war camp at Camp Butner, North Carolina, 26–27 April 1945, RG 59, Entry 1353, Lot 58D7, Box 23.

33. Disciplinary Punishment, March 1945, Prisoner of War Camp, Camp Butner, document accompanying report by 1st Lt. Burton Spear, S-2 Officer, Prisoner of War Camp, Camp Butner, North Carolina, to Office of the Provost Marshal General, Prisoner of War Division, Washington, D.C., 27 April 1945, RG 59, Entry 1353, Lot 58D7, Box 23.

34. Smith memorandum for the Director, Prisoner of War Operations Division, 23 March 1945.

35. Ibid.

36. "POW's to be Taken from NC Industries," *Durham Morning Herald*, 24 November 1945, 2.

## Chapter 7. Escapes

1. The evolution of the government's public relations policy regarding the POW camps is the focus of a chapter in an excellent early study of the German POW phenomenon: Pluth, "The Administration and Operation of German Prisoner of War Camps in the United States during World War II," especially 239 and 242–43.

2. See Billinger, *Hitler's Soldiers*, 99, for a discussion of Florida and early assessments of national POW escape percentages compared to the percentages at maximum security federal penitentiaries.

3. Report of visit by Verner Tobler, Swiss Legation, and Carl Marcy, Department of State, to the prisoner of war camp at Camp Butner, North Carolina, on 11 December 1944, RG 59, Entry 1353, Lot 58D7, Box 23.

4. Thanks to the provisions of the Freedom of Information Act and the cooperation of the Federal Bureau of Investigation, 163 pages of FBI files pertaining to the Karl Haeberlein case were made available to this author in January 2005. The files contain documents that include a set of photographs of the escapee, Helmut Karl Haeberlein, filed by the FBI on 5 July 1944 and internal FBI correspondence concerning the search for Haeberlein and the finding of the body. There is also some final paperwork from February 1959, which called for the review and disposal of no longer relevant bulky laboratory exhibits of materials found on the body and earlier attached to Haeberlein's file.

5. SAC, Charlotte, to Director, FBI, 14 July 1944, Subject: Helmut Haeberlein, Federal Bureau of Investigation, "Haberlein, Karl. FOIPA no. 1002090-000."

6. Martin J. O'Donnell, FBI Agent, Charlotte, 22 July 1944, Report on Helmut Karl Haeberlein, Federal Bureau of Investigation, "Haberlein, Karl. FOIPA no. 1002090-000."

7. Ibid.

8. Agent McKee, Newark, N.J., to Director [Washington] and SAC [Charlotte], 4 October 1944, Federal Bureau of Investigation, "Haberlein, Karl. FOIPA no. 1002090-000."

9. John Edgar Hoover, Memorandum to Mr. Charles Malcolmson, Director of Public Relations, 7 October 1944, Federal Bureau of Investigation, "Haberlein, Karl. FOIPA no. 1002090-000."

10. "Escaped German Prisoner Drowns: Body of Corp. Haeberlein, Who Fled Camp Davis Stockade, Found," *Sunday Star-News* [Wilmington, N.C.], 8 October 1944, 1.

11. Edmond J. Kennedy, FBI Agent, Newark, NJ, report on Helmut Karl Haeberlein, 15 October 1944, Federal Bureau of Investigation, "Haberlein, Karl. FOIPA no. 1002090-00."

12. Ibid.

13. James P. Martin, FBI Agent, Report on Helmut Karl Haeberlein, 11 December 1944, Federal Bureau of Investigation, "Haberlein, Karl. FOIPA no. 1002090-00."

14. Martin J. O'Donnell, FBI Agent, Charlotte, report on Helmut Karl Haeberlein, 9 April 1945, Federal Bureau of Investigation, "Haberlein, Karl. FOIPA no. 1002090-00."

15. Col. A. M. Tollefson, Assistant Director, Prisoner of War Division, to Legation of Switzerland, Department of German Interests, 18 October 1944, RG 389, Entry 451, Box 1338, File 704.

16. Maj. Stephen M. Farrand, Prisoner of War Operations Division, to Special War Problems Division, Department of State, Attention: Bernard Gufler, 13 March 1945, RG 389, Entry 451, Box 1340, File 704.

17. A. M. Tollefson, Colonel, CMP, Director, Prisoner of War Operations Division, to Commanding General, Fourth Service Command, Atlanta, Georgia, 5 June 1946, RG 389, Entry 461, Box 2598, File Envelope: Escapes.

18. Sherman L. Watts, Lt. Colonel, Infantry, Acting Provost Marshal, HQ Seventh Army, Atlanta, Georgia, to The Provost Marshal General, Washington, D.C., 12 June 1946, RG 389, Entry 461, Box 2598, File Envelope: Escapes.

19. Report of visit by Dr. Bubb, International Committee of the Red Cross, and J. L. Toohey, State Department, to the prisoner of war camp at New Bern, North Carolina, 11 June 1945, RG 389, Entry 461, Box 2657.

20. "Recaptured Nazi Helps Look for Partner in Lake Michie: No Trace of Rudolf Streinz Found in Lake; Gerd Roempke Tells about Swimming Attempt," *Durham Morning Herald*, 19 April 1945, 9.

21. For more about the story of Werner Friedrich Meier's escape and death, see Chapter 3.

22. This interesting point is discussed more thoroughly in Reiss, "Bronzed Bodies behind Barbed Wire."

23. "Two Nazi Prisoners of War Escape from Compound at Butner," *Durham Morning Herald*, 16 April 1945, 10.

24. "Three War Prisoners Captured Here after Escape from Camp, "*Durham Morning Herald-Sun*, 24 September 1944, 1.

25, Ibid.

26. "Recaptured Nazi Helps Look for Partner in Lake Michie," *Durham Morning Herald*, 19 April 1945, 9.

27. "Gerd Roempke, Nazi Prisoner, in Third Break for Freedom," *Durham Morning Herald*, 12 September 1945, 12.

28. "German Prisoner Is Taken at Gibsonville," *Durham Morning Herald*, 27 September 1945, II:1.

29. Entry for November 1945 in "Escaped Prisoners of War" (a notebook), RG 389, Entry 461, Box 2598.

30. "Two Nazi Prisoners Make Another Break; Butner Guards: Gerde [sic] Roempke Flees for His Fourth Time since Reaching U.S." *Durham Morning Herald*, 2 November 1945, II:1.

31. For dates of escapes and captures, see "Escaped Prisoners of War," note 29.

32. Krammer, *Nazi Prisoners of War in America*, 115–16, makes the point that the German government reminded its soldiers to be aware of their Geneva Convention rights, including the right and duty to attempt escape, through the International Committee of the Red Cross and the American War Department.

33. Krammer, *Nazi Prisoners of War in America*, 140–42.

34. "German Recaptured," *Durham Morning Herald*, 14 March 1945, 2. The newspaper reported that "Wilhelm Jendricke, 19, German prisoner of war who escaped from Seymour Johnson Field Monday, has been recaptured by Wayne County officers. The fugitive was captured in downtown Goldsboro some eight hours after his escape." See also 1st Lt. Burton Spear, S-2 Officer, Camp Butner, North Carolina, to Office of the Provost Marshal General, 27 April 1945, Washington, D.C., RG 59, Entry 1353, Lot 58D7, Box 23.

35. Krammer, *Nazi Prisoners of War in America*, 138–39.

36. "Hunt Being Pushed for Escaped German," *Durham Morning Herald*, 11 August 1945, 10.

37. Krammer, *Nazi Prisoners of War in America*, 138.

38. Copy of handwritten note enclosed with Max Reiter to the author, 3 December 2002.

39. "Escaped German Prisoner Returns Here Voluntarily: Lt. Guido Graffield Rides to Camp Butner in Taxicab after Being Free since Jan. 6," *Durham Morning Herald*, 26 March 1946, 5.

40. National number of escaped German POWs from Krammer, *Nazi Prisoners of War in America*, 146.

## Chapter 8. Reorientation Programs at Camp Butner, Camp Mackall, and Fort Bragg

1. See Krammer, *Nazi Prisoners of War in America*, 195; and Article 17 of the Geneva Convention, in Bevans, *Treaties and International Agreements of the United States of America*, 2:942.

2. Krammer, *Nazi Prisoners of War in America*, 197. Robin's thesis is that "no plan for education would have made any meaningful difference"; Robin, *The Barbed-Wire College*, 9.

3. Major Paul A. Neuland, CMP, Chief, Field Service Branch, Memorandum for Director, Prisoner of War Special Projects Division, Subject: Field Service Report on Visit to Prisoner of War Camp, Camp Butner, North Carolina, 7–10 April 1945, by First Lieutenants Joseph H. Waxer and Richard Mayer, RG 389, Entry 461, Box 2657.

4. Ibid.

5. Ibid.

6. Ganzberg, *Stalag: U.S.A.*, 93–94.

7. Ibid., 99.

8. Ganzberg, *Stalag: U.S.A.*, 100.

9. Transcript in German of lectures by Professor Helmut Kuhn of University of North Carolina, Chapel Hill, delivered at Camp Butner and its side camps, sent with a cover letter from 2nd Lt. Joseph E. Patman Jr., Assistant Executive Officer, to Office of the Provost Marshal General, Special Projects Division, Washington, D.C., 18 April 1946, RG 389, Entry 459A, Box 1635.

10. Fritz Teichmann remembered that Professor Kuhn lectured on democracy and politics several times. Fritz Teichmann, Unterleinleiter, Germany, to the author, 11 February and 10 March 2003. See also a report by H. Sommerbrodt on the lecture Dr. Kuhn presented at Camp Butner on 13 July 1945: "Gedanken und Wirklichkeit im Deutschen Politischen Leben," *Der Lagerfackel*, 22 July 1945, 6. The article notes that Dr. Kuhn taught in Berlin until 1937 and then at Chapel Hill. See also "Amerika, Du hast es besser," and the themes for Kuhn's ten-week series in *Der Lagerfackel*, 28 October 1945, 7, 9. See also the positive review of Dr. Kuhn's efforts in "Bericht der Freizeitgestaltung ueber das Jahr 1945," *Der Lagerfackel*, 1 January 1946, 8–11. The article said: "The greatest impact was had by the lectures of University Professor Dr. Kuhn. He, a native German, immediately made contact with his listeners and his discussions were always followed with great interest. The theses of the lecture evening were always chosen such that Germany in today's world was always the focus. The success was great and the work of enlightenment within the camp was most effectively supported by the lectures of Professor Kuhn. We particularly value his tireless

involvement. The discussion at the end of each lecture contributed much to clarification." *Der Lagerfackel*, 1 January 1946, 9. [My translation.]

11. Robin, *The Barbed-Wire College*, 86.

12. Robert Kern, "Pfingsten," *Die deutsche Insel*, 15 May 1945, 8.

13. H. Schweiger, "Rückblick auf Pfingsten," *Die deutsche Insel*, 15 June 1945, 9.

14. For the announcement of the change to a monthly edition, see the 15 June 1945 issue, page 6.

15. Kurt Granichstaedten-Czerva und Gerald Kummer, "Das Leben in Österreich nach dem 13. März 1938," *Die deutsche Insel*, July 1945, 5.

16. Albert Resch, "Die Zeitung: Teil I: Ihre Bedeutung und politische Auswirkung auf das Volksempfinden" *Die deutsche Insel*, July 1945, 10–11.

17. "Etwas fuer Alle," *Die deutsche Insel*, July 1945, 15.

18. Willy Bartik, "Wir Neuen," *Die deutsche Insel*, 1 August 1945, 7.

19. Kurt Niezel, "Ich liebe den Verrat und hasse den Verraeter," *Das Freie Wort*, 15 August 1945, 5.

20. First Lieutenants Joseph H. Waxer and Richard N. Meyer, Memorandum for Director, Prisoner of War Special Projects Division, 13 April 1945, Subject: Field Service Report on Visit on 5–6 April 1945, RG 389, Entry 459A, Box 1617.

21. See Chapters 1 and 4.

22. Gustav Bieck, "Ziel,"*Der Drahtberichter*, 1 April 1945, 3–4.

23. "Der Unterricht in unserem Lager," Der Drahtberichter, 1 April 1945, 9.

24. "Konzert zum Heldengedenktag," Der Drahtberichter, 1 April 1945, 17.

25. "Kurz Nachrichten," *Der Drahtberichter*, 15 April 1945, 58.

26. "Strick drunter!" *Der Drahtberichter*, 22 April 1945, 1.

27. Leo Josef Bylicki, "Gedanken zur Filmvorfuehrung, Greueltaten in deutschen Konzentrationslagern,'" *Der Drahtberichter*, 10 June 1945, 163–64.

28. Leo Josef Bylicki, "Der deutschen Mensch im Aufbruch," *Der Aufbruch*, 24 June 1945, 2–3.

29. "Unterrichtswesen: Ein deuer Lehrplan," *Der Aufbruch*, 22 July 1945, 18–19.

## Chapter 9. Winding Down: Late-War and Postwar Reactions

1. Krammer, *Nazi Prisoners of War in America*, 240–42.

2. "DCV-3023 report."

3. Krammer, *Nazi Prisoners of War in America*, 240; and Jung, *Die deutschen kriegsgefangenen in amerikanischer Hand, USA*, 46–62.

4. Report of visit by Dr. Werner Bubb, International Committee of the Red Cross, and Mr. J. L. Toohey, State Department, to Monroe Side Camp, Camp Sutton, North Carolina, 15 June 1945, RG 389, Entry 461, Box 2657.

5. Jung, *Die deutschen kriegsgefangenen in amerikanischer Hand, USA*, 52.

6. "Nazi Prisoners Feast on Ham at Easter Meal," *Charlotte Observer*, 5 April 1945, 1.

7. "Why the Contrast?" *Charlotte Observer*, 5 April 1945, 8.

8. Pluth, "The Administration and Operation of German Prisoner of War Camps in the United States during World War II," 259. The perception that POWs were coddled

both in a national setting and with particular reference to Florida is the subject of Chapter 7 of Billinger, *Hitler's Soldiers in the Sunshine State*.

9. For statements by the provost marshal general and the House Military Affairs Committee, see Billinger, *Hitler's Soldiers in the Sunshine State*, especially 138–39.

10. "Allied Prisoners Suffered Brutality to Shock World on Forced March in Snow," and "Striking Nazi Prisoners Get Their 'Smokes,'" both in *Charlotte Observer*, 12 April 1945, 1. For more on the strike in Belle Glade, see Billinger, *Hitler's Soldiers in the Sunshine State*, 129–39.

11. J. W. Davis, "Well, Well, At Long Last: U.S. Warns Reich of Prisoner Crimes," *Charlotte Observer*, 13 April 1945, 6.

12. "Study in Startling Contrasts," *Charlotte Observer*, 15 April 1945, 8.

13. James F. Reynolds, "War Prisoner at Bragg Treated Strictly, Fairly, Justly," *Greensboro Daily News*, 29 April 1945, 4:1.

14. James F. Reynolds, "War Prisoner at Bragg Treated Strictly, Fairly, Justly," *Greensboro Daily News*, 29 April 1945, 4:1–2.

15. James F. Reynolds, "Prisoner of War Spokesman Keeps in Contact with Camp Authorities," *Greensboro Daily News*, 30 April 1945, 10.

16. James F. Reynolds, "No Coddling Given Nazis at Ft. Bragg," *Greensboro Daily News*, 1 May 1945, 4.

17. Report of visit by Dr. Bubb of the International Committee of the Red Cross, to Fort Bragg, North Carolina, 10 July 1945, RG 59, Entry 1353, Lot 58D7, Box 23.

18. Report of visit by Guy S. Métraux, International Committee of the Red Cross, and Louis S. N. Phillipp, State Department, to the prisoner of war camp at Camp Butner, North Carolina, and branch camps, 3 April 1946, RG 59, Entry 1353, Lot 58D7, Box 23.

19. While Métraux and Phillipp's report of 3 April 1946 indicated that POWs buried at Camp Butner would be moved to Fort Bragg, that is not what finally happened. On 13 March 1947, their remains were buried at the National Cemetery in Chattanooga, Tennessee. Confirmation of the graves of the eleven former Butner POWs, along with the date of their internment at the National Cemetery Chattanooga, Tennessee, was obtained from Mary Jett, Program Support Assistant, Chattanooga National Cemetery, in an e-mail to the author on 11 August 2004. Information on the locations of individual graves, dates of death, and dates of interment can be found under the individual POW's name through the Nationwide Gravesite Locator of the U.S. Department of Veterans Affairs at http://gravelocator.cem.va.gov/j2ee/servlet/NGL_v1 (accessed March 14, 2007).

20. Report of visit by Guy S. Métraux, International Committee of the Red Cross, and Louis S. N. Phillipp, State Department, to the prisoner of war camp at Camp Butner, North Carolina, and branch camps, 3 April 1946, RG 59, Entry 1353, Lot 58D7, Box 23.

### Chapter 10. It's Not Over Until It's Over: Memories of France and England

1. For the British capture of the Germans in North Africa and a November 1942 agreement that turned them over for custody in the United States, see Jung, *Die*

*deutschen kriegsgefangenen in amerikanischer Hand, USA*, 7. For an August 1943 agreement with Britain that reduced the number of "British-owned" POWs in the United States from 170,000 to 130,000, a September 1944 agreement with France to furnish German POWs for postwar labor, and the resulting return of about 178,000 German POWs from the United States to Britain, France, and Belgium, see pages 242–48.

2. Ibid., 252–53. The denunciation of American "slave-trading" was common among German POWs, who faced prolonged labor in Europe before repatriation. See, for example, Reiss, *"Die Schwarzen waren unsere Freunde,"* 307-8.

3. Günter Bischof and Stephen E. Ambrose, eds. *Eisenhower and the German POWs: Facts Against Falsehood* (Baton Rouge: Louisiana State University Press, 1992), 5, suggest that there were 5 million German soldiers in American hands in Europe in June 1946. Earlier contemporary figures cited by Pluth estimated that the United States held about 2,100,000 German prisoners in Europe in June 1945. See Pluth, "The Administration and Operation of German Prisoner of War Camps in the United States during World War II," 405.

4. Krammer, *Nazi Prisoners of War in America*, 248, quoting from "Retaining of War Prisoners May Imperil Future Peace," *World Dispatch*, 8 October 1946, 10–11. The *World Dispatch* mentions "Scandinavia," but that is a bit vague. Norway requested at least 25,000 German POWs from American forces. See Brian Loring Villa, "The Diplomatic and Political Context of the POW Camps Tragedy," in Bischof and Ambrose, *Eisenhower and the German POWs*, 68. The total number of German POWs America turned over to its Allies given in Reiss, *"Die Schwarzen waren unsere Freunde,"* 307, differs from Krammer's figure. Reiss says that about 740,000 German POWs ultimately were sent to France, 123,000 to Great Britain, 30,000 to Belgium, 14,000 to Holland, and 5,000 to Luxemburg for reparation labor. Krammer says 700,000 were sent to France, 40,000 to Belgium, 10,000 to Holland, and 7,000 to Luxemburg. See Krammer, *Deutsche Kreigssgefangenen*, 264. Neither Krammer nor Reiss mention American-owned POWs turned over to Norway.

5. For Article 75, see Bevans, *Treaties and International Agreements of the United States of America, II,* 954.

6. Pluth, "The Administration and Operation of German Prisoner of War Camps in the United States during World War II," especially 403-10.

7. Bethell, *The Last Secret*, xii.

8. Ibid., 166-70.

9. Pluth, "The Administration and Operation of German Prisoner of War Camps in the United States during World War II," 392-93.

10. Reiss refers to a *New York Times* article of 19 May 1945 and the response by the provost marshal general that appeared in *Der Ruf*, 1 July 1945, 1. Major General Archer L. Lerch assured disheartened cooperative POWs that the Nazis who were to be returned early to Germany would "be prisoners still, prisoners in their own land, eating less, earning less, and working harder." See Reiss, *"Die Schwarzen waren unsere Freunde,"* 308,

11. Max Reiter, Schwertberg, Austria, letter to the author, 14 April 1999; Erich

Moretti, telephone interview with the author, 1 May 2004; and Erich Moretti, interview with the author, Graz, Austria, 4 June 2004.

12. "WKG 012 Report."

13. "WKG 012" said that the guards were Poles, but Reiter said they were Yugoslavs. Max Reiter, interview with the author, Schwertberg, Austria, 24 January 2004.

14. "DCV-3023 report."

15. Ibid.

16. Ibid.

17. Matthias Buschheuer, interview with the author, Brühl, Germany, 22 August 1980.

18. Fritz Teichmann, Unterleinleiter, Germany, to the author, 2 March 2003.

19. Photocopy of front page of *The Yorkshire Post and Leeds Mercury*, 30 December 1946, enclosed in Teichmann to the author, 2 March 2003.

20. Helmuth Schimmelpfennig to Arthur Ezold, 16 October 1946, in author's possession.

21. A useful Web site that lists the POW camps in Great Britain and their official numbers and locations has been put together by Brett Exton. See "Map Showing Location of POW Camps and List of Camps," at "Other POW Camps In Britain," http://www.islandfarm.fsnet.co.uk/LIST%20OF%20UK%20POW%20CAMPS1.htm, accessed 14 March 2007.

22. Klaus Bockhacker to Arthur Ezold, 21 May 1946, in author's possession.

23. Rudolf Haynk to Arthur E. Ezold, 14 December 1946, in author's possession. For Haynk's service as spokesman at Wilmington, see English translation of report on visit by G. Métraux, International Committee of the Red Cross, to the prisoner of war camp at Camp Davis and the work detachment at Wilmington, N.C., 23 and 24 September 1944, RG 59, Entry 1353, Lot 58D7, Box 25.

24. Rudolf Wellein to Mr. A. E. Ezold, 22 December 1946, in author's possession.

25. Gerhard Bachmann to Mr. Arthur Ezold, 22 January 1947, in author's possession.

26. Krammer, *Nazi Prisoners of War in America*, 262, citing Costelle, *Les Prisonniers*, 242.

## Chapter 11. Graves and Memories

1. Mark Price, "They Were Our People," *Charlotte Observer*, 23 June 1995, 1A.

2. Deutsche Dienststelle für die Benachtrichtigung der nächsten Angehörigen von Gefallenen der ehemaligen deutschen Wehrmacht [German Office for the Notification of the Next of Kin of the Deceased of the Former German Armed Forces] to the author, 3 August 2004. This letter included four pages of information on the names, birth dates, ranks, dates of capture, death dates, and final resting places of eight POWs buried at Fort Bragg; eleven POWs formerly buried at Camp Butner and reinterred at the National Cemetery Chattanooga, Tennessee; and one former *U-352* man who, though he was wounded and captured off the North Carolina coast, was buried at the National Cemetery in Beauford, South Carolina, while his shipmates were sent to internment at Fort Bragg. Confirmation of the graves of the eleven for-

mer Butner POWs, along with the date of their internment at the National Cemetery Chattanooga, Tennessee, was obtained from Mary Jett, Program Support Assistant, Chattanooga National Cemetery, in an e-mail to the author on 11 August 2004.

3. Quotation and statistics here from Provost Marshal General's Office, "Supplement to Historical Monograph," 26.

4. Maj. Stephen M. Ferrand, CMP, Prisoner of War Operations Div., Provost Marshal General's Office, to Special War Problems Division, Department of State, Washington, D.C., 8 March 1945, RG 389, Entry 452A, Box 1403.

5. Maj. Stanley L. Richter, Memorandum for General Lerch, General Bryan, and Colonel Tollefson, 15 June 1945, RG 389, Entry 451, Box 1340, File #14.

6. The army told the State Department that the death of one prisoner was caused when he intentionally threw himself in front of an oncoming truck. See Colonel A. M. Tollefson, Director, Prisoner of War Operations Division, to Special War Problems Division, Department of State, 10 October 1945, RG 389, Entry 451, Box 1340. The army reported that the POW "had been in a depressed mental state for some time, due to the bombings in Germany and to his being troubled about the welfare of his family" and that it was felt that he had committed suicide.

7. Transcript of telephone conversation between Col. William M. Everett Jr., Chief Intelligence Branch, Security and Intelligence Division, Atlanta, Georgia, and Captain Fralick, PMGO Duty Officer, 16 January 1945, Subject: Kernsberger, Killian [sic], ISN 271502, Company 10, PW Camp, Camp Butner, North Carolina, RG 389, Entry 451, Box 1340.

The murder case at Aiken, South Carolina, involved the investigation and conviction of two German POWs for their murder of a comrade at the Aiken Branch Camp of Camp Gordon on 5 April 1944. The two convicted prisoners were sentenced to death and later hanged on 14 July 1945 at the detention barracks at Fort Leavenworth, Kansas. Provost Marshal General's Office, "Prisoner of War Operations," Reel 2, "Enemy Prisoners of War under Sentences of Courts-Martial" (Through 31 August 1945), Table 115. Copy of original in RG 389, Entry 439A, Box 25. Microfilm available through Library of Congress.

8. Maj. Stephen M. Ferrand, Prisoner of War Operations Division, to Special War Problems Division, Department of State, Washington, D.C., 8 March 1945, RG 389, Entry 452A, Box 1403.

9. Maj. Stephen M. Ferrand, Prisoner of War Operations Division, Provost Marshall General's Office, to Special War Problems Division, State Department, 26 March 1945, RG 389, Entry 451, Box 1340.

10. Lt. Burton Spear, S-2 Officer, Camp Butner, to Commanding General Fourth Service Command, 12 September 1945, RG 389, Entry 451, Box 1340.

11. "Wincenty Bednarski geb. 23 Maerz 1914 gest. 8 September 1945," *The European*, 16 September 1945, 1.

12. Maj. Stanley L. Richter, Prisoner of War Operations Division, Provost Marshal General's Office, to Special War Problems Division, Department of State, 18 July 1945, RG 389, Entry, 451, Box 1340.

13. "Berichte aus dem Lager," *Der Aufbruch*, 8 July 1945, 14.

14. "Unfallverhuetung," *Der Aufbruch*, 24 June 1945, 13.

15. Report of visit by Verner Tobler, Swiss Legation, and Carl Marcy, Department of State, to Prisoner of War Camp, Fort Bragg, North Carolina, on 9 December 1944, RG 389, Entry 461, Box 2656.

16. Ibid.

17. Maj. Leslie E. Griffith, Prisoner of War Operations Division, to Eugene Hoffer, 6 March 1946, RG 389, Entry 451C, Box 1355.

18. Thanks to Matthias Reiss for this insight.

19. Roberson, "Our Friends the Enemy," 12.

20. John Mattfeldt, Bokel, Germany, to mayor of the town of Monroe, 3 January 1947, in possession of Edith Long, Indian Trail, North Carolina. Ms. Long's father worked as a civilian with German POWs.

21. Robert Pittman, "D-Day Spotlights the Power to Forgive," *St. Petersburg Times*, 3 June 1984, D1.

22. Jack Horan, "Friendship Born of Wartime Kindness," *Charlotte Observer*, 30 January 1994, 1A, 8A.

23. "Former German POW Returns to Fort Bragg for First Time since '46," *Charlotte Observer*, 26 May 1989, 4C.

24. Dennis Rogers, "German POW Camps in N.C. Have Distinguished History," *News & Observer* [Raleigh, North Carolina], 8 June 1987, C1.

25. Horan, "Friendship Born of Wartime Kindness"; and Jack Horan, "Former Enemies Share Memories," *Enquirer-Journal* [Monroe, North Carolina], 10 May 1992, 6A.

26. "Transfer of Prisoners of War, 31 July 1942," Maj. Gen. Geo. V. Strong, G-2, to Provost Marshal General, by Direction of the Secretary of War, RG 389, Entry 461, Box 2476.

27. "German POW Visits R. J. Reynolds," *Caravan*, 29:2 (March 1995), 23.

28. Christopher Quinn, "Trip Back: German POW Remembers Winston Fondly," *Winston-Salem Journal*, 28 March 1997, B1, B6.

29. Ibid., 6.

30. Ibid., 6. The good feelings between American blacks and German POWs is the thesis of Reiss, *"Die Schwarzen waren unsere Freunde."*

## Appendix. The Jakob Fischer Case

1. This letter, the accompanying autobiographical essay, and the letter from General Bryan to the Special Projects Division are all found in RG 389, Entry 461, Box 2570, File: State Department.

2.Information in parentheses is in the English "original" archival document. It seems to be clarifications inserted by the original translator.

# BIBLIOGRAPHY

## Archival Materials

Bundesarchiv, Militärarchiv, Freiburg, Germany
    DCV-3023, B205.1541 (anonymous interviewee, former POW)
    WKG-012, B205, v. 45 (anonymous interviewee, former POW)
    *Das Freie Wort* [Camp Mackall] B205/312
    *Der Ruf*, B205/333
    *Die deutsche Insel* [Camp Mackall], B205/360
    Mitteilungsblatt für die österreichischen Kriegsgefangenen [Camp Butner], B205/452
    *The European* [Camp Butner], B205/493
    *Der Aufbruch* [Fort Bragg], B205/523
    *Der Drahtberichter* [Fort Bragg, B205/527
Deutsche Dienststelle für die Benachtrichtigung der nächsten Angehörigen von Gefallenen der ehemaligen deutschen Wehrmacht [German Office for the Notification of the Next of Kin of the Deceased of the Former German Armed Forces, formerly the Wehrmachtauskunftsstelle, or WASt], Berlin. Letter to Robert Billinger, 3 August 2004, containing four pages of information on the names, birthdates, ranks, dates of capture, death dates, and final resting places of eight POWs buried at Fort Bragg, eleven POWs formerly buried at Camp Butner and reinterred at the National Cemetery Chattanooga, Tenn., and one former *U-352* man buried at the National Cemetery Beaufort, S.C.
Federal Bureau of Investigation. "Haberlein, Karl. FOIPA no. 1002090-000." Materials sent by David M. Hardy, Section Chief, Record/Information Dissemination Sections, Records Management Division, Federal Bureau of Investigation, Washington, D.C., to Robert D. Billinger Jr., 24 January 2005. Files accessed through Freedom of Information Act.
National Archives and Records Administration, College Park, Maryland
    RG 59, General Records of the Department of State
    Entry 1353, Lot 58D7, Special War Problems Division, Inspection Reports on Prisoner of War Camps, 1942–1946
        Box 23, Fort Bragg and Camp Butner
        Box 25, Camp Davis and Branch Camp Wilmington
    RG 211, Records of the War Manpower Commission, Series 176, Civil Archives Division, Industrial and Social Branch

Box 1422, File: Weekly Reports on Prisoners of War. July 1944–June 1946; File: POW Camps by Location ad Principal Types of Work; RG 389, Modern Military Branch, Office of The Provost Marshal General

Entry 434, Administrative Division, Mail & Records Branch, Unclassified Decimal File

    Box 422, Ft. Bragg

Entry 439A, Historical File

Entry 451, Prisoner of War Operations Div., Operations Branch, Unclassified Decimal Correspondence File 1942–1946

    Box 1338, File 704: General P/W/ #6, 11 Sept 1944–19 Oct. 1944: Deaths and Suicides

Entry 451C, Prisoner of War Operations Div., Operations Branch, Unclassified Decimal Correspondence File, 1946–1948,

    Box 1355, File #704: Deaths and Suicides

Entry 452, Prisoner of War Operations Division, Operations Branch, Classified Decimal File 1942–1945

    Box 1370, File 250.1 General P/W #2

Entry 452A, Prisoner of War Operations Division, Operations Branch, Classified Decimal File, 1942-1946

    Box 1403, File 704: General #2 Deaths, suicides, etc.

Entry 459A, POW Special Projects Division, Administrative Branch, Decimal File, 1943–1946

    Box 1596, File 000.75 [Newspaper clippings on reoriented POWs]; and File 000.76: General [Publications allowed in POW camps, Reports and evaluations on camp papers and books, and Reactions, POW Camp Papers]

    Box 1608, File 255, General

    Box 1609, PMG Inspection Reports, Camp Ashburn to Fort Bragg, File: Fort Bragg

    Box 1617, PMG Inspection Reports, Camp Lamont to Fort McClellan, File: Camp Mackall

    Box 1622, PMG Inspection Reports, Camp Shoemaker to Camp Turner Field, File: Camp Sutton

    Box 1635, File 350.001: Lectures and Speeches, Camp Butner, General

Entry 461, Enemy POW Information Bureau, Reporting Branch Subject File 1942–46

    Box 2476, Camps—Beal to Butner: Transfers of POWs

    Box 2478, Camps—Crossville to Devens, File: Camp Davis

    Box 2481, Camps—Indianola to Maxey, File: Camp Mackall

    Box 2485, Camps—Sam Houston to Swift, File: Camp Sutton

    Box 2493, Camps Inactivated—4th Service Command, Labor Reports, Files: Davis; Edenton

    Box 2494: Camps Inactivated—4th Service Command, Labor Reports, Hendersonville, Mackall, Seymour Johnson Field,

Box 2495, Camps Inactivated—4th Service Command, Labor Reports, Files: Scotland Neck; Whiteville

Box 2520, Camp Labor Report—4th Service Command, North Carolina, Files: Ahoskie; Bragg; Butner; Greensboro; Monroe; Moore G.H.; New Bern; Roanoke Rapids; Winston-Salem; Williamston; Wilmington

Box 2570, File: Deaths and Escapes

Box 2578, Detention Rosters—File: #43, Camp Butner

Box 2598, Envelope: Escapes

Box 2604, Prisoner of War Graves Location File

Box 2656, Inspection and Field Reports—Fort Bragg

Box 2657, Inspection and Field Reports, Camp Butner and Branch Camps

Box 2660, Inspection and Field Reports, Camp Davis

Box 2666, Inspection and Field Reports, Camp Mackall

Box 2673, Inspection and Field Reports, Camp Sutton

Entry 467C, Provost Marshal General, Prisoner of War Operations Division, Labor and Liaison Branch, General Correspondence 1942–1946

Box 1574, File: Fourth Service Command

North Carolina Office of Archives and History, Raleigh, North Carolina, Archeology and Historic Preservation Section

## Interviews (Notes and Tapes in Possession of the Author)

### Interviews with Former German POWs

Buschheuer, Matthias. Brühl, Germany, 22 August 1980.

Lobback, Werner. Raleigh, North Carolina, 21 May 2004. Video interview with Sion H. Harrington III, North Carolina Office of Archives and History.

Moretti, Erich. Graz, Austria, telephone interview, 1 May 2004.

———. Interview in the Hotel Grossherzog Johann, Graz, Austria, 4 June 2004.

Reiter, Max. Schwertberg, Austria, 24 January 2004.

### Interviews with American Civilians

Funderburk, Harold C. Monroe, North Carolina, 12 February 1980.

Griffin, Elbert. Unionville, North Carolina, telephone interview, 21 June 1980.

Hill, Douglas. Former paperboy in Monroe, North Carolina, 1 April 1980.

Nicholson, N. B. Monroe, North Carolina, telephone interview, 17 June 1980.

Rogers, Margaret. Wilmington, N.C., 2 December 1998, available at http://capefear w2.uncwil.edu/voices/rogers_margaret019.html (accessed 18 March 2007).

### Newspapers

*Der Aufbruch* [Fort Bragg]

*Caravan* [Published for employees and retirees of R. J. Reynolds Tobacco Co.]

*Charlotte Observer*

*Die deutsche Insel* [Camp Mackall]

*Der Drahtberichter* [Fort Bragg]
*Durham Morning Herald*
*The European* [Camp Butner]
*Das Freie Wort* [Camp Mackall]
*Greensboro Daily News*
*Der Lagerfackel* [Camp Butner]
*Mitteilungsblatt für die österreichischen Kriegsgefangenen* [Camp Butner]
*Der Ruf*

## Other Primary Sources

Bachmann, Gerhard, 276 G.P.W.W. Camp, Nissen Creek, Pinhoe, Nr. Exeter, Devon, Great Britain, to Mr. Arthur Ezold, 22 January 1947, in possession of R. Billinger.

Bockhacker, Klaus, No. 116 POW Camp, Great Britain, to Mr. Arthur Ezold, 21 May 1946, in possession of R. Billinger.

German P.O.W. Camp Papers. Washington, DC. Library of Congress Photoduplication Service, 1965, 15 microfilm reels. A microfilm guide and index by Karl John Richard Arndt, *German Prisoner of War Camp Papers Published in the United States from 1943 to 1946*, is on the first reel. The *European* [Camp Butner], Der *Lagerfackel* [Camp Butner], and *Mitteilungsblatt* [Camp Butner] are on Reel 2.

Haynk, Rudolf, P.O.W. Camp 19, Happendon, Douglas Lanarkshire, Great Britain, to Arthur E. Ezold, Holyoke, Mass., 14 December 1946, in possession of R. Billinger.

Mattfeldt, John, Bokel, Germany, to mayor of Monroe, North Carolina, 3 January 1947, in possession of R. Billinger.

Mutter, Willy. "Amerikafahrt Deutscher Landser. Ein Erlebnisbericht." Stuttgart, 1948. Unpublished 322-page typescript. (Copy shared with author by Matthias Reiss.)

Provost Marshal General's Office. Prisoner of War Division. "Prisoner of War Operations." 4 vols. Unpublished historical monograph, Historical MSS File, Office of the Chief of Military History, Dept. of the Army, Washington, D.C. 31 August 1945. Copy of original in RG 389, Entry 439A, Box 25. Available on microfilm through the Library of Congress.

———. "Supplement to Historical Monograph." April 1946. Copy of original in RG 389, Entry 439A, Box 25. Available on microfilm through the Library of Congress.

Reiter, Max, Schwertberg, Austria, letter to the author, 14 April 1999; e-mail to Robert Billinger, 4 February 2003; and letter to Billinger, 19 February 2003, in possession of R. Billinger.

Schimmelpfennig, Helmuth, Stuttgart, Germany, to Arthur Ezold, Holyoke, Massachusetts, 16 October 1946, in possession of R. Billinger.

Teichmann, Fritz, Unterleinleiter, Germany, letters to the author, 11 February, 2 March, 10 March, and 9 April 2003, in possession of R. Billinger.

Wellein, Rudolf, No. 101 German PW Working Camp Newton-Mont, Great Britain, to Mr. A. E. Ezold, Holyoke, Massachusetts, 22 December 1946, in possession of R. Billinger.

## Articles, Books, and Dissertations

Bethell, Nicholas. *The Last Secret: The Delivery to Stalin of over Two Million Russians by Britain and the United States*. New York: Basic Books, 1974.

Bevans, Charles I., comp. *Treaties and International Agreements of the United States of America, 1776–1949*. 12 vols. Washington, D.C.: Government Printing Office, 1968–1976.

Biess, Frank. *Homecomings: Returning POWs and the Legacies of Defeat in Postwar Germany*. Princeton, N.J.: Princeton University Press, 2006.

Billinger, Robert D., Jr. "'Austrian' POWs in America, 1942–1946." *Zeitgeschichte* [Vienna] 29 (May–June 2002): 113–22.

———. "Behind the Wire: German Prisoners of War at Camp Sutton, 1944–1946." *North Carolina Historical Review* 61, no. 4 (October 1984): 481–509.

———. *Hitler's Soldiers in the Sunshine State: German POWs in Florida*. Gainesville: University Press of Florida, 2000.

———. "Mysterious Nazi Prisoners Next Door." *Tar Heel Junior Historian* (Spring 1986): 10–12.

Bischof, Günter, and Stephen E. Ambrose. *Eisenhower and the German POWs: Facts against Falsehood*. Baton Rouge: Louisiana State University Press, 1992.

Böhme, Kurt W. *Geist und Kultur der deutschen Kriegsgefangenen im Westen*. München: Verlag Ernst und Werner Gieseking, 1968.

Bykofsky, Joseph, and Harold Larson. *The Transportation Corps: Operations Overseas*. Washington, D.C.: Department of the Army, Office of the Chief of Military History, 1957.

Carlson, Lewis H. *We Were Each Other's Prisoners: An Oral History of World War II American and German Prisoners of War*. New York: Basic Books, 1997.

Coll, Blanche D., Jean E. Keith, and Herbert H. Rosenthal. *The Corps of Engineers: Troops and Equipment*. Washington, D.C.: Department of the Army, Office of the Chief of Military History, 1958.

Cook, Ruth Beaumont. *Guests behind the Barbed Wire: German POWs in America: A True Story of Hope and Friendship*. Birmingham, Ala.: Crane Hill Publishers, 2007.

Costelle, Daniel, *Les Prisonniers*. Paris: Flammarion, 1975.

Fickle, James E., and Donald W. Ellis. "POWs in the Piney Woods: German Prisoners of War in the Southern Lumber Industry, 1943–1945." *Journal of Southern History* 56 (November 1990): 695–724.

Fiedler, David. *The Enemy Among Us: POWs in Missouri During World War II*. St. Louis: Missouri Historical Society Press, 2003.

Gaertner, Georg, with Arnold Krammer. *Hitler's Last Soldier in America*. New York: Stein and Day, 1985.

Ganzberg, Judith. *Stalag: U.S.A.* New York: Thomas Y. Crowell, 1977.

Jung, Hermann. *Die deutschen kriegsgefangenen in amerikanischer Hand, USA*. Munich: Ernst and Werner Gieseking Verlag, 1972.

Koop, Allen V. *Stark Decency: German Prisoners of War in a New England Village.* Hanover, N.H., and London: University Press of New England, 1988.

Krammer, Arnold. *Deutsche Kriegsgefangene in Amerika 1942–1946.* Tübingen: Universitas Verlag, 1995. Expanded edition of *PW-Gefangenen in Amerika*, 1982, first German edition of *Nazi Prisoners in America.*

———. *Nazi Prisoners of War in America.* New York: Stein and Day, 1979.

Lerch, Archer L. "The Army Reports on Prisoners of War." *American Mercury* 60 (May 1945): 536–47.

Lewis, George G., and John Mewha. *History of Prisoner of War Utilization by the United States Army, 1776–1945.* Washington, D.C.: Department of the Army, 1955.

Moore, John Hammond. *Faustball Tunnel: German POWs in America and Their Great Escape.* New York: Random House, 1979.

Pluth, Edward J. "The Administration and Operation of German Prisoner of War Camps in the United States during World War II." Ph.D. diss., Ball State University, 1970.

Reiss, Matthias. "Bronzed Bodies behind Barbed Wire: Masculinity and the Treatment of German Prisoners of War in the United States during World War II." *Journal of Military History* 69 (April 2005): 475–504.

———. *"Die Schwarzen waren unsere Freunde": Deutsche Kriegsgefangene in der amerikanischen Gesellschaft 1942–1946.* Paderborn, Germany: Ferdinand Schöningh, 2002.

Robin, Ron. *The Barbed-Wire College: Reeducating German POWs in the United States during World War II.* Princeton, N.J.: Princeton University Press, 1995.

# INDEX

illness, 183, 184; intellectual diversions for, 149, 152; Jewish guards and camp personnel, 44–45; Jewish POWs, 199–206 (*see also* Fischer, Jakob); labor (*see* Farm labor; Labor); memories, 19, 188–95; memories, American, 49–50, 191, 192; murders, 43, 182; nationalities of, 64 (*see also* "Allied" prisoners; Alsatians; Arabs; Austrians; Belgians; Czechs; Dutch; Luxembourgers; Polish; Russians; Soviet-ruled nationalities); naval POWs, 20–24; Nazis, 57, 230n10; with horns, 7, 208n10 (*see also* Nazis and Nazi compounds); newspapers in POW camps (*see Aufbruch, Der* [Fort Bragg]; *European, The* [Camp Butner]; *Freie Wort, Die* [Camp Mackall]; *deutsche Insel, Die* [Camp Mackall]; *Drahtberichter, Der* [Fort Bragg]; *Lagerfackel, Der* [Camp Butner]; *Mitteilungsblatt für österreichischen Kriegsgefangenen im Camp Butner*); postwar reactions to, 156–60, 171; pranks by, 194; press coverage of, 122, 133; probationary battalions (Bewährungsbataillone), 17, 19 (*see also* Punishment Division 999); public awareness of and reactions to, 14, 59, 74 (*see also* Prisoners of War, German: postwar reactions to); punishments for (*see* Prisoners of War, German: discipline and punishment); rations of, 74, 157, 163–64, 166–67, 217nn26,27; reactions to, 115 (*see also* Prisoners of War: German: postwar reactions to); recreation for, 38, 73, 76–77, 88; reeducation (*see* Prisoners of War, German: reorientation); religion, 28, 38, 52, 77, 79, 88, 153; reorientation of, 68–69, 141–55, 227n2; repatriation of, 171–73, 175, 177, 180; restrictions on, 74, 83; sabotage by, 120; segregation of Nazis and anti-Nazis, 43, 151; serial numbers of, 217n37; shootings of, 39–40, 53, 133, 182; stereotypes of, 133–34; strikes by (*see* Labor, strikes by POWs); suicides by, 182–84; "traitors/turncoats," 42, 60; transport to United States, 4, 5, 6, 13, 15, 42, 214n22; work by, 105–21 (*see also* Farm Labor; Labor: refusal or unwillingness to, 80, 109)

Prisoners of War, Italian, 58–60, 61, 75–76, 105; conflicts between, 75
Pullium, Maj. Vernison G., 58
Punishment Division 999, 19

R. J. Reynolds Tobacco Company, 16, 84, 193
Reeducation, program of. *See* Prisoners of War, German: reorientation
Rathke, Helmut, 21,
Reiss, Matthias, 9, 114, 189
Reiter, Max, 2, 7, 12–14, 99, 100, 138–39, 173, 231n13
Reussel, Gerd, 21, 196
Reorientation. *See* Prisoners of War, German: reorientation of
Repatriation. *See* Prisoners of War, German: repatriation of
Resch, Albert, 148, 228n16
Reynolds, James F., 160–66
Rich, Lt. Albert H., 80
Richter, Maj. Stanley, 183, 186, 232nn5,12
Roanoke Rapids, 2, 27, 70, 91–92, 167
Robertson, Onward and Verona, 77
Robin, Ron, 145
Rockingham, 29
Roempke, Gerd, 133, 134, 136–37
Rogers, Margaret Sampson, xiii
Rommel's Corps. *See* Afrika Korps
Rossmeisel, Kurt, xiv, 10, 104, 137–39
Roth, R. W., 29, 52, 109
Rothkegel, Adolf, 112–14
Rüter, August, 198
*Ruf, Der* (Fort Philip Kearney, Rhode Island), xvi, 141, 145
Russians, 34, 60, 64. *See also* Soviet-ruled nationalities

Sampson, Margaret, xiii. *See also* Rogers, Margaret Sampson
Schaeffer/Schäffer, Willi, 110–11, 186, 197
Schiedt, Edward, 54, 124
Schikora, Gunter, 193
Schimmelpfennig, Helmuth, 177
Schmidt, Paul, 79, 133, 182, 183, 197
Schweiger, H., 147
Scotland Neck, 2, 27, 59, 70, 80–81
Segregation in the United States, racial, 213n6

Robert D. Billinger Jr., the author of *Hitler's Soldiers in the Sunshine State: German POWs in Florida*, is Ruth Davis Horton Professor of History at Wingate University in North Carolina.